W9-CNB-010

The International Political Economy of Work
and Employability

International Political Economy Series
General Editor: **Timothy M. Shaw**, Professor and Director, Institute of
International Relations, The University of the West Indies, Trinidad & Tobago

Titles include:

Pradeep Agrawal, Subir V. Gokarn, Veena Mishra, Kirit S. Parikh and Kunal Sen
ECONOMIC RESTRUCTURING IN EAST ASIA AND INDIA
Perspectives on Policy Reform

Leslie Elliott Armijo (*editor*)
FINANCIAL GLOBALIZATION AND DEMOCRACY IN EMERGING MARKETS

Diane Ethier
ECONOMIC ADJUSTMENT IN NEW DEMOCRACIES
Lessons From Southern Europe

Jeffrey Henderson (*editor*)
INDUSTRIAL TRANSFORMATION IN EASTERN EUROPE IN THE LIGHT
OF THE EAST ASIAN EXPERIENCE

Gary McMahon (*editor*)
LESSONS IN ECONOMIC POLICY FOR EASTERN EUROPE FROM
LATIN AMERICA

Phoebe Moore
THE INTERNATIONAL POLITICAL ECONOMY OF WORK
AND EMPLOYABILITY

Ann Seidman, Robert B. Seidman and Janice Payne (*editors*)
LEGISLATIVE DRAFTING FOR MARKET REFORM
Some Lessons from China

International Political Economy Series
Series Standing Order ISBN 978–0–333–71708–0 hardcover
Series Standing Order ISBN 978–0–333–71110–1 paperback
(*outside North America only*)

You can receive future titles in this series as they are published by placing a
standing order. Please contact your bookseller or, in case of difficulty, write
to us at the address below with your name and address, the title of the series
and one of the ISBNs quoted above.

Customer Services Department, Macmillan Distribution Ltd, Houndmills,
Basingstoke, Hampshire RG21 6XS, England

The International Political Economy of Work and Employability

Phoebe Moore
Lecturer in International Relations, University of Salford, UK

First published 2010 by
PALGRAVE MACMILLAN

Palgrave Macmillan in the UK is an imprint of Macmillan Publishers Limited, registered in England, company number 785998, of Houndmills, Basingstoke, Hampshire RG21 6XS.

Palgrave Macmillan in the US is a division of St Martin's Press LLC, 175 Fifth Avenue, New York, NY 10010.

Palgrave Macmillan is the global academic imprint of the above companies and has companies and representatives throughout the world.

Palgrave® and Macmillan® are registered trademarks in the United States, the United Kingdom, Europe and other countries.

ISBN 978–0–230–51794–3   hardback

This book is printed on paper suitable for recycling and made from fully managed and sustained forest sources. Logging, pulping and manufacturing processes are expected to conform to the environmental regulations of the country of origin.

A catalogue record for this book is available from the British Library.

A catalog record for this book is available from the Library of Congress.

10   9   8   7   6   5   4   3   2   1
19   18   17   16   15   14   13   12   11   10

Printed and bound in Great Britain by
CPI Antony Rowe, Chippenham and Eastbourne

*This book is dedicated to my families: the Moores,
the Van Somerens, and the Carters.*

Contents

List of Figure

1
Introduction: The International Political Economy of Work

> *Knowledge can make the difference between sickness and health, between poverty and wealth. Governments that adopt policies to make the most of knowledge will have major advantage in improving the lives of their citizens.*
>
> —*Carl Dahlman*[1]

Where is the study of *work* in the discipline of International Political Economy (IPE)? If the discipline aims to break away from International Relations (IR) (Watson 2005: 14) by establishing its own categories of analysis that differ from the questions that originally drive the discipline of IR, that is, security and war; then we have to establish exactly which questions IR is not addressing and, furthermore, the issues IPE must address to become a defensibly contrasted, albeit complementary, entity to IR.

Mainstream IPE finds its home in classical and neoclassical political economy theory, and often the focus of this discipline can be linked to the myths of Adam Smith and David Ricardo. These classical political theorists' tenets resound within the halls of neoliberal decision making with the song of the free market. But neoliberal free market capitalism is no longer a hegemonic political economic model, and so neither are these classical political economists' ideas. The works and ideas of Antonio Gramsci are more relevant to understand how hegemony is being challenged in the contemporary context. Gramsci based his ideas on Marx's theses but his work is far more advanced in his analysis of what happens within the superstructure and how these happenings allow capitalism to endure.

Through the analysis of three countries' cases across the world in the contemporary context of globalising neoliberal capitalism, I identify an increasingly international *hegemonic project* of skills reform that occurs within the superstructure, or in this case at the level of ideas and human subjectivity. This international project aims to accommodate and perpetuate what is perceived as the status quo, and so I propose we put the focus of IPE on the study of work, to understand how hegemonic struggle affects people's lives, and to take note of how people explicitly resist these changes in unprecedented ways.

Social change is usually, though not exclusively, seen as a top-down project in the current climate. The dominant elite-led drive towards corporate restructuring and labour market flexibilisation since the 1980s, has had a dramatic impact on the perception of exactly what makes people 'employable' in the ever-changing global context. From 2008, the global crisis has inspired an acceleration of a range of employment and skills policies that reveal striking resemblances across hemispheres in their contradictory convictions towards inclusion and emancipation in the exciting, new, knowledge-based economy (KBE), which often do not match the impact that flexibility and corporate restructuring has had on workers who are rapidly finding themselves out of work. A globalising breed of what appears to be a kind of 'third way' politics and neoliberal economic decision making towards skills expectations in employment and education policy transcends borders and cultures, and this hegemonic struggle is in need of extensive research and thought to bridge the divide between International Relations and Industrial Relations, and to provide the basis for what I proposed should be called the International Political Economy of Work (IPEW).

Policymakers, business figures, and union representatives across the world have discussed the transformation of what makes workers 'employable' as industrial revolutions give way to information and knowledge revolutions. This book looks at ways in which the policies related to employment, education and training programmes, and workplace expectations are placing pressures upon workers to manage their subjectivities and to equip themselves to remain employable in preparation for the post-industrial world, in three specific locations. South Korea, the UK, and Singapore hold different economic and social histories, but their respective national skills revolutions have occurred at a similar pace, and in a pattern that I argue has a tendency towards simultaneity. Comparisons between national skills enhancement projects show a transformation in ideas that define the way skill is understood. As a concrete strategy governments have introduced the ideal type of a new kind of worker, the learner/worker, who can become *employable* rather than necessarily *employed*.

Burnham stresses that politicised labour management involving tripartism and inflation control, while prevalent before the 1980s, took a turn towards seemingly depoliticised management styles. This shift demonstrates a globally prevalent attempt to 'marketise aspects of state activity and publicly shift responsibility for management onto external regimes and independent organisations' (Burnham 1999: 60). But the analysis should not be isolated to transnational corporate/organisational transfer, as this dramatic shuffle has begun to impact directly upon people due to expectations of their individual responsibility for national economic prosperity and development, and the concept of self-management was arrested from any semblance of autogestion for employability.

While in the 1980s the Conservative government in the UK was privatising transportation and overhauling manufacturing industries, South Korea and Singapore were busily industrialising and simultaneously investing heavily in education and training. Coates (2000: 107–11) writes that government spending on education is often an inadequate and a simplistic link to the status of employment. For example, in comparison to other developed nations, considering its industrial and imperial history, Coates claims that the UK still manifests a misdirected education and training curriculum that cannot construct the kinds of 'attitudes and values' necessary for ongoing success. So in this respect, South Korea and Singapore have bypassed this past empire, making the lines of forces difficult to rank between nations, and policy transfer a tricky delineation to isolate. Nonetheless convergence is noted within training programmes and with the rhetoric and intentions of nations' skills revolutions and training curricula towards lifelong learning and skills development.

A shift to a supply-side strategy became apparent in all three nations from the 1980s, which further demonstrates the case of attempted convergence and/or policy transfer, depending on which directional lines of force one wants to analyse among the international expansion seen at the level of ideas, material capabilities, and institutions in response to changes to world orders, struggles between social forces, and the forms of state that can be theorised (Cox 1981: 136, 138). However, in this account, I do *not* aim to identify specific power relationships because the process of restructuring management and control of labour markets across three nations is a complex analysis, involving social forces engaged in hegemonic struggles in specific locations that are, by virtue of their policymaking initiatives, connected through their intention to become neoliberal global competitors in the theatre of the knowledge economy.

The empirical reasoning for choosing these three countries for analysis, despite their contrasting 'models of capitalism', is as follows. Within the context of neoliberal globalisation, all governments have devised a 'utopian' vision that could be claimed to emerge from a conservative, radicalised modernity (Apple 2004). Tenets within each vision are intended to become axiomatic and a universal common sense that somehow legitimises the upsurge of temporary contracts and flexibilisation of work. These supposedly visionary projects promote skills reform and offer 'concessionary' skills programmes that aim to prepare workers for the flexible world,[2] but are a characteristic of the Gramscian understanding of passive revolution in the sense that they are organised to prevent workers' uprising, in a distinct *trasformismo* style, in the face of the dramatic instabilities that flexibilisation incurs. Whereas subordinated groups are most often considered to contain 'revolutionary' motives in Marxism, where the exploited working class would find solidarity and class consciousness, Gramsci's conceptualisation of passive revolution holds that a dominant class enacts its own type of revolution that aims to circumvent the multitude. In the contemporary phase of neoliberal capitalism, this technique is seen by public–private partnerships, wherein governments join hands with the elite in the private sector to enact top-down, wide-scale changes that are often decorated with emancipatory overtones and promises for bright futures, that in fact Gramsci would maintain hold the underlying intentions for power and social control. Passive revolution creates an ambiguity between resistance and rule by merging ideologies of both in a manner less obviously coercive but coercive all the same, using the technique that Gramsci called *trasformismo*. Passive revolution is a transnational project and cannot be seen otherwise in the contemporary age.

Examples of *trasformismo* are seen within South Korea's vocational education and training (VET) campaign that has been titled an 'Edutopia' and has been explicitly named the Skills Revolution. The UK has seen a 'Renaissance for a New Britain'. Singapore, in a similar vein, aims to become a 'Talent Capital'. Each site of development in this regard experiences control of labour with these soft touch programmes of limited safety-net capacity. Rather than devising strategies to reintroduce a concept of workers' rights in the quickly changing world, where knowledge is a form of property, governments are busily increasing the personal and reflexive responsibilities of workers and dispossessing responsibility for their welfare.

Where is work in IPE?

This project applies an eclectic approach because the concepts I explore and points I make are known in a range of disciplines in the social sciences, and their investigation is required to fully delineate a strand of IPE that looks at work. As Davies points out, the two core UK journals that publish articles almost exclusively in the area of IPE, *New Political Economy* and the *Review of International Political Economy*, have published just 36 articles about work, labour or production out of an aggregate of 446 articles (Davies 2009: 2). Clearly, IPE is missing something, which is shocking not least because political economy was originally a study, in many ways, of work. While Smith was interested in promoting productivity through efficient production methods, and Ricardo sought methods to reduce labour in geographical locations by identifying countries' comparative advantages, these theorists could not fathom the role of the state beyond a limited intervention that could encourage these ideals, and saw these modes as having the perhaps unintended, but very convenient liberal outcome of social harmony perceived in a way that perhaps only a middle-class white male in this time period could have done. Marx was very critical of these classical arguments and based his arguments on the point that the value of labour is exploited by those who own the means of production, and looked at work as a commodified entity in the circulation of capital. For the arguments in this book, I incorporate specific Marxist theory that makes the most convincing 'critique of political economy', by operationalising the concept of passive revolution as introduced by Gramsci and built upon by the neo-Gramscians. I also build on labour process theory, integrate models of capitalism arguments, and resource sociological and comparative politics methodologies. These are literatures to which IPE owes tribute, and they are investigated in the following chapter. Within IPE today, researchers are devoted to discussions of the internationalisation of finance, foreign direct investment (FDI), and currency fluctuations; and methodologies are often focussed on econometrics in the developing world, supply and demand chain statistics, and related quantitative methods. Interest in the fluctuations of global capital in mainstream IPE rises in the context of crises, such as the 1997 Asian economic crisis and the 2008 emerging global crisis. But alongside mainstream research, critical, transnationalised IPE should become committed to understanding how the collapse of neoliberal banking and corporate systems and restructuring of labour markets is affecting people and struggles for the hegemony of discourses that affect how people live and work, and thus consider literatures that diverge from the mainstream quantitative bias. In response to the onslaught of mainstream theory, areas of research conducted, and methodology in IPE, this book looks at what is expected of people for their survival in neoliberal capitalist markets.

IPE is often divided into the English school and the American school (Cohen 2008: 16–65). The application of qualitative versus quantitative research is often the core rift between the schools but, in general, the English school is more sympathetic to research that is not dedicated to finance and banking; see, for example, Amoore (2002), Davies and Ryner (2007), and Harrod (1987) for research that is committed to analyses of work, production, and poverty. These works apply methodologies from the qualitative genre, such as interviewing and text research, and address issues that fall outside of a mainstream agenda and the American school of IPE.

As Jeffrey Harrod (1997) stresses in an under-acknowledged piece 'Social Forces and International Political Economy: Joining the Two IRs', the incessant devotion to specialisation in our disciplines across the social science is grounded in methodological and epistemological *choices*, and is thus not some accident, and may even look like a 'crutch for intellectual cripples' (ibid.: 107). Industrial Relations as an academic discipline has taken a serious blow across the UK. The threatened job cuts and restructuring of departments at the University of Keele in 2008 instigated some of the most 'vigorous campaigning in opposition, the biggest in our nearly 60-year history' (Darlington 2009: 1). I participated in the campaign, which involved a march across Keele's campus in protest of threatened cuts of 38 of the 67 academic posts in the Economic and Management Studies School, and to contest the reintroduction of the degree programmes offered in the previously separate Industrial Relations department within the new Business School. Ralph Darlington has highlighted the need to rescue Industrial Relations in his recent work *What's the Point of Industrial Relations? In Defence of Critical Social Science* (2009), and points to the fact that the campaign he led with the British Universities Industrial Relations Association (BUIRA) was successful in preventing compulsory redundancies and in improving severance packages. Nonetheless the fight has not been won, and many aspects of positive radical thinking in social life are being threatened and subsumed by seemingly emancipatory rhetoric, such as policy to do with skills revolutions. Industrial Relations is increasingly classified as a form of human resources management, and mainstream economics has nearly eliminated any form of critical political economy within the academy (Spencer 2009: xvii).

The research of Darlington, Spencer, and Harrod demonstrates that Industrial Relations, a school that emerges from heterodox economics, is becoming increasingly underrepresented in the academic arena. IPE is perhaps the new home for this discipline. The developments within Industrial Relations must be protected, and must be absorbed within IR and IPE for a 'full understanding of the construction of world orders' (Harrod 1997: 106). To fully incorporate the study of social forces, there should be a marriage of the 'two IR's': *'International Relations* dealing with world orders and *Industrial Relations* [my italics] dealing with social forces created from the sociological, psychological, and political effects of the power relations surrounding the universal occupation of work and production and the universal preoccupation with its distribution and allocation' (ibid.:105). Harrod suggests the introduction of an International Political Economy of Labour (2002), and I would like to extend that to a discussion of work (see the next chapter for a discussion regarding the nuances between the concepts of 'work' and 'labour'), and a discourse of employability as a technique for the micromanagement of the productive self, in the form of the transnationalised concept of a forced subjectivity.

Neo-Gramscian conceptual navigations to do with passive revolution are advanced and developed here, then, via a survey of a range of policies across hemispheres, and by identifying an emerging discourse that aims to create a comprehensive transnational mural of the types of subjectivities that are necessary for survival in the global information era. A struggle for the hegemony of ideas is identified in the global expansion of 'employability'-related education and employment policy, which seeks to construct a particular subjectivity. This is a global passive revolution, since it is not identified as being hegemonic in the Gramscian sense. The manner in which hegemony is disputed and resisted is particularly documented in the final chapter of this book with the analysis of workspaces found in both virtual and physical arenas.

Gramsci himself succeeded in developing an idea (in the dark cells of prison during Mussolini's fascist Italy) that managed to overcome some of the weaknesses of Marx's thesis on the labour process. Marx's observations of the exploitation of surplus value inherent to capitalism accurately represented industrial production. This German exile neglected to look at episodic resistance, however, and to theorise how these episodes are managed by dominant classes and forces, and how powerful leaders continue to hold positions of power and to convince dissenters to desist. Gramsci reshaped the originally Greek idea of hegemony to devise a hypothesis for the reasons resistance appears futile, by viewing it as an elite project that requires not just coercion of the masses, but in fact gains a level of consent. Hegemony is absent within the context of passive revolution, which must be a *globally* perceived construct in the contemporary age.

Global passive revolution

Antonio Gramsci is read across these disciplines and his work has been 'internationalised' by the neo-Gramscian school,[3] which is placed within the school of IPE. Neo-Gramscian authors are dedicated to applying Gramsci's ideas of hegemony to global historical struggles in the context of production. However the neo-Gramscian literature neglects research on work and employment policy, as well as comparative research. Several authors have used and adapted Gramsci's ideas, including, but not exclusively, within cultural studies Stuart Hall (1986), and in IPE, Cox (1981, 1983, 1987, 1989, 2000,

2001); Worth (2005); Rupert (1995, 2000); Gill (1990, 1993a, 1993b, 1995); Morton (2007); and van der Pijl (1984, 1997, 2002). Neo-Gramscians' empirical work include analyses into the emergence of transnational capitalist class by van Apeldoorn (2002); mass production and its relation to the United States' hegemonic status in the post-wars era (Gill 2003); the emergence of a transnational capitalist class and global civil society (Robinson 2005); law and civil society in Cambodia and Vietnam (Landau 2008); the case of Russia in the context of political and economic change after 1989 (Worth 2005); neoliberal hegemony in Chile (Davies 1999); passive revolution in Mexico (Morton 2003); European social relations (Bieler and Morton 2001); Taylor's work (2001) that looks at the brand of democracy which emerged in South Africa; and my own work (Moore 2006, 2007) on the battle for hegemony of ideas to cultivate certain workforces who are increasingly expected to protect themselves, rather than rely on state welfare in the era of neoliberal flexibilisation of all aspects of the corporate world.

Several authors remind us that neo-Gramscian thought is not without its faults. Criticisms have been levelled at the school's danger of empirical pluralism (Burnham 1991) and also include Drainville's observation (1994) that theorists have not engaged with the repertoire of creative resistance towards global capitalism; Panitch's comments (1994) on the way in which Cox appears to reduce state activity to a level of mechanistic response to what are presented as global economic demands; Worth's comments on the tendency recent neo-Gramscians have to revert to structuralist accounts of class struggle (2008); as well as the noted lack of rigorous analysis in historical and practical contexts (Germain and Kenny 1998; Morton 2003). Furthermore, neo-Gramscian interpretations of hegemony have been largely state-centric and are not able to take the *coercion plus consent* model outside of these parameters:

> Cox employs Gramsci's concepts of hegemony and historical bloc to show how dominant states inspire an order which is conditioned through conducive ideas and a specific form of production. Yet, despite this, Cox's Gramscian model of 'international' hegemony is still one that is largely state-centric and one that does not offer a significantly different account from that of its realist counterpart.
>
> (Worth 2009: 34)

Worth points out that Hall and Williams understand the workings of hegemony as not being confined to analyses of the general consent across classes, that they look at 'highly complex' processes, and understand these processes as 'continually being renewed, recreated and defended' (Williams 1980: 38, cited in Worth 2009: 46). 'In applying these complexities to the international arena hegemony thus should be developed as a concept that is more open, multilayered and less rigid in its understanding of the relationship between capital and production and the highly complex issues of culture, identity and class that are played out at different levels within international society' (ibid.).

An account of emerging discourses centred on specific ideas that target workers' subjectivity and employability in a wide range of contexts provides the wider collection of neo-Gramscian analysis with the empirical and comparative work that it lacks, partly as a result of its state-centric tendency. Gramsci was interested in how particular powerful ideas become hegemonic and begin to control people, so to speak, by way of inculcating any potentially threatening ideas to their leadership through *trasformismo*.

As previously stated, neo-Gramscian authors have not written explicitly about work or the ideas of what allows people to work and to know measurable labour time, so to write about work in the context of passive revolution is also unprecedented. Over the past decade, a range of authors have looked at Gramsci's theory of passive revolution in the context of property reform (Williams 1998; Morton 2003); 'direct engagement with Gramsci's own writings and the contextual issues that embroiled the Italian thinker' (Morton 2007: 76); religious absorption (Tugal 2009); the media (Landy 2008); and culture and the use of irony (Barfuss 2008). A series of 'new voices' assembled by *Capital and Class*[4] is being gathered to revive this important idea in the context of global challenges to any perceived hegemony. In the light of a dearth of research into specific policy that affects people's everyday lives and work, I advocate the inclusion of a new category of analysis in critical IPE that is in fact focussed on 'work' and brings neo-Gramscian research into the present. So I intend to advance neo-Gramscian and IPE research by using a comparative approach to policy change on work and the new realities demonstrate that people are expected to behave as passive subjects who are *employable* for work in the context of international competition.

So the proposed research framework involves a theoretical approach using Gramscian concepts and transnationalising these concepts by assessing the relevance of what I call a *global passive revolution*; but I have not restricted myself to the typical avenues taken by neo-Gramscian authors who tend to construct theoretical fences rather than promote theoretical mergers. In this work, I aim to understand how the global 'revolutionary' project is promulgated by national instances of *trasformismo*, as seen in this context through education and training, and employment policy. Chapter 2 theorises the idea of work, labour, and employability, advocating the use of empirical data as well as resourcing a variety of literatures to understand this phenomenon in the current context of globalisation. A global passive revolution exists in the absence of hegemony, which means also that spaces for resistance exist, and are becoming genuinely challenging for the hegemonic struggle for transnational capital.

The international expansion of powerful and influential ideas that are intended to consolidate a 'world view' is characteristic of global hegemonic struggle. Associates and members of a burgeoning transnational capitalist class[5] seek to advocate particular ideas and to define and dictate workers' employability as seen in government and educational discourse. Discourses embedded in training policy across nations have emerged in a significant way since the 1980s and bear remarkable resemblances across three historically and economically different locations: South Korea, the UK, and Singapore, particularly focussing on skills that appear necessary to promote employability of workforces. This transnational phenomenon is seen as a demonstration of the global political economic crisis of capitalism, or what I consider to be a global passive revolution.

Gramsci's understanding of hegemony requires more than dominance of leadership, and needs more than determinist frameworks of hegemonic leadership as related to economic growth and material conditions of power as neorealism imagines; but its 'decisive' elements are ideological, and are recognisable through educative discourses. The General Secretary of the Italian Communist Party (PCP) was informed by the Third International regarding strategies of the creation of the Soviet state and the Bolshevik Revolution, by Machiavelli's ideas of consent and coercion, and by Lenin's revolutionary ideas on hegemony of the Russian Labour Movement in the late nineteenth century. Gramsci's innovation was not just an unprecedented concept of hegemony, but a completion of others' analyses through a commitment into looking at elite behaviour that occurs during crises of hegemony, which is seen in the plight of passive revolution, seen as the elites' aim of recapturing hegemonic power. Whereas subordinated groups are most often considered to contain revolutionary motives, Gramsci considered that dominant classes enact revolutions with power-seeking motives too: a *passive revolution* (Gramsci 1995, 1985, 1971).

Neo-Gramscian writers (in particular, Cox 1987) utilise the concept of historical blocs, a term originally created by Sorel to understand the dynamic between various forces in specific periods of time to identify how forms of state, material configurations, and social forces interact to identify whether hegemony has prevailed, or not. 'Structures and superstructures form an "historic bloc". That is to say the complex contradictory and discordant ensemble of the super-structures is the reflection of the ensemble for the social relations of production' (Gramsci 1971: 366). Cox states that this concept is, in fact, dialectical, 'in the sense that its interacting elements create a larger unity. Gramsci expressed these interacting elements sometimes as the subjective and the objective, sometimes as the superstructure and structure' (Cox 1993: 56).

> Bourgeois hegemony presupposes the dichotomy of leaders and led, of dominant and subordinate classes, and strives to reproduce this condition in the economy, in the political states and in the cultural institutions of civil society. 'Passive revolution', in which the dominant group takes the initiative in making concessions (of an 'economic corporate' type) to subordinate classes, thereby fore-stalling more comprehensive challenges from them, may serve to disable effective social action on the part of the subaltern groups and hence to reproduce the conditions of capitalist domination.
>
> (Cox 1993: 81)

Cox sees hegemony in a dialectical sense, whereas the nuances pro-duced within the superstructure and within civil society as identified in these quotations make it difficult to remain so reliant on what in the extreme sense could be considered a Cartesian paralysis (reducing the dialectic to a dual structure rather than focusing on the eman-cipatory potentials upon which the model relies). While Gramsci himself wrote in the early part of the twentieth century and did not theorise the impact that globalisation would have on societies in the sense of hegemonic struggles, neo-Gramscians look at contemporary struggles for international hegemony, building on earlier conceptual developments envisioned by world systems theory for a broad division of labour. But what neo-Gramscians have not fully theorised is what happens in the non-hegemonic historical periods, and whether, for example, global passive revolution may be in operation. My aim is to make a case for a global passive revolution that is evidenced through nationally specific but globally relevant skills revolutions; rather than the tendency of neo-Gramscians to analyse only specific instances throughout history to judge whether or not they have been hegemonic, but not to explain what happens in the case of absences of hegemony.

Local *trasformismo*

Passive revolution creates an ambiguity between rule and resistance by consolidating ideologies from contrasting perspectives, through what Gramsci called *trasformismo*. The Gramscian concept of hegemony is an idea that overall represents leading ideas and assumptions held by leaders and leading class cadres within societies, but leadership is not sustainable unless the hegemonic ideas saturate society to the extent that it 'constitutes the limits of common sense for most people under its sway' (Williams 1980) and *trasformismo* controls 'common sense'. In the current trend of neoliberal capitalist societies, common sense is increasingly hard to separate from good sense, and it is the project of this book and of the critical theorist to disentangle these, and to get to the heart of 'emancipatory' projects that are as restricting and isolating as the processes of Taylorism and piecework management of the industrial age. *Trasformismo* is enacted by managers, politicians, civil servants, and educators who can be seen as members of the transnational capitalist class (van der Pijl 1984, 1997; Sklair 1997, 2001a, 2001b). *Trasformismo* is seen in policy discourse and application that appears to give power to workers, in a way that might impress the *autonomists*, except that in practice, this discourse looks nothing like the *operaismo* movement as envisaged by Paolo Virno, Antonio Negri, Mario Tronti, and others.

The employability policy revolution is a passive revolution because it has allowed the ideas of these types of socialist movements to become incorporated into the hegemonic discourse, and these ideas are expected to become part of people's practice as well as their very subjectivity or self-understanding. These projects are not self-valorising and do not allow for the self-management as perceived and advocated by the *workerists*, but these projects are evidence of *trasformismo* at work. The appeal to workers' subjectivities included in the 'promise' for employability is framed in such a way as to appear to provide tools for workers' survival in an increasingly uncertain world. Training programmes appear to offer worker empowerment or authority, such as limited self-management of worker associations, but are ultimately managed by pre-existing power structures or formal discussion platforms. These provisions have been designed to tackle the needs of workers to remain or to become newly employable through the cultivation of workers' subjectivities, but do not meet fundamental needs, which include basic humane working conditions and involve the need for secure employment in the more recent years in every country of the world.

Gramsci, as I have stated, was a pre-'globalisation' thinker, but the pressing question fuelling his work was Marx's and Lenin's unresolved prediction for the overturning of the oppressive class. He reasoned, without explicitly making links across nations/areas, that powerful groups within civil society play a role in the consolidation of hegemony, and in the contemporary context of globalisation this role has become increasingly interlinked across nations. It is for this reason that I aim to look at particular ideas contributing to the process of *trasformismo* and common sense towards what makes a person 'employable' that is prevalent within not only education and research institutions but is increasingly corporate-established and financed by institutions discussed in Chapters 3 and 4 of this volume.

Hegemonic struggle within the contemporary neoliberal bloc of history involves consent as well as some amount of coercion at the international level. Since ideological leadership and consolidation is the cohesion that maintains hegemonies, ideological impotency must be a condition for passive revolution at a global hiatus. A class becomes hegemonic when it effectively transcends its corporate phase of solely representing its own interests but succeeds in representing universally, at least in rhetoric, the main social forces that form a nation. Organic intellectuals or the missionaries of dominant ideas work very hard to keep these ideas at the forefront of people's lives, meaning that ideas become a kind of tool for leadership and the control of potentially dissenting populations. Gramsci notes that ideas are 'real historical facts which must be combated and their nature as instruments of domination exposed ... precisely for reasons of political struggle' (Gramsci 1995: 395). Increasingly, management and policymakers' interest in providing curricula for worker training requiring lifelong learning for continued employability of workforces designed during the skills revolutions of the past few years is projected towards a larger framework of economic and social reform initiatives designed to build nations' competitiveness based around norms within a neoliberal hegemonic struggle. Political and business leaders recognise knowledge economies as the most competitive but, despite the commitment to an internationalising regime of ideas, appear to overlook workers' sustainable welfare in the process. Organic intellectuals' undivided belief in empowerment through self-managed, self-directed learning relies on unlimited and sustainable lifelong learning. These beliefs also require subjective identities that in many ways replace what could be expected in the era of a welfare state, which replaces any semblance of lifelong employment. Individuals are increasingly being held responsible for the success of the organisations that hire them, to the point that this relationship is taken as a given, as will be seen in Chapters 3 and 4.

Researchers have become interested recently in the relationship between the labour market, employability, lifelong learning, and individual workers, and often conclude that self-directed and workplace learning are the key for workers' survival in an increasingly unstable world wherein they are held responsible not only for their own ability to become gainfully employed through self-training and preparation, but also for the success of employers' businesses and even university programmes. Experts have measured employability as a unit of analysis and found that the general perception tends to be more optimistic that people are generally employable during times of prosperity, but that dual labour market and human capital factors also affect the level of perceived employability of workers regardless of structural factors (Bernston et al. 2006). International competition and skills gaps left in the wake of technological advancement have raised a set of issues previously unseen. Responsibility is increasingly transferred to workers themselves, as the relationship between employers, workers, and the government is reorganised by the capitalist class. Critics of the hegemonic management discourse note that 'companies have emphasised employability in an attempt to shift the responsibility for jobs, training and careers onto the individual' (Brown, Hesketh, and Williams 2003: 114).

Comparative case studies

One obvious question to be raised in any comparative analysis is why the selected case studies have been chosen and how they can adequately address the issues raised. The countries of the UK, Singapore, and South Korea differ in their systems of capitalist organisation and governance, including the degrees of control of labour and cultural forces, as well as the organisation of capital and the way that the state is deployed (Coates 2000: 148). But I argue that all three of these nations look increasingly like neoliberal capitalist models. While the UK case is obvious in this respect, South Korea and Singapore have been classified as state-led East Asian ideal types during the period of industrialisation of a large part of the Southeast and East Asian region. However, each of the three nations has been enthusiastic about the use of education as a direct instrument for growth and prosperity in conjunction with economic policy, and the resulting skills revolutions can be legitimately analysed and compared as attempted neoliberal capitalist hegemonic projects.

As the world continues to 'shrink' in the age of globalisation, it has become increasingly vital for researchers from all enclaves of the social sciences to think about the variety of expressions of capitalist expansion and to find both convergence and divergence in their consolidation. The pressures to 'flexibilise' labour markets have seen strikingly similar responses from governments, civil societies, and business forces. This is a crisis that has had a similar impact on workers through the expectations placed upon them to reskill in very specific ways to maintain individual employability, as evidenced within an emerging master discourse revealed in training curricula, government white papers, and policy.

But what kind of methodology is appropriate for IPEW analyses? How can I reconcile this with a comparative project I have pursued when IR and IPE research is so often accused of lacking empirical and comparative analysis? Political scientists, sociologists, and IPE specialists have carried out research projects in the spirit of comparison, but there is no single methodology for comparative analysis seen within the IPE literature, so I propose, for IPEW, that comparative analysis as utilised within the discipline of Sociology is appropriate.

Oyen asks whether 'comparisons across national boundaries represent a new or a different set of theoretical, methodological and epistemological challenges ... or whether doing comparative research involving two countries is any different from research involving three or more countries, and how different the countries to be compared can be allowed to be before they are no longer comparable' (Oyen 1990: 4). She writes that there are four tendencies in the humanities in the ways researchers carry out cross-national case studies.

First, the 'purists' assume that cross-boundary research is not at all different from other kinds of research and thus researchers are not reflexive about their positions as researchers, relying strictly on theory and methodology for multi-level research.

The 'ignorants', on the other hand, are not ignorant in the commonly understood sense of the word, but forget that cross-boundary research, because of geographical and cultural differences, inherently adds to the complexity in understanding and extracting information from the data.

'Totalists', as another category of comparative researchers, ignore the scientific assumptions for sourcing and coding data to reach basic validity and reliability standards. They may encounter 'unmaneuverable problems' in research projects, but ignore them and choose to make compromises, to continue with research that may not completely or adequately reflect cross-national comparison.

The final category as defined by Oyen is the 'comparativists'. Researchers with this point of view highlight the difference between non-comparative and comparative work. Comparative work looks at macro-social units as real entities, whereas non-comparative analysts see units to be analysed as abstract concepts that do not require operationalisation. Overall, comparative analysis intends to meet the 'twin goals of comparative social science – both to explain and to interpret macrosocial variation' (Ragin 1987: 1, in Oyen 1990: 6).

Perhaps because Oyen is a sociologist, she does not discuss trends in political science or IPE. Comparative politics has historically adamantly set itself apart as having a separate set of methodologies and epistemologies, but to a large extent it has been monopolised by theorists in the American school who imagine that any study that does not focus on the US, must be considered *comparative*. Studies have typically attempted to explain differential change in dependent variables through observing differing independent variables within conditions across environments, which are usually countries, but do not look at relationships *between* countries in the same way that IPEW can be committed to doing. Orenstein and Schmitz (2006) are correct to direct comparativists' attention to a 'new transnationalism' that refers to interactions that link people beyond the borders of nation states.

The *models of capitalism* literature, on the other hand, gives distinct comparative measures for growth performance of advanced capitalist economies as influenced by public/private relationships, management of labour and regulation of the labour market, and organisation of capital, and the types of economies that embody capitalism. Coates' models of capitalism (2000: 9–10) are summarised here:

1. *Market-led*. The private business sphere is given a large proportion of power and autonomy. This is evident with corporate-led, short-term decisions made with the intention to protect open financial and product markets. The US and UK are perhaps the most powerful of these entities.
2. *State-led*. This type of capitalism is also called East Asian developmentalism. Private corporate authority is still recognised, but is reliant on public discussion and liaison. Labour movement still lacks 'rights', though some company-provided welfare provisions are evident. This model is led by 'conservative nationalist' cultural forms for the most part. [South Korea and Singapore can be classified as such until more recently, and are also in the 'trust-based' category.]
3. *Negotiated/consensual capitalism*. There is some state regulation of capitalist accumulation, but also worker rights and welfare provision. Cultural forms are usually Christian/social democratic, as seen in the post-war West German and Scandinavian models.

(Coates 2000: 9)

The literature on varieties of capitalism (Crouch and Streeck 1997; Hall and Soskice 2001; Berger and Dore 1996; Coates 2000; Bruff

2008) looks at the responses of growth-theory scholarship to the rise of seemingly dominant models within specific historical periods. When the US lost its world market share in accumulation in the 1970s and 1980s, the scholarly lens turned to the consensual models seen in Europe, and gradually to accelerated development under statist models found in East Asia until the 1997 crisis. In terms of growth, each model has had varying levels of success over time. But the literature seeks to identify the diverging state and private sector strategy rather than convergence at other levels of state initiative, not to mention its 'subjectivity and inconsistency in applying these labels to particular countries' (Casey 2004). Casey claims that the point of encounter for the models of capitalism literature in the era of globalisation is the convergence–diversity debate, but he claims globalisation has not resulted in a significant level of convergence. I dispute this claim, noting that education and training initiatives in several nation states (or city state in the case of Singapore) have been coordinated to accommodate perceived success stories for varying models of capitalism. Regardless of whether each nation I will investigate is a complete representation of the highest-growth rate model in the contemporary global neoliberal historical bloc, I can note their aims to become members of a 'convergence club' (Magariños 2001) for prosperity, and even according to this literature's own policy transfer measures, have seen a level of 'success' in this regard.

Increasingly, workers in all of the Organisation for Economic Co-Operation and Development (OECD) nations are faced with a global flexibilisation crisis that appears to require a kind of transformation of labour markets as well as individual workers. The preparation of the self (Rose 1999) and expectations for workers' subjectivities to match flexible job markets and firms, as companies restructure to accommodate technology and innovation, is a contemporary innovation celebrated by a range of management gurus and specialists (Peters and Waterman 1982). This project is applicable within the varying models of capitalism, and the aggregation of policy across nations can be understood as a global passive revolution.

The focus is upon a new management or, to be precise, a required *self*-management surrounding workers' perceived employability, because the rapid transformation of what this means for workers, particularly after episodes or periods of crisis, throws people's lives into tumult and disarray. This symptom of the globalisation of capitalism as a global passive revolution must be addressed by the IPEW literature if we are to remain both responsive and reflexive to our contemporary world. The debate about globalisation is not just semantic (Robinson 2004: 1) but is a real question of whether this political and economic set of changes can be understood as a finished project and/or condition, or as a process that has potential for transformation. The transformative question of change within the idea of globalisation takes place at two levels, firstly, whether globalisation can be said to have a positive or negative impact for the majority of the world's people, and then, whether it is an immutable feature of global political economy or whether it is possible to overcome or overthrow the characteristics involved in what Robinson sees as capitalist globalisation:

> In theoretical terms, globalization can essentially be seen as the near culmination of a centuries-long process of the spread of capitalist production around the world and its displacement of all precapitalist relations, bringing about a new form of connection between all human beings around the world.
>
> (Ibid.: 2)

Many versions of globalisation theory have emerged, from the hyperglobalists, globalisation sceptics, orthodox, and transformative theorists. Regardless of a theorists' impression of the nature of capitalist globalisation, David Harvey says capitalism is *not* unfettered and neither is it disorganised as Lash and Urry claim (1987). Nor is it as definitive and categorical as the models of capitalisms require for economies' distinct paths. Harvey's flexible accumulation thesis of globalisation maintains that capitalism

> is becoming ever more tightly organised through dispersal, geographical mobility, and flexible responses in labour markets, labour processes, and consumer markets, all accompanied by hefty doses of institutional, product, and technological innovation.
>
> (Harvey 1994: 159)

However, globalisation is never separate from capitalist expansion. Capitalism has demonstrated its ability and in fact its inherent quality to colonise and perpetually accumulate. Skills campaigns, as seen within education and employment policy, have centred on the idea of 'employability' and have been used to organise the disorganised and contradictory elements of capitalism. As a form of supposedly necessary subjectivity, flexible, 'employable' (but not necessarily employed) workforces are seen to allow the ongoing neoliberalisation of states, and to permit the ongoing rolling back of welfare and support for workers. Education, within previous historical periods, was not seen as a tool for capitalist competition for profit, but was to provide something that people needed for survival as well as personal self-fulfilment and identity. The privatisation of education can be seen as an example of the commodification of social relations.

Chapter breakdown

The book's chapters review the increasing semi-proletarianisation of labour, the emerging transnational 'precariat' class, the propaganda of the emancipation of labour by way of membership in the 'creatives' club, and the impact of technological development on labour who are increasingly expected to become self-managing lifelong learners in both hemispheres. This is achieved through the analysis of what is seen to make people 'employable' according to government employment and education policy, and then I ask what exactly this will mean for workers.

The second chapter, therefore, deals with the idea of *employability as subjectivity* in the context of the discrepancy between conceptions of work and, alternatively, of labour. 'Employability' as an increasingly hegemonic idea is usually used uncritically across industries, and has not been adequately challenged in much of the literature that looks at how workers can survive globalisation and the new work culture it requires. Employability and skills campaigns are rooted in particular philosophies and could be seen as an ascribed state of being, manipulated to suit specific economic development initiatives. Workers' survival and workers' ability to stay 'employable' has become appropriated within the rapidly globalising international political economy and the way this has been adjusted over time is noted throughout a series of training programmes internationally, domestically, and regionally. In this context, Chapter 2 sets out the parameters for how 'employability' must be investigated as a concept whose remit should not be taken as a given, but must be understood in the context of capitalist expansion and elite-led economic growth.

Innovation, flexibility, entrepreneurialism, and reskilling are all concepts that sound quite adaptable and user-friendly. But this book looks at the way in which the contemporary stage of 'knowledge-based' capitalism is progressing through a series of manifestations of some *very organised* attempts to institutionalise particular types of labour markets with particular skills and competencies postured towards technological development.

While it will be impossible to touch on every element of the institution of the process of flexibilisation of the labour force and its relation to technological development, Chapters 3 and 4 look at certain 'skills revolutions' with quite impressive similarities across the UK, in the context of deskilling and reskilling and the recent Leitch Report; and South Korea and Singapore. The rapid process of flexibilisation of the labour force is having a dramatic impact on forms of employment that workers can expect, as well as an impact on subjectivities for *employability* – a term that places emphasis on people's ability to tolerate instability and to take as a given the lack of commitment from employers in the employment relationship. Internationally, policy has begun to encourage direct links between education and industry, subordinating 'learner-workers' to the state and to unstable labour markets, in an unprecedented manner.

After a detailed look at how subjective elements of employability are portrayed in these relevant skills revolutions across the world, in the final section of the book I analyse what has become a very interesting resistance movement that I argue can provide an alternative to the transnationalised governments' view of what makes people employable, to wit, the peer-to-peer movement, which transcends geographical boundaries and challenges the basic activities and premises of competitive capitalism. In the critical IPE literature, we are too reliant on traditional perceptions of time and space and the physical nature of labour markets. For IPEW to be a reality, we need to start thinking about new sites for producers' revolution, sites that are in tune with technological change and development, such as cyberspace, which provides the platform for a shared wisdom such as Marx referred to in his depiction of the 'general intellect'. Producers of what was termed in the early days of the movement 'free software', and increasingly hardware and sustainable infrastructures in open source or peer-to-peer communities, operate to some extent on a similar ethos than is seen in the rhetoric of the skills revolutions I depict in the preceding chapters. While they are a form of entrepreneurs and are some of the most precariat workers in the contemporary world of work, open source and peer-to-peer producers are also some of the most revolutionary in their ideas for production. Rather than focusing on the industrial relations of worker struggle in South Korea as I have done in previous work (2006); simmering unrest in the UK, which itself is interesting in the context of the January 2009 strike action at the Lindsey Oil Refinery in North Lincolnshire; or the nascent signs of resistance in Singapore; to battle an idea of subjectivity of the proposed subordinate learner worker, I want to investigate actual producers' involvement in unpaid production. In the arena of open source software, we find a production model that appears to be a voluntary, interactive, and very much enjoyed space of resistance to dominant models of capitalism.

The final chapter thus explores what it *can* mean to be a 'lifelong learner' outside of the skills revolutions rhetoric discussed in Chapters 3 and 4. I look at case studies of one project, Sooda, based in South Korea and run by Dr Chun Soonok, whose brother is Chun Tae Il the labour activist in the 1970s who in fact became posthumously famous for incinerating himself in protest of sweatshop labour conditions that he and his sister endured in the Peace Market where they toiled. The chapter then introduces a discussion of peer-to-peer production, which is a political economic ecology formed by people who aim to transcend all strictures of capitalist production by introducing new forms of value and through the explicit ownership of means of production and formulations of unprecedented collective subjectivities.

The key to the argument is that the production of knowledge occurs within a rapidly changing arena and holds the potential to become a site for contestation, or for a reconsideration of how subjectivities as well as intersubjectivities are formed. Because the value of labour is increasingly difficult to measure quantitatively with the developments of technology and with the transformation from the reliance on full time employment to a flexibilised notion of employability, workers are thrown into a completely new playing field. Demands on labour and conditions of production have a tendency to change rapidly and unpredictably and, thus, often remain uncontested.

This volume looks at how people's personal ability to *be* employable, or employ*ability*, has been consistently highlighted throughout government policy in a way that exploits the subjective nature of people's skills through universalisation of certain ideas, in particular through education and training policy reform, and therefore through perpetual reform of the discourse that informs concrete policy initiatives. The volume demonstrates empirically grounded case studies of skills revolutions in the form of employability campaigns in both hemispheres. But to resist geographical parameters, I look at a resistance movement that is based on Marx's concept of the general intellect which may, I argue, overcome class struggle and empower people in ways that labour struggle previously has not been able to do.

The hypothesis is that the 'new' employability as portrayed in government policy will *not* transform power relations between workers, management, and the government, but is an elite-led political project which works to subordinate workers through a language of self recognition and legitimation that appears to provide emancipation from the Dickensian work floors of industrialisation. In this book, I aim to exhume the internationally expanding 'lifelong learning' mantra to explore its demonstrable impact on workers' everyday lives. I have also set a framework for the introduction of a new body of research that can be classified an IPEW, which puts people in the centre of the research and rescues studies of work and labour from the mainstream. The IPEW accommodates critical political economy research in the globalised age, opening more doors than it closes; and also genuinely looks for production models that are created and owned by workers, as is hoped through social enterprise projects such as is seen in the Sooda textiles project in Seoul, and the virtual and real-time peer-to-peer communities identified in the final chapter.

2
Work, Employability, Subjectivity

This chapter explores a variety of literatures that deal with the question of the meaning of 'work', and I look at the ways that people are impacted by changes to how work is viewed, and how these views are processed by governments that influence particular political strategies intending to create employable, objectified subjects. I compare traditional views to more contemporary, modern, and even postmodern conceptualisations, to identify how common sense, discourses, and the hegemonies of ideas in a Gramscian understanding take shape in conjunction with social change and assumptions of human capabilities in the new and 'flexible' world of work.

The analysis and comparison of cross-national education and employment policy is particularly important in the context of a contemporary crisis of capital. Starting in 2008, the world was faced with an international economic crisis with unprecedented implications for the sustainability of capitalism as a global economic model. Although Europe had had an economic slump in the 1980s and East Asia experienced a regional crisis from 1997, a truly international crisis had not emerged with the same implications for the operation of the modern global financial architecture since its first incarnation at Bretton Woods in 1944. The November 2008 forecast set by the IMF indicated that global unemployment was going to rise to 6.1 per cent in 2009, as compared to 5.7 per cent in 2007 (ILO Jan 2009). In 2009 in the UK, unemployment rose to 6.3 per cent.[1] In South Korea, the rate of joblessness rose from 3.1 per cent to 3.3 per cent from November to December 2008, which was the only contraction within the previous three years for job growth. A sharp rise in applications for unemployment benefit was seen in January 2009 in South Korea. Also in January, 128,000 people went on the books for 'unemployment insurance', which was the biggest figure since 1996, just before the Asian economic crisis (AsiaPulse 2009). Singapore enjoyed five years of a consistent fall in unemployment from 2003 to 2008, during which time unemployment fell from 4.6 per cent to 2.1 per cent (Index Mundi 2009). However, Singapore was the first of the Asian economies to face a recession in the context of the global economic crisis, and in January 2009 the Finance Minister Tharman Shanmugaratnam announced that a stimulus package of USD13 billion would be applied to the Singaporean economy, since the recession had hit most of the sectors of Singaporean industry and manufacturing. Non-oil domestic exports fell by 7.9 per cent in 2008 particularly in the final months of that year, and the number of new jobs dropped by 26,900 net in the fourth quarter. Gross domestic product (GDP) growth dropped continuously over the year, and unemployment rose to 2.6 per cent (*International Herald Tribune* 2009). The rate of unemployment in Singapore was predicted to rise to 4 per cent and Singapore's National Wages Council announced that layoffs would be significantly higher in 2009, and advised firms to apply freezes or cuts on wages to save jobs (Lim 2009). International symptoms of the recession began to affect workers first, which is typical of economic contraction, but this recession was perhaps different from any previous downturn.

Neoliberalism is a peculiar offspring of liberalism, one that aims to stalk and control an increasing arena of social experience, and these intentions begin to invade policy that in turn affects day-to-day lives. This chapter sets up a theoretical framework to understand the use of a term which has become critical to discourse affecting work, employment and the workforce, or 'employability'. The terms 'employability', lifelong learning, and skills and competencies are increasingly seen in labour market policy reports and various binding statements across the three case studies identified in this book. These concepts are very much *subjectively* derived states of being and mind, and diverge dramatically from employ*ment*, and begin to affect people's experiences of the world and most importantly, subjectivities.

To build the foundation for the argument of the following chapters, both the notion of employability and, at its core, the idea of *work*, are negotiated, in the post-industrial era and in the context of our new 'knowledge based' global economy. Labour process theorists, sociologists, and psychologists have researched the evolution and significance of the concept of work as it has emerged in various epochs of specific production models and management strategies as well as production relations. The first section of this chapter looks at how *labour* has become *work*, and how this has impacted people's ability to have autonomy over their lives in a variety of guises. My argument is that work has taken a different significance for people with regard to identity formation in the climate of consumerism and rhetorical freedom of choice that has less to do with society and the family and more to do with individualism and accumulation. A seeming shift to new forms of work and creative 'play-bour' (in place of 'labour'),[2] usually discussed in the context of work in the entertainment industries, is heralded as emancipatory and generally liberating for workers. However, I argue that there is not yet an emancipatory angle to this new world of work stemming from the Quality of Working Life (QWL) model in the 1970s and emerging into the current KBE. Reasons for this lack of fulfilment of the 'promise' for workers have to do with what is done with the product of 'play-bour'. While workers cannot expect a guaranteed wage within this new world of work (Gorz 1999; Braverman 1974; Burawoy 1979; etc.), people are still expected to produce. Production or 'product', whether it is a form of commodified cognitive output or traditional physical items, is viewed and measured in light of others' production and presumably can be used to alter the employee relationship depending on its measure, but increasingly, at the macro-level people's productiveness with relation to people's employability and competency, is also viewed in light of company productivity and international competitiveness. So, simultaneous to the government-led skills revolution that places responsibility for workers' employability directly into the hands of those workers through personal self-management and lifelong learning abilities, workers are ironically being held accountable for nations' economies and economic health. Therefore the position of the worker is not only unstable according to supposedly immutable conditions of capital but, increasingly, is unstable unless personality and drive are freely available to all from some unknown resource found within subjective congruities.

The second section of this chapter then looks at the implications this has for the changing meaning of what it is now to be 'employable', in the context of the rapidly changing world of work and the new expectations of enterprise to become involved in increasing avenues of social life and society's institutions, such as education. To be generally 'employable', but not necessarily 'employed', means that people are required to take a new form of subjectivity and self-awareness as well as responsibility for learning and self-education in the form of lifelong learning. The study of employability as a newly relevant form of subjectivity is an under-researched area. The significance of its meaning is often used in such a way that it appears authors would like this idea to be taken for granted. However, as globalisation becomes an increasingly questioned idea in the context of the Asian economic crisis of 1997, and the global recession starting in 2008, and as people find themselves increasingly out of work for reasons that are attributed to a global problem, people's self awareness and identities are becoming increasingly removed from their physical workplaces. If people were identified previously by the work they did, now they are being forced to understand themselves as workless people, but still as labourers in the wider sense with a growing responsibility for their own identity creation as employable subjects.

So the chapter identifies 'employability' as a form of subjectivity that is intended to complement the contemporary, post-Fordist interpretations of work, work that is apparently more self-managed and creative and 'immaterial', but that has not yet eliminated the government and management structures that tend very successfully to undermine and control workers. In fact, the 'employability' revolution of subjectivities is one that governments have tried to incorporate and manipulate as part of a supposedly commonly accepted discourse, by way of the 'skills revolutions' they have initiated. So within this chapter I take an interdisciplinary approach to understand the ideas I have outlined, with the intention of looking at how skills revolutions are in fact passive revolutions in the Gramscian sense, in our current world of less-measurable labour time. In this sense, this seeming global 'skills revolution' is elite-led.

Labour and work

'The notion of work [*travail*] is an invention of modernity or, more exactly, of industrial capitalism' (Gorz 1994: 53). Indeed, work only becomes work as we know it today in the context of commodity production. After people did not toil, drudge, construct, prepare (ibid.), or attend to subsistence production in villages there was no measure for production that could be used for all outputs and for all types of workers, in the same way that management had thought during the Fordist era. Hannah Arendt's distinction between labour and work is reflected in Gorz's insights. These authors are not ashamed to point out that Marx and Marxists paid/pay scant attention to the difference between manual and intellectual work, and focus on relations of production in a way that does not allow for historical updates. Rose points out that 'in nineteenth century capitalism – in mine, mill, and manufactory – work seems easy to picture in these terms. But over the course of the present century, types of work and conditions of working have radically changed' (Rose 1999: 56). This is particularly the case in the twenty-first century, during which time we are seeing the rise of post-industrial forms of labour and organisations of work, and increased flexibilisation and precarious forms of labour on the rise. In earlier times, that which was performed in the household was the basis for survival, and 'work' was considered a very negative, intrusive, and annoying matter to be avoided. Perhaps this view is romantic and gendered in a way that can no longer be accepted in the feminist line of reasoning. But, nonetheless, it allows insight into the transformation of how activities can be perceived in the different historical periods.

Arendt, and later Gorz, reasoned that work becomes a separate category of activity when production is no longer solely for the self, but fulfils a wider function for society, and is necessarily seen as having value outside the labour in and of itself. Work is done in the public eye, and is done for the greater good of society rather than private individuals. These two characteristics were apparently always the defining points of work, but one more has been added with the rise of industrial capitalism:

> Work must have a recognized social validity or value, and this will be attested by the possibility of exchanging it for a determinate quantity of any other kind of work whatever – or, in other words, by the possibility of selling it, of presenting it as a commodity. It is by its commodity form that it becomes social work 'in general', abstract work, participation in the overall social process of production.
>
> (Ibid., 54)

In the nineteenth century, a class of skilled industrial workers emerged, and 'work' took on a creative dimension, as the supposed road to prosperity and wealth, and the way to dominate nature. It is with this rise of a 'poietic' framework that work was considered to be a creative and productive act for the greater social good, an act that would ultimately provide mastery over nature. Work is supposedly now only to be carried out publicly, thus underplaying all traditional private sphere production, despite the fact that reproduction is clearly as relevant and necessary for the survival of social life.

As workers become increasingly skilled and management structures increasingly place emphasis on such activities as team working, mobile working, and flexibility (more often seen than flexisecurity, a set of policies applied for the Scandinavian workforces), the private sphere for some forms of work and production becomes public. The question becomes obvious: how does one separate *work* from free time, leisure time, and genuine creativity? Gorz talks about work as production in the contemporary workplace as a 'false work'. This new inheritance of the model of *work-as-poiesis* is being applied to new forms of work such as are seen within the service industry. Gorz points out that this work has very little to do with the types of work conducted by 'toolmakers, boilermakers, metal-turners, masons and rolling-mill workers' (1994: 56).

Rose (1999) is concerned with the changed face of work and the impact this has on workers' subjectivities. He outlines the way in which transformations to the 'conception, organisation, and regulation of work and the worker over this century involve relations between many aspects of thought and practice ... human technologies, and the techniques of the self have been brought into being by [these] new ways of thinking and acting on the economy, the workplace and the worker' (1999: 60). Particular networks of power were evident within Taylorist design and later post-Fordist management structures. Like Yahoda (1932/2002), Rose writes that, in times past, work gave people a sense of self-fulfilment, social identity, and personal satisfaction. However, a shift from the Protestant work ethic emerged particularly in the 1980s and we no longer see ourselves as merely producers, but we are now consumers with a choice of work and professions. We can choose how to live our lives, we can even choose our own 'selves' from a range of choices set out for us through various media.

Work is no longer something that allows social satisfaction and a type of inclusion with origins in the family/marriage or wider social structure. It is now seen as a tool for individual identity formation. Workers are not, in this subjective appearance, simply seeking financial gain through work, but are seeking to discover themselves. There is, Rose claims, no emancipation *from* work, but there should be emancipation *in* work in our new world of work. A new management style, or perhaps movement, emerged in the 1970s called QWL, probably originating from the US. This movement emphasised 'excellence' and 'humanising work' (Rose 1989: 102), and really took force in the 1980s. What we see now is an unprecedented psycho-technology of work, one that requires a specific psychology and subjectivity, as well as a management psychology. Peters and Waterman outline conservative management styles and associated required behaviours in their best-selling book, *In Search of Excellence: Lessons from America's Best-Run Companies* (1982). The authors suggest behaviours that seem almost like adages to the contemporary management guru, having to do with the fostering of innovation, teamwork, and so on. This influential text relies on a supposedly typical human psyche or human nature, and has a sub-text for how these behaviours would increase productivity of the humans it was intending to represent. This type of subjectivity must be held by the individual who craves security but is also in love with change, one who is competitive but also longs to work in groups, longs for success and achievement, and so on. This was to be a new kind of citizen who longs for self-fulfilment through work, but in a way that is not complementary to the society of the industrial age. What is now generally taken out of the equation is a guaranteed wage, and union involvement at the level of human resources, and the commitment from governments to provide anything but a resolve to inculcate higher education and training by way of a particular process that could produce such subjectivities.

Theorists of the emerging IPEW can learn much from a wide range of authors who are often overlooked in traditional IPE, such as seen in the work of Beynon et al. on the 'new realities of work' (2002); Rifkin on the 'end of work' (1992); Burawoy on work conditions and monopoly capitalism (1979; 1985); Spencer's *Political Economy of Work* (2009); Fine and Milonakis on 'the social' in economic theory (2008); and Fine (2001) on social capital versus social theory. Moreover, theorists who are interested in the world of work in the digital 'playground' are searching for new ways to measure work and labour in our new information economy, such as Cubitt (1998), and have begun to make investigations into how society is constructed objectively, subjectively, and the importance of inter-subjectivities (building on the work of Berger and Luckmann 1967). IPE has very few critical theorists to offer in the contemporary moment, although the work of Abbott and Worth (2002), Worth and Moore (2009), and others aims to rectify this. Montgomerie (2008) attempts to build bridges between competing 'critical' political economy perspectives by arguing for an end to the obsessive attacks on mainstream 'economic' approaches in favour of more collaborative efforts to offer an alternative theoretical and empirical method of evaluating the changing dynamics of present day capitalism. With reference to work and wages, Montgomerie demonstrates how individuals who rely on inflation-indexed wage increases have been drawn into global labour market dynamics as low-cost consumer goods produced in the Global South affect wage-growth of workers in the Global North through diffuse mechanisms of global trade relations and consumer-price index measures.

However, no IPE theorists are investigating the relevance of the contemporary 'necessary' subjectivities of the worker. Typically, sociologists or work psychologists have taken the lead in analyses of the subjective elements of work, such as Clark and Oswald (1996), and Clark (2005) (cited in Spencer 2009: xvii) who aim to find ways to identify life satisfaction as associated with subjective participation. The 'economics of happiness' (Layard 2005) thesis claims that happiness can be found through work, a philosophy that informs New Labour's unemployment and welfare-to-work policy in the UK, but Spencer (2009) is critical of this homogenising platform. A handful of mainstream work psychologists, including Holman et al. (2009, 2008), advocate well-being through specific work design models and goal-setting strategies. But these authors completely ignore the implications for why resistance is happening in the workplace and are interested only in reforming it according to pre-determined 'rules'. The emotional labour literature looks at emotion work and emotion labour as forms of alienation that occur particularly in the context of service labour, that is, hotel and shop work that forces people into 'suppression of the real self' (Brook 2009: 533). Hochschild distinguishes between emotional labour, which is the 'management of feeling to create a publicly observable facial and bodily display (1983: 7) and emotion work, which is the 'process of managing and presenting emotions in the private sphere of our lives such as among family and friends' (Brook 2009: 533).

The 'labour process' literature, on the other hand, is based around a category identified by Marx that referred to 'the simple elements of the labour process [which] are 1) purposeful activity, that is work itself, 2) the object on which that work is performed, and 3) the instruments of that work' (1976: 284). Littler states that the labour process is a category that lies in 'contradistinction to the valorisation process' (1990: 77). Valorisation (translated from the word *Kapitalverwertung*) is vital for the labour process, but this is often overlooked. While the translation of this term is not completely precise, valorisation is understood as the process of value creation and of the surplus value of work. So the labour process is not a theory in and of itself, but it is a process of production that Marx critiqued in his *Critique of Political Economy* (1976). The activity that makes this process affiliated with capitalism is the seemingly endless search for profitable accumulation, including profit for the capitalist, from workers' output. Paying a worker less for her work than the value that is added to the labour process as a result of that work, is at the heart of the capitalist employment relationship (Knights 1990: 4).

The literature associated directly with the 'labour process' starts with Harry Braverman's *Labour and Monopoly Capital* published in 1974. Braverman's work was the first to analyse systematically the employee/employer relationship and the management structures of control to manage this relationship through deskilling workers; and, separating manual from mental labour, Braverman famously identified how scientific management separates conception from execution.

Several debates across academics were triggered by Braverman's groundbreaking book, to do with:

1. questions about deskilling and the attempt to construct a satisfactory model of skills changes;
2. questions about labour markets and the attempt to construct a satisfactory model of capitalist labour markets; and
3. questions about managerial strategy and control.

(Littler 1990: 46)

Littler notes these as the 'core' areas of the debates after *Labour and Monopoly Capital* was published. While Braverman's work caused significant discussion across the fields of industrial relations, sociology, and politics, it was not entirely above reproach, and perhaps the most important critique is that Braverman was too committed to structures, rather than with workers' subjectivities and their own experiences of the workplace. Several authors, most prominently Burawoy, voiced concern regarding the issues that were overlooked by Braverman. Braverman was concerned with '"objective" aspects of the labour process' (Burawoy 1985: 25) but did not consider the 'day-to-day impact of particular forms of "control", and specifically Taylorism, so the same one sided perspective leads him to compound Taylorism as ideology and as practice ... He makes all sorts of assumptions about the interests of capitalists and managers, about their consciousness, and about their capacity to impose their interests on subordinate classes' (ibid.). Burawoy aims to indemnify this lack of investigation and conducts extensive fieldwork in the factory to disclose how regimes of control operate. Where Burawoy builds on Braverman's influential analysis is his application to the workplace of Gramsci's thesis on hegemony and the absorption of workers' needs and interests through what he calls *concrete* coordination (ibid.: 10). Political and ideological research is crucial for the understanding of what actually occurs in the workplace, of how management structures of control are operationalised and how they are sustained, and why workers have not overthrown these structures of control. Braverman did not look at the 'subjective dimension' of class, and is restricted by an economistic view of externally defined class and one that predominantly looks at people's contribution to capital-accumulation processes despite his claims that classes are 'not fixed entities but rather *ongoing processes*' (1974: 409).

So, considering the absence of adequate analyses of subjectivity, how could this father of the labour process literature theorise resistance or dissent? While Braverman led the American Socialist Party, which had been a splinter group from the Socialist Workers' Party, he defended slaves' rights, and wrote in 1956 about American radicalism with the insight that, after the Second World War, there had been a crisis of the left (Braverman 1956). The following quotation indicates Braverman's earlier dedication to looking at resistance to the expansion of capitalism which he predicted:

The Communist Party's number one dictum for years has been that 'socialism is not the issue,' but that confuses two things. If it is taken to mean that at present no direct struggle for socialism is possible in the form of mass activities or a broad national election campaign, that is quite true. But if it is taken to mean that on this account it ought to be discarded or shelved to a future millenium [*sic*], that is dead wrong. Exactly because now is not a time when the Left can move masses into struggle either for immediate demands or for socialism, its role as an educator, posing fundamentals and recruiting a serious following on a fundamental basis, comes to the fore. ... But organized labor in this country is a massive and slow-moving body where politics is concerned, and tends to move as a unit, out of timidity and conservatism, and fear on the part of each leader of getting out too far in front. This means that groups inside and outside the labor movement will tend to outrun it in pioneering attempts, as happened in Britain as a prelude to the organization of the Labor Party there. We will probably see many third-party attempts of various sorts before the twin-headed monopoly is finally broken. Radicals can and should take an active part in these advance-guard movements.

(Ibid.)

With this in mind, Nikolas Rose explores the connections between material, social and economic changes, and workers' subjectivities:

The changes in the conception, organisation, and regulation of work and the worker over this century involve relations between many aspects of thought and practice: the history of the large corporation, the changing relations of manufacturing and non-manufacturing industry; the elaboration of an expertise of management; innovations in the rationale and techniques of accounting to incorporate the human resources of the enterprise; transformations in macro-economic policy and much more ... the relations between governmental rationalities, social strategies, human technologies and techniques of self [that] have been brought into being by these new ways of thinking and acting on the economy, the workplace, and the worker ... new networks of power have been established, a web of calculations and technologies connecting macro-economic policy, the management of the enterprise, and the design of the labour process with human subjectivity itself.

(1999: 60)

So what scholars have not yet done is to look specifically at how policy is affected by the policy and workplace changes that link with 'human subjectivity itself' (ibid.). Education has been targeted as a site for reskilling, and industry is repeatedly welcomed to take part in curricula development in an increased number of countries internationally.

In all of this, Michel Foucault cannot be overlooked. Foucault's groundbreaking work on power relations, governmentality, and subjectivation offers a great deal to the exploration of policy and its impact on people. Power is conducted through a multiplicity of forms, and Foucault identifies several ways this is applied, not least in the realm of the subject. The state is seen not simply as 'government', though government is often the form that we see at the helm of the objectification of the subject, in particular through the uprooting of the individual in a number of ways. The struggle against 'government of individualisation' is seen in a 'series of oppositions that have developed over the last few years: opposition to the power of men over women, of parents over children, of psychiatry over the mentally ill, of medicine over the population, of administration over the ways people live' (Foucault 2000: 329). The latter comment here is the area of interest for research into employability as a form of subjectivity and of subjectivation. Postmodern struggles are those that revolt against a 'technique, a form of power' (ibid.: 331) rather than perhaps a revolt against the elite, or against an institution as such. 'Where there is power, there is resistance, and yet, or rather consequently, this resistance is never in a position of exteriority in relation to power. Should it be said that one is always "inside" power, there is no "escaping" it, there is no absolute outside where it is concerned' (Foucault 1990: 94).

Employability as discourse and as subjectivity

Employability within this supposedly 'excellent' world of work is a seductive term as it seems to provide a one-size-fits-all safety net for people's survival in an increasingly unstable labour market. But what does the rise in an 'employability' rhetoric seen across social policy and education programmes mean for workers, as well as jobseekers?

Starting in the 1960s and picking up considerable pace in the 1980s, leaders decided that change would be inevitable as a response to pressure to 'outsmart' rivals in the global political knowledge economy, and began to focus on ways to prepare labour markets and to promote workers' employability as a policy target for the sake of economic prosperity.[3] Despite the industry/education link has never been proven to be an effective or successful approach and a way to understand 'employability', governments have adopted it increasingly since the 1980s.

Garsten and Jacobsson (2004) offer several definitions for employability and note the transformations of the concept over time. In a series of 'waves' (2004: 7–9), the meaning of employability has responded to different forces. In the 1900s, someone was either available for employment and was thus employable or, alternatively, they were not. During the Great Depression, *dichotomic employability* was seen as a statistical measure to explain people's ability to work and get into employment. Modern versions emerged during a 'second wave' occurring in the 1950s and 1960s, and were more inclusive of ideas beyond the predominantly Anglo-Saxon model. Garsten and Jacobsson outline three different versions of employability developed and used by labour market policymakers and public sector professionals. The first wave genre is apparently 'socio-medical employability', which emphasises a range of qualities observed by potentially employable individuals with an emphasis on physical and mental health. The second version is more general in that it identifies social 'health', that is, whether someone has a criminal record or has a driving licence, and rehabilitation centres on these apparent detriments towards employability. This is called the 'manpower policy employability' because it by definition 'measures the distance between the individual's characteristics and the production and acceptability requirements on the labour market' (7). Both these versions assume authority of markets and do not question employer prejudice or forced social change. The third variation, developed in France in the 1960s, takes a more collective dimension but concentrates on *un*employability rather than employability through an observation of the amount of time it takes for unemployed groups to find work.

But over time, employability has become increasingly defined as the ability to *adapt* to flexible patterns of employment more than anything else, and has often been conflated with the idea of lifelong learning (Hillage and Pollard 1999; Tamkin and Hillage 1999; Worth 2003), rather than the ability to work in a socially sustainable

and meaningful way. Companies were seen as unreliable for comprehensive training in economies that have begun to commodify
knowledge, and government programmes appeared to focus on
training people to achieve 'greater individual self-sufficiency over
job stability and career advancement' (Worth 2003: 608; Walker and
Kellard 2001). Experts have also measured employability as a unit
of analysis and found that the general perception of employability
tends to be higher during times of prosperity but that dual labour
market and human capital factors also affect the level of perceived
employability of workers regardless of structural factors (Berntson
et al. 2006). What this means is that training is no longer associated
specifically with job-related tasks, but consists of a more seemingly
holistic preparation forum, with education/learning at the forefront
and with individuals' self-improvement and a certain kind of self-
management as a crucial value.

As a result, governments in each country reviewed in this volume have made explicit attempts towards building a high-skilled,
value-added production capacity to accommodate technology-heavy
industries through building links between education and industry.
Policies in each case have demonstrated a people-centred or supply-
side agenda and have made 'employability' a top priority rather than
using the demand-led approach that uses a different set of criteria
to interpret how industries are kept in 'business'. Contemporary
skills revolutions, as this volume names them, have followed the
human capital approach, which prioritises employability. The British
government from 1997 to 2010, Labour, has also been claimed to
increasingly follow the American model at many levels as well, or the
welfare to work, 'workfare' model (Daguerre 2004: 20–4).

South Korea, the UK, and Singapore all made the effort to openly
and publicly shift responsibility for decision making to external factors, from international organisations, to individuals, and to the not
always tangible 'authority' of the market. International networks and
regimes of responsibility include Korea's involvement with UNESCO
Vocational Education and Training Council (UNEVOC), Singapore's
ongoing relationship with foreign capital, both of these entities
with the Association of Southeast Asian Nations (ASEAN), and the
UK's ongoing membership of the International Network for Quality
Assurance in Higher Education as well as the pressures of EU membership to adapt to the Lisbon Agenda. The nature of choices towards

supranational governance involves frameworks of 'rules, institutions and practise at a level above the nation-state whose authority extends beyond just one state' (Kennett 2001: 31–3).

Marxist analyses have revealed inequalities and power relations as based on labour regulation within an industrial model, but new models of production and labour processes appear to differ from those of the industrial age. Labour process theory had been criticised for failing to address the importance of the subjectivity of the worker and the way in which exploitation of the surplus value of labour is not always explicit, but is a lived process that becomes internalised to the point that a version of 'consent' can replace the assumption of worker compliance (Burawoy 1979). Braverman had noted even earlier that 'as human labour becomes a social rather than an individual phenomenon, it is possible – unlike in the instance of animals where the motive force is inseparable from action – to divorce conception from execution' (Braverman 1974: 113). While 'conception' relied on management's exclusive power to define and manage work, responsibility was gradually transferred to workers themselves in unprecedented production environments, or what are now understood as work cultures. The cultural turn in this topical age throws a new light on the management of business and organisations (Lash and Urry 1994: 108), and has inspired a shift from bureaucratic, mechanistic, rationalist systems that constitute the firm of old. The term cultural economy is associated with the grand claims towards economies of signs, the network society, and the knowledge economy, highlighting a turn to culturalised organisational and economic life (DuGay and Pryke 2002: 6).

Employability is increasingly described in the discourse as though it is a skill in its own right, which is a frightening development when this tenuous term is viewed as supposedly the most important/viable way to maintain employment. Historically, someone's employment, or waged relationship to his/her employer on its own, did not mean that the worker was employable strictly and exclusively according to market terms, in the way that the contemporary neoliberal marketplace demands. People are subjected to labour processes in the same way as they were before Post-Fordism supposedly overturned this static waged relationship. Workers' labour becomes a commodity when sold to the capitalist, but in the case of the employability discourse, it is more than the work alone playing a role in this relationship. The worker who can demonstrate employability has begun a relationship of subordination to capital before even necessarily being employed, meaning that capitalism is successfully becoming integrated into increasing levels of people's everyday lives. But what is even more interesting is that this phenomenon looks increasingly similar in a widening territorial context, as capitalism continues its ascent to hegemonic status. 'Employability' is a highly subjective term, and requires the productive woman/man to become a citizen/worker, who is also labelled a learner worker (Williams 2005) and an 'incurable learner' (Harding 2000). Rather than specific skills and abilities alone, workers are expected to have particular 'labour attitudes' (Worth 2003: 608). The employable worker appears to demonstrate the following characteristics:

- Flexibile personality
- Incurable learner
- Learner worker
- Enriched communicator
- Entrepreneur
- Employable
- Self-managed/directed
- Innovator
- Independent thinker
- Individual
- Adaptable
- Job sharer

(Ibid.)

A perception of the 'employable' individual appears to be gradually replacing or at the very least, challenging, discussions for 'employment' or job creation. The ambiguity of the emerging debate seems to require a marriage of the productive individual (what Lefebvre calls 'productive man') with a contemporary form of idealised citizenship (or Lefebvre's 'political man') that in practice requires people to become entrepreneurs of their own fates in unprecedented campaigns, apparently triggered by unregimented globalisation.

Contu (Contu et al. 2003: 943) is very critical of the 'common *imaginaire*' that has emerged in the construction of a particular kind of learning discourse; one that aims to create an 'incurable learner' (Harding 2000) with campaigns that construct a certain set of standards for individuals' employability, and the campaign's crucial companion, lifelong learning. The campaign marginalises more than it includes, as it places a homogeneity of expectations on all people, demanding certain types of capabilities for learning, excluding for example autistics, manic-depressives, schizophrenic people, and perhaps 'eccentrics', just to name a few. Britain's, South Korea's, and Singapore's employability campaigns all demonstrate a significant shift in what is expected of citizens via the formulation of their subjectivities in a normalisation process that is consolidated by the private sector's renewed demands for skills.

Skills and subjectivity

The transformation of skills expectations is increasingly becoming internationalised, and is considered crucial for knowledge production and workers' employability, which includes methods of learning that require creativity, and andragogical learning capabilities that must become subjectively inculcated and personally developed for 'learner-worker's' (Williams 2005) ongoing employability. Sturdy et al. (1992) contrasts the concept of a manual worker who stops working when 'coercion is removed' (Mann 1973: 23 quoted in Sturdy et al. 1992: 116) and socialisation literature that discusses work ethics and other worker characteristics, which are somewhat indoctrinated via external training sources. Sturdy comments that the labour process literature has neglected discussions of 'subjective action' (1992: 117), as well as emerging cases of workers' resistance even in the forms seen in absenteeism, 'making out' (Burawoy 1979: 27), and day-to-day evidences of rebellion (de Certeau 1984).

As I describe in the following chapter, for example in the UK, the Learning and Skills Council (LSC) has begun to work towards a project that intends to

> transform the way people think, feel and act about learning and skills ... we will achieve this ambition through a lasting, memorable and actively supported campaign which will be used and developed by everyone in Further Education.
>
> (LSC 2007)

The highly personal and invasive language used in the campaign begins to move stealthily into the territory of subjectivities and people's lives. 'Everyday life' has been ascribed by elite voices to working classes or to the supposed types of people/workers who are incapable of understanding or living in the enlightened and perhaps postmodern world, an assumption that has been heavily critiqued on the left. How does the employability campaign deal with 'everyday lives' but as a criticism of the way people may have traditionally chosen to live, that is, in a way that is not all-consumed with preparing oneself for the supposedly immutable instability of the labour market? Employability of the *self* is a concept that holds absolutely no meaning if it is not an experience lived and constructed by people whose relationship to their work is increasingly subordinated to global and local changes to labour markets.

Scientific analyses of creative processes stem from the 1960s, at which time psychologists even referenced late nineteenth century authors to explore the idea of creative thought in comparison to other knowledge processes. Campbell noted the conditions for general inductive gain, involving a process of the evolution of mechanisms for introducing variation, added to consistent selection processes, which finally was expected to reveal a mechanism for reproducing and preserving selected variants emerging from the former conditions. So knowledge production emerges from 'blind-variation-and-selective-retention'. Creative thought, on the other hand, requires 'substitute exploration of a substitute representation of the environment' (Campbell 1960: 384) by way of an exploratory thought process. This author cites Bain (1874) in this discussion of trials and errors for theorisation of the accurate and successful process termination, or the 'aha-erlebnis' of a final idea. Bain condones originality, emotion, adventurism, and energetic character traits for the success of creative thinking. More recently, sociologists and management specialists have begun to consider membership of the 'creative class' (Florida 2004) as important for workers' knowledge production capabilities and thus for employability, but still limit the final outcomes of creative thinking to assessment within an unwritten curricula. Furthermore, andragogy may be seen to have taken the place almost of pedagogy, which removes the metaphorical instructor from the workplace nearly completely. These shifts represent a transformation of hegemonies for knowledge production both within models for business interaction, and within the concept of workers' employability in the post-industrial KBE.

However, the 'skill' of creativity has now become a tool to divide classes. The Richard Florida Creativity Group has divided percentages of 'classes' of workers and wage shares. People with 'creativity' make the most money, according to the Creativity Group, a project founded by Richard Florida, a Carnegie Mellon economist. Creative capital is 'even more important to regional growth than human capital or high-tech industries', since the latter two items are 'shaped' by the former. Regions' economic gain can be specifically linked to the 3T's: Technology, Talent, and Tolerance; these items will attract creative talent in the emerging global competition for talent. The Creative Class demonstrates:

- Individuality: Members of the creative class exhibit a strong preference for individuality and self-statement. They do not want to conform to organisational or institutional directives and resist traditional group oriented norms.
- Meritocracy: The creative class favours hard work, challenge, and stimulation. Its members have a propensity for goal setting and achievement. They want to get ahead because they are good at what they do.
- Diversity and Openness: Members of this class strongly favour organisations and environments in which they feel anyone can fit in and get ahead.

(Florida 2002)

The action of creativity is understood generally as the creation of an idea, whereas innovation is a more complex concept. A group of researchers at the Institute of Work Psychology, University of Sheffield, critique their own discipline for advancing the generation of ideas without examining their implementation, which requires an extended range of skills and most importantly, innovation (Axtell et al. 2000). Employee role orientation and self-efficacy are linked to innovation (Farr and Ford 1990; Bandura 1982; Anderson and West 1998) though innovation itself requires 'approval, support and resources of others' (Axtell et al. 2000: 269), and assumptions of individualism and rationality lie at the core of skills and production capacities.

But this line of reasoning still relies on unwritten curricula and on the epistemological 'truths' that determine and design measures for success. Workplace expectations for knowledge production are becoming normalised within the KBE and rely on employability of workers, revealing contradictions within this transformation. If employability is dependent on the 'accidental circumstances' (Mach 1896) that must be instigated by workers' energetic trial and error, how can potential employees possibly defend themselves and their abilities in a meaningful sense, or in a way that protects jobs and job security? Furthermore, experts rely on the assumption that the process as a whole externally provides foresight for overt behaviour; otherwise, the results could not be measured for success as the production of truly 'new' thought.

Resnick and Wolff (1987) claim that knowledge is a process and a conceptual response that 'continually extends, elaborates, and revises its conceptual apparatus according to the ever-changing determinations of its environment'. Responses demand creations of new concepts, rejections of other concepts, and a 'systematic ordering' of a growing body of accepted concepts. These authors credit Marx for this depiction of knowledge creation, citing *Critique of Political Economy*, in which Marx writes that 'it is not the consciousness of men that determines their existence, but on the contrary, their social existence determines their consciousness' (ibid.: 54). But these authors also rely on a line of reasoning that restricts the line of knowledge production as originating from the structure.

Jessop discusses critical semiotic analysis for a better understanding of knowledge production that critiques the variation, selection, and retention model understood within the aforementioned psychology circles. Jessop is interested in the way in which capitalism reproduces itself via social and, to a lesser extent, material constructions of historically specific networks of social relations and aggregations of institutions. He initiates a discussion of CPE that marries critical political economy with semiotics, which specifically looks at 'argumentation, narrativity, rhetoric, hermeneutics, identity, reflexivity, historicity and discourse', and Jessop looks at the 'intersubjective production of meaning [semiosis] to cover them all' (2004). It is thus appropriate to look at the production of knowledge regarding what makes employees employable and an investigation of the value ascribed to knowledge produced in the workplace from the CPE perspective, which allows for a critique rather than a reification of understandings. If OS is a site for the attainment of employability, then does it succeed in creating an alternative economic imaginary?

Or is it reinvention, indeed redemption of the capitalist mode of production?

Theorising 'Employability'

The Bologna Declaration emphasises employability and encourages the 'adoption of a system of easily readable and comparable degrees, also through the implementation of the Diploma Supplement, in order to promote European citizens' employability and the international competitiveness of the European higher education system' (European Ministers of Education 1999). Employability is a term that is becoming accepted internationally and is thus part of an international discourse that encourages a particular form of power over subjectivities and bodies. It has, as is shown in subsequent chapters, become almost a matter of common sense that informs policy-making. The difference in theorising discourse in the Foucauldian framework and common sense from a Gramscian perspective is that Gramsci imagined a 'correct' way of thinking that is not evident in cases of common sense (in fact he designated the correct way of thinking as 'good sense'). The idea of discourse and power is that there are multiple ways of thinking that could become discourses, and Foucault was not committed to identifying the 'correct' way.

Often, confusion regarding definitions and interpretations of what employability represents is evident, and one study looks at the employability of geography graduates in Estonia, the US, Chile, Greece, the UK, Italy, and Spain. Employability is linked with education in these studies and countries' curricula are discussed to incorporate strategies to enhance graduates' employability (Rooney et al. 2006). The unemployable in the late nineteenth and early twentieth century were simply those who were unable to work (Welshman 2006) but the concept has altered dramatically to almost unrecognisable proportions as a result of globalisation and the changing relationship between industry and education.

Two threads run through the literature on employability: (1) a human capital approach and (2) an approach that stresses labour market attachment or work-first (Daguerre 2004). Overall, employability has shifted from the simple notion of those who are 'able' to work, to a reliance on workers' capabilities to adjust to changing labour markets, and how workers can be trained into this mentality

is an issue discussed at increasing levels of government and governance alike. Employability is a concept that appears now to stretch
beyond solely personal factors, but must include the awareness that
individuals encounter a range of barriers to prevent access to the
labour market due to 'globalisation'.

Braverman argued in his groundbreaking work (1974) that the
deskilling of workers has always been a management imperative
designed to maintain hierarchies and subordinate workers. Several
authors with left political leanings aim to resurrect Braverman's
ideas into present analyses, and look at the transposition of Taylorist
employment relations into the present day. Clearly, dedicated orthodox management theorists see exploitation of labour as being simply
that, that is, the extraction of value through workers' productive
capability for the good of organisational aims, and absolutely see
no need for normative explanations (Reilly 2001). Labour process
literature has been critiqued for neglecting to fully engage with
and explore the important subject of the subjectivity of workers
(O'Doherty and Willmott 2001; Knights 1990; Willmott 1990; Sturdy
1992). Within Marxist literature, too much emphasis has been placed
on the structure of management control and objective conditions
that are viewed over and above 'workers' subjective feelings and
identities' (Glenn and Feldberg 1979: 52). To restrict research to
structural conditions is to offer an incomplete view of the labour
process and of important relations of production, that is, employment relationships in the contemporary context wherein policy
discourse relies on the gospel truths of what must be done in the neoliberal, globalised world. Lazzarato points out that in our new world
of work, 'the worker's personality and subjectivity have to be made
susceptible to organization and command' (1996: 133). Burawoy and
several others began to attempt to put some meat on the bones of
the corpus of ideas started by Braverman, with the understanding
that what happens on the shop floor and production more widely
are events that are formed around political and ideological factors
(Smith 1990: 233).

But 'skill' has become more than specific knowledge about the
execution of a job, but nonetheless it has become a competitive
advantage within supposed knowledge economies, and contemporary governments have tended to forget their own rules for neoliberal
laissez faire-ism and have begun to intervene through investment

into education. A 'high skills approach' is thus taken in policymaking to remain competitive in the global knowledge economy. The concept of skill is increasingly concurrent with education, while industries have begun to operate a 'skills approach' (Pascail 2006). Pascail notes that higher education is no longer devoted to the transmission of knowledge alone, but has become a training ground to create a workforce that will directly become involved in the development of economies (ibid.).

The debate surrounding the extent to which higher education can or even should engage itself in this way seems to position itself on two sides. First, authors like Cranmer (2006) began to doubt that employable skills can be acquired in the classroom, and advocate a return to on the job training and learning by doing or, on the other hand, actual involvement of employers into curricula. One study by the Higher Education Funding Council for England (HEFCE) (Mason et al. 2006) throws doubt on the idea that educators in the classroom of higher education can actually have an impact or improve the chances for graduates' employability, but encourages increased direct involvement and investment of employers into education to aid in graduates' obtaining of employment.

The following chapters look at the impact of skills revolutions in both the 'West' and the 'East', through the institutionalisation of certain ideas towards employability that are becoming hegemonic and realised through specific policy. This book thus highlights the urgency of discussions of work and production and looks at how in our supposed post-industrial world, in the context of global recession, subjectivity is less affiliated with people's work and employment and is more about a supposed core ability to posture oneself towards the market in a way that ultimately disallows creative self identification and self-realised and managed subjectivity. The following chapters include case studies looking into the policies that affect the way people are being told that they can cultivate their own market-postured 'employability', and include discussions of employment and education strategies and policy in the drive towards knowledge based production development in three locations, and then look to the peer-to-peer model for production as the possible arena for the realisation of subjectivity through work.

3
Skills Revolutions in the 'West'

With pressures from employers, government ministries, and the new paying student/customer, New Labour has began to restructure higher education and worker training in the UK supposedly to accommodate global markets, in the context of increasingly intimate relations between business and the public sector.

Simultaneous to flexibilisation of the labour market, New Labour increasingly sought private sector involvement in an increased range of avenues towards education of the 'citizen', or the 'learner worker', to become accustomed to, and reproductive of, the vagaries of neoliberal capitalism in everyday life. This project had a lineage perhaps with origins in the Robbins Report of the 1960s, which gave technological institutes 'university' status, and encouraged the continued expansion of universities. A series of Teaching and Higher Education acts and education White Papers followed, which perhaps came to a head with the strong recommendations for private sector involvement in the public, as dictated within Lord Sandy Leitch's Review of Skills 2006, which is a strategy intending to transform education in the UK that would result in market liberalisation and market-led 'progress', despite claims for a demand-driven transformation in policy. The impact this would have on workers reflects growing insecurities resulting from the rolling back of the welfare state and in the context of increasing rates of hidden unemployment as depicted by Beatty et al. (2007) and dramatically rising unemployment in the contemporary economic 'credit crunch'. The present chapter is positioned from the Western view, and looks at how an Anglo-Saxon country has responded to the increase of global dependencies.

The UK looked for ways to internationalise its labour market, and as such has deployed higher education to create an army of employable subjects who would be able to participate effectively in the increasingly privatised global chains of commodity production and services. However, as Terry Wrigley (2007) states, 'capitalism needs workers who are *clever enough to be profitable, but not wise enough to know what's really going on'*.

The scenarios discussed in this book reveal a striking resemblance across hemispheres by way of their contradicting messages of *emancipation* which are simultaneously saddled with promises of *inclusion*. The overriding rhetoric of skills revolutions is contradictory in the sense that related projects do not fully take into account the impact of the full range of expectations that will be placed upon workers, which includes agilities of subjectivity. Personal availability and flexible ability to adapt to quite explicit requirements for employability is the unspoken missing dimension to the campaigns analysed. The chapter is thus a critique of the perceived forced inclusion of the inculcation of self-inventions of employability into everyday life.

The citizen

> has become a political fiction ... the externality of the citizen in relation to his own everyday life becomes a necessity projected outside of himself; in models, in fanaticisms, in ideolisations, in fetishisms. Wherever it appears, the cult of personality has a political sense and can never be reduced to a peripheral ideology; it is bound up with the nature of the State ... the externality of the citizen and his projection outside of himself in relation to his everyday life is part of that everyday life.
>
> (Lefebvre 1958/1991: 89)

The LSC worked closely with the newly formed Department for Innovation, Universities and Skills (DIUS), Jobcentre Plus, the Sector Skills Development Agency (SSDA), and the Department for Work and Pensions (DWP) to

> transform the way people think, feel and act about learning and skills ... we will achieve this ambition through a lasting, memorable and actively supported campaign which will be used and developed by everyone in Further Education.
>
> (LSC 2007)

To demonstrate these points, the first section of this chapter looks at the process of restructuring of education in the UK as part of a global hegemonic project towards the expansion of neoliberal capitalism in the sense that education is becoming a service that is no longer public, but is becoming increasingly subordinate to capital, and is thus being put under a process of liberalisation to supposed market demands. This is seen in the developing relationship between education, which was, historically, a public service, and the private sector; a relationship that imposes a managerial regime onto subjects towards 'objectification of subjectivity' in a process of governmentality that points towards what Foucault termed 'biopower', or a subordination of bodies through particular means of social regulation under conditions of domination (Beckmann and Cooper 2005).

The idea of 'employability' as discussed in the previous chapter is seen in conjunction with labour market flexibilisation, and claims that while it is presented as a one-size-fits-all escape clause from the insecurities of the market, it can also be seen as a management technique over workers' everyday lives, and for the management of any potential social unrest resulting from increased instability of the economy and the resulting ambiguities of employment, and the escalation of unemployment. The reliance on private vice that is necessary to become and remain competitive on the job market for the supposed maintenance of public virtue is encouraged by the 'Private Vices by the dextrous Management of a skilful Politician [which] may be turned into Publick Benefits' (Mandeville 1714: 369).

The second section then looks closely at the developing relationship between business and education in the UK, with an examination of the Leitch Report and requisite recommended relations between business and education. The long-awaited and highly influential Report, commissioned by the New Labour government in 2004 and published in December 2006, demonstrates that the UK significantly lagged behind other post-industrial nations in skills levels as well as productivity levels, and the report encourages a demand-led initiative to compensate. Leitch suggests various ways to restore the UK's international status in the general categories of basic skills improvement through the increase in people's aspirations and the awareness of the 'value' of skills, and the creation of an integrated employment/skills service; all with accelerated private sector relationships. The campaign, and the de facto privatisation of education, implicates a very different relationship between the citizen and the state, as well as a reformation of what is expected of workers' subjectivities as a means towards the colonisation and microregulation of workers' everyday lives. The relationship requires a 'hands-off' approach on the part of the state, but a far more 'hands-on' attitude that must become adopted and incorporated into the subjectivities of each worker and of each unemployed individual alike. These nuances contribute to the perpetuation of hegemonic struggle.

Employability of worker, flexibility of work

New Labour intended to guide the process of integrating the private sector into the public to develop and to promulgate a high skills project in response to Leitch's recent criticisms. The national Employability Skills Programme and the related 'Our Future. It's in our Hands' campaign launched in August 2007, and the deployment of the Sector Skills Councils (SSCs) seemed to offer a rosy hue of mobility and prosperity to people whether employed or not, with enormous value placed upon education. To remain employable, one must be a self-imposed, lifelong, incurable learner (Harding 2000). The incurable learner is the character sought within key skills modules at the level of Higher Education, and employability is the 'keyest of concepts'. Harding suggests a cross-university key skills module that would become implemented over a two year process; one whose implementation, she realises, could be perceived as a 'loss' or a top-down imposition onto other course designers, but she does not once question the ethics of this 'real life need' for academics to work together to put this kind of module into place. Harding talks about a range of 'unicorn' concepts, which are 'flexibility, imagination, ability to ask good questions, to hypothesise what a situation might be like under other circumstances, and all our "C" words, creativity, confidence, challenge, curiosity, connecting, and communication' (ibid.: 83–5). These skills can perhaps function as a formula that people can adopt, in order to maintain personal employability, and apparently have replaced specific job related skills and are superior to all other abilities.

'Employability' has huge resonance for the individual, and requires a productive person to also become a specific kind of citizen as well as a worker, one who is devoted to remaining a lifelong learner, or learner worker (Williams 2005).[1] While the *unemployable* were in previous eras simply seen to be people who could not work (Welshman 2006) or were generally demonised and put into various derogatory categories (Foucault 2001; Berend 2005), now, to not work, is not seen as a lifestyle or behaviour choice, or set of attitudes, in the contemporary era of competitive globalisation. On top of the skills expected for jobs obtained, workers need to acquire the right 'labour attitudes' (Worth 2003: 608).

Employers have begun to place emphasis on work ethics and soft skills like communication, to the extent that in 2006, employers cited communication skills, worth ethic, and personality as the top three desirable skills, placed above literacy, qualifications, and numeracy (CIPD 2006). Only 26 per cent of the 1400 employers surveyed in the Chartered Institute of Personnel and Development (CIPD/KPMG) quarterly *Labour Market Outlook* placed literacy and numeracy at the top of rankings. The August 2006 report indicates that UK employers emphasise soft skills over literacy and numeracy in spite of the concern regarding public examination standards in recent years. 40 per cent of employers indicated that a key attribute they seek is excellent communication skills, and 32 per cent even emphasise *personality* as a crucial factor (Phillips 2006)!

Also in 2006, the Pedagogy for Employability Group recommended a specific pedagogy that could suffuse across the entire UK higher education curriculum to teach students how to prepare themselves for the job market from day one, and that intends to 'make the links with employability [and education] explicit' (ibid.: 15). This report, prepared by the Higher Education Academy/Enhancing Student Employability Team emphasised that teaching was now not to be simply about teaching, but was to include *task design*, and should aim to work towards 'providing cognitive scaffolding to help students towards achievement currently beyond their unaided capability and progressively removing it as that capability develops', and encouraging students 'to evaluate their achievements with respect to the expectations of employers and the broader society' (ibid.: 12–13). This cognitive scaffolding encourages a straightjacket for the hegemony of the assumption of homogeneity of levels of ability to compete, through the mastering of certain supposedly universally attainable skills seen in this group's report, with the ideal type of employable subject demonstrating the following characteristics:

- Imagination/creativity
- Adaptability/flexibility
- Willingness to learn
- Independent working/autonomy
- Working in a team
- Ability to manage others
- Ability to work under pressure
- Good oral communication
- Communication in writing for varied purposes/audiences
- Numeracy
- Attention to detail
- Time management
- Assumption of responsibility and for making decisions
- Planning, coordinating, and organising ability

(Ibid.: 4)

The 'Skills Plus Project' related to the Employability group's report involved 17 University departments across the UK who tested whether 'it is possible to take a programme approach to fostering employability even in highly-modularised curricula' (ibid.: 7). This project involved strategies to create specific links between 39 'desirable characteristics' for employability and the 'fine tuned' curricula. Related to this was also the Personal Development Profile (PDP) as promoted by the QAA in 2002, which was to note 'the development of students' self-awareness' as employable subjects to the market. This was to involve 4 'broad, interlocking constructs':

- Understanding (of disciplinary material, and, more generally, of 'how the world works')
- Skilful practices in context (whether the practices are discipline-related or more generic)
- Efficacy beliefs (under which are subsumed a range of personal qualities and attributes)
- Metacognition (including the capacity for reflection, and that of self-regulation)

(Ibid.: 8)

Perhaps, if there were no economic 'question', these initiatives would look like some kind of game or time-wasting exercise for technocrats. In the UK the recent emerging debt crisis has had implications for the magnitude of the problem of rising unemployment. The average UK consumer is GBP3008 in debt compared to an average figure of GBP1558 across the rest of Western Europe. The UK is responsible for a third of all unsecured debt in Western Europe and, over the past decade, many families owning homes suffered record mortgage arrears, negative equity and a high number of repossessions. Britain's escalating personal debt crisis is exacerbated by the readings of the total figure for personal debt in Britain in June 2007 at GBP1355bn with the growth rate increasing to 10.1 per cent in the previous 12 months. Including mortgages the average household debt for the UK is GBP56,000; excluding mortgages the figure is GBP8856; and if based on households with some form of unsecured loan, the average amount is GBP20,600. Every four minutes the UK's personal debt rose by 1 million pounds in 2008 (Nouse 2008). This issue shows no sign of slowing down and is now in a situation of urgency with the imminent credit crisis.

So the CIPD's June 2008 report has resonance when it demonstrates that the economy is generating too few jobs to 'prevent the dole queue from starting to lengthen', simultaneous to continued strong growth in the number of people entering the labour market and shows that the rate of growth in employment is much slower than in preceding quarters. The finance and business sectors showed obvious signs of strain, and the CIPD's Chief Economist John Philpott stated that 'the economy is now generating too few jobs to prevent the dole queue from starting to lengthen. The finance and business services sector remains in the eye of the storm, shedding 20,000 jobs in the first quarter, and is now easily outstripping manufacturing as the principal sector experiencing job cuts. ... For the time being, however, it looks as though contract staff – the self-employed and temporary workers – are bearing the brunt of the jobs slowdown'.

How can this travesty be explained? Is it a result of market failure? Is it a problem resulting from overvaluation and manipulation of finance statistics? Is it because markets are burdened with individuals' debt? Or is it because people are simply *unemployable*? Too often, employability is used as a mediator that fails to address the extent to which deregulation and governments' willingness to allow markets to govern themselves overlooks unequal access to job markets and is merely a performance indicator that neglects to note 'how social structures such as gender, race, social class and disability interact with labour market opportunities' (Morley 2001). Generally, though, employability has increasingly become defined as the ability to adapt to flexible patterns of employment and the ability to become lifelong learners (Hillage and Pollard 1999; Tamkin and Hillage 1999).

The demands for adaptability and self-management have actually been critically deemed an 'ethic of employability' for unemployed youth (Worth 2003). This ethic is increasingly evangelised in a judgemental tone that appears to be encroaching on the lives of all age groups.

This discussion is prevalent particularly in the context of rapid shifts in internal labour market patterns. Ireland has lost more than 10,000 jobs due to outsourcing of manufacturing and service work, and has also lost 200 professional accountancy jobs to Poland. In the US, 2.1 million manufacturing jobs have been shipped overseas. McQuade and Maguire (2005) write about the impact that migration of all types of work will have on the employability of Irish nationals, and in particular the impact that this will have on its wealth of skilled and experienced manufacturing workers. People who constitute the Irish manufacturing workforce predominantly hold more higher and further education qualifications than British workers and this type of disparity may be part of the impetus for reskilling seen in the UK. Nonetheless the issue remains the same. As long as capital investors seek out the cheapest sites of production, there will be competition for low cost workers at all levels of the game, and thus pressures will be placed on workers in developed, post-industrial economies to keep afloat with all levels of competition.

Debates across Europe in the discussion towards employability, particularly in the pursuit of the common European Higher Education Area as defined by the Bologna Process, urge member nations to integrate the teaching of skills into a higher education curriculum that is not just vocationally driven, but involves 'holistic development of the individual' (Harvey and Bowers-Brown 2004). Globalisation and the rapid renewal of information and technology apparently mean that graduates must be capable of behaving with 'flexibility to operate in a changing environment ... graduate employability is not only the technical skills and competences to do the task, but, also, such endemic competences as are necessary to manage the modern labour market' (EURASHE 2003). At the 'Bologna Seminar on Employability in the Context of the Bologna Process' in 2004, a range of stakeholders were challenged to work towards incorporating a model of employability to suit social and economic changes. 'Society, the labour market and individuals demand from higher education to make a significant contribution in order to help achieving sustainable employability, including continuous self-development ... lifelong learning should be understood as a meaningful way of enhancing one's employability' (Bologna 2005).

Harvey and Bowers-Brown identify four broad areas of activity that higher education institutions have sought across Europe, for the development of students' employability:

- Enhanced or revised central support (usually via the agency of careers services) for undergraduates and graduates in their search for work. To this can be added the provision of sector-wide resources.
- Embedded attribute development in the programme of study often as the result of modifications to curricula to make attribute development, job-seeking skills, and commercial awareness explicit, or to accommodate employer inputs.
- Innovative provision of work experience opportunities within, or external to, programmes of study.
- Enabled reflection on and recording of experience, attribute development and achievement alongside academic abilities, through the development of progress files and career management programmes.

(Harvey and Bowers-Brown 2004)

These responsibilities are thus shared across various institutions and groups within society, in an increasingly coherent project towards producing employable subjects via education strategies in EU member states.

In the UK, the Committee of Vice-Chancellors and Principals as well as the Department for Education and Employment attempted to express employability in terms of 'knowledge, skills and attributes that graduates are expected to be able to demonstrate that they have acquired in higher education' (ibid.). This preceded New

Labour's modern welfare reform project within the 2007 Budget, titled 'Employment for All', which is, in effect, a modified version of Keynes' vision for full employment that promises to deliver all the 'support [that citizens] need to find, retain, and progress in work, and adapt to a benefit from a global labour market' (UK Budget 2007). New Labour's principles of welfare reform were set forward in the Budget as two related goals:

- To ensure employment opportunity for all, giving everyone the opportunity to fulfil their individual, social, and economic potential. Achieving this requires effective labour market policies set against a background of macroeconomic stability.
- To foster a world-class skills base, equipping everyone with the means to find, retain, and progress in work, and the ability to adapt to and benefit from a globalising labour market. Integrating the employment and skills agenda is central to achieving this.

These goals are underpinned by several key principles, including the relatively conservative mantra of 'rights and responsibilities', which apparently means that 'everyone should have the opportunity to work and for this to be effective, [reform] needs to be supported by access to appropriate training, information and advice ... these responsibilities on the part of the government are matched by the responsibility of individuals, where possible, to prepare for, look for and engage in work' (ibid.). So the government has adopted an eclectic blend of the human capital and work-first models, propped up with a terminology that fits with New Public Management ideas and agendas as private sector techniques begin to dominate public sector management in the name of neoliberal social progress. Labour's version of 'rights' thus became transformed to construct an outer frame of 'community' expectations and supposed needs rather than an outer frame that allows for alternative personalities/types of individuals with certain needs. Government programmes therefore are now aiming to prepare workers for international competition and have begun to focus on training people to achieve 'greater individual self-sufficiency over job stability and career advancement' (Worth 2003: 608).

In 2000, HEFCE commissioned research into teaching and learning of employability skills and its relation to graduate employment based on 34 departments in eight universities. Results demonstrated a positive association between graduate employment within six months of graduation and participation in sandwich placement during studies, or 'participation in work experience', as well as 'employer involvement in course design and delivery' (HEFCE 2003). In later years, HEFCE promised subsidies to universities proving their commitment to an employability agenda. However, tensions lie within this agenda, because 'employability' in the context here is difficult to define, to measure, to develop, and furthermore, to transfer. Thus the 'elusive quality of employability makes it a woolly concept to pin down' (Cranmer 2006: 172).

Inherent to the employability campaign is a suggestion of a kind of link towards emancipation from the drudgeries of everyday work and production. Will workers become entitled to producing 'works' rather than 'products'? Or is this campaign another feature of the ongoing survival of capitalism (Lefebvre 1973) in its invasion into people's everyday lives? Is this characteristic of the subsumption of lives to capitalism (Negri 2003)? Is this campaign in fact a criticism of life choices and of people's decisions regarding how to manage their own personal time and energies? The latter appears to be the case, considering the recommendations towards private sector involvement into education, as work becomes less and less separate from accepted definitions of 'life' and the flexibilisation of work and of people's lives.

Private sector involvement into education and skills development

The Secretary of State for Education and Skills 2005–6 grant letter written to the LSC states that 'we need a real determination to change the way training is designed and delivered to meet the priorities of employers. In the Skills Strategy, we set out the Government's intention to rebalance public and private contributions to the cost of learning, so that they better reflect the benefits and financial returns to learners and employers'. Pressure has thus been applied to both employers and public sector institutions to cultivate an environment that will facilitate a particular type of worker who, regardless of skills level, will be able to survive unstable job markets.

The case of the UK is particularly relevant in debates that look for the most appropriate ways to prepare workforces for the globalising world and for ways to navigate reskilling of a curiously underprepared labour market. As this scenario has unfolded, the SSDA, which in 2008 merged with the National Employer Panel to become the Commission for Employment and Skills, is the latest evidence of growing corporate power and strengthened networks between business and education with the intention of creating a workforce that is subject to the contemporary 'demands' of capital.

New Labour claimed that its responses to the Leitch Report, and related shifts in policy, were a 'demand side' initiative (DIUS 2007: 7) which supposedly would uproot the leftovers of the dramatically deregulated market-driven supply side, monetarist economics that were definitive of Thatcher's government. But New Labour should have been careful in its liberal use of the term 'demand side', as from 1997, its policy typically demonstrated a mixture of monetarist and Keynesian supply side aims, nicknamed the 'third way'. The only adjustment that the later set of initiatives seemed to make towards a demand side initiative was to actively invite employers and the private sector to become more involved in the articulation of the types of skill needed for its world-class skills 'ambition' (ibid.). In fact, monetarist ideas, which usually inform supply side policy, hold that the market should be free from government intervention and that private enterprise and entrepreneurialism should be encouraged. In particular these latter two ideas were embraced by New Labour, and so a dedication to demand side policy was approximate at best.

But to support claims towards a 'demand' side scheme, several institutions and programmes were established by the New Labour government to arrange the involvement of the private sector in education and skills development. These institutions were part of an 'Entrepreneurial Spirit [that] Sweeps the Nation' that the LSC News Release site declared in July 2007. Entrepreneurialism is apparently something that can be cultivated in the classroom, and the learner worker with a spirit of individualism and self-improvement ideologies would be best served by the following set of initiatives created in the supposed drive towards a demand side economy. This system is sought through the following objectives:

- Transform incentives of providers to react to employers and individuals rather than meeting supply side targets.

- Streamlining the LSC with the main role being to manage the Train to Gain programme (support to employers for training) and individual learning accounts (support to individuals for training).
- Funding should be routed through mechanisms that put effective purchasing power in the hands of the customers. [Demonstrating a] move away from funding the provider to funding the customer.

(Seex 2006)

Perhaps the most relevant institutions for the UK's contemporary skills campaign were those involved in the Skills for Business network, which was made up of the 25 SSCs. These were independent employer-led training and research organisations that also functioned as policy consultants for relevant policymakers (this type of organisation has been called a 'quango'). The SSCs were funded, supported and monitored by the SSDA, and existed solely to 'boost the productivity and profitability of the UK'. The SSDA worked to identify and tackle skills gaps on a sector by sector basis. 'In short', the Agency's website read, 'we're trying to get the right people with the right skills in the right place at the right time'.

In 2002, responsibility for the SSCs was handed over from the Department for Education and Skills to the SSDA, which worked very hard to appropriate a 'powerful role for employers in the skills agenda across the UK' (Salmon 2002). Complementary proposals, beginning in the 1990s when the Labour Party Manifesto deemed Britain's future as a 'high skill, high wage and high technology' nation (1992), included a National Investment Bank, enhanced allowances for related investment, increasing tripartite influence on economic policy, and a training revolution that was intended to contribute significantly to enhancing skill. These initiatives are indicative of the not-so-gradual shift from old labour to 'New Labour', which was originally a Labour party conference slogan used in 1994, and became definitive within the Party's manifesto 1997 rhetoric towards 'personal prosperity for all', setting the stage for the 'welfare-to-work budget', which was expected to be 'funded by a windfall levy on the excess profits of the privatised utilities, introduced in this Budget after we have consulted the regulators' (Labour Party General Election Manifesto, Dale 2002, 356). Over the following years, a range of policies were put into place to support these aims and to encourage increased partnerships between the private sector, the public sector, and the individual. In 2007, as an indication of these relationships, the *Universities UK* network boasted 131 UK university heads as members. This network highlighted 'knowledge transfer' in response to the Government's promise for an additional GBP450 million (recurrent funding) for universities' establishments of community and industry links, which would provide a 'route to innovation and development at all levels' and inspire a 'renewed drive for entrepreneurialism and wealth creation' (Universities UK 2007).

Another justification of the restructuring of education and the corresponding involvement of industry as was seen by the introduction of SSCs only requires a hearing of Lord Leitch's revelation that the UK, despite being the fifth richest economy in the world, was in danger of lagging significantly behind many of the advanced OECD nations. Productivity failure is depicted as a direct result of education and training failures (Leitch Report: 10). In this Report, the UK is ranked seventeenth on low skills, twentieth in intermediate and eleventh in high skills. The number of adults lacking functional numeracy has reached 7 million; and 5 million lack functional literacy. Skills are not just *a* driver in becoming an internationally competitive nation, but this research demonstrates that it is *the* driver and thus, the reasoning goes, education must begin to respond directly to employers. The Report demanded a tangible policy response and the Government seems to have absorbed its advice whole heartedly, as is seen in the DIUS publication *World Class Skills: Implementing the Leitch Review of Skills in England* (DIUS World Class Skills 2007).

In a formal semi-structured interview I conducted with two policy consultants at the SSDA on 9 May 2007, it became clear that the precise reason for the formation of the Agency was to garner information directly from employers as well as to put pressure on employers to train staff to prepare the labour market for contemporary changes. Perceived changes will reduce state input into telling the unemployed which skills they should have in order to go and get a job, as the SSDA, which merged with the National Employer Panel in 2008 to become the Commission for Employment and Skills, is committed to getting this information from employers. According to the two consultants, the hardest workers to recruit in late 2006 were managerial, skilled trade, and sales and customer services staff. This could be a result of inadequate training, as can be gathered from the Leitch report, or, as one employer told the CIPD, 'there's reluctance for the average British employee to change jobs ... and do things they don't particularly like. There's more willingness among Eastern Europeans to do these jobs' (Philpott and Davies 2006).

The consultants I spoke to at the SSDA also stated that some of the biggest skills gaps are in entry level jobs that do not require technical skills, such as cleaners, and hence this has been linked to immigrant labour issues. Employers are saying they are not as concerned about qualifications as they are for qualities such as attitude, punctuality, and flexibility to change job positions. Even these qualities contract themselves within their own remit. Negri discusses the temporal features of the hegemony of neoliberalism generally, whereby capitalism requires the measure of time to prevail although subjectivities require the space to expand in multiple 'times' (Negri 2003). Furthermore, the very idea of time as confined to the restrictions of punctuality seems to contradict the basis for flexibility.

One of the SSDA consultants was furthermore wary of the flexibilisation debate for reasons to do with union rights, and asserted: 'I just have one question in my mind about flexibility, which reminds me of the Thatcher years, i.e. does flexibility mean a decline in union rights? Is that where we are going with flexibility?' Or, does flexibility refer to the ambiguities of the structure of social class in the contemporary economy? Brown and Hesketh note that the way managers see employability of workers is not an exact science, but is dependent more on a managerial 'science of gut feeling', combined with applicants' reputational and social capital, associated with class and background (Brown and Hesketh 2004). This is an important claim as Western job markets become increasingly unstable, and as flexibility is becomes increasingly accepted as the norm.

A crucial question in this discussion, of course, is who is going to pay for what, and what the implications of this relationship are.[2] Employers, the government, and workers alike are expected to participate in financing European-wide campaigns towards lifelong learning, as is stated in the Report of the Employment Taskforce chaired by Wim Kok, who was commissioned by the European Council held in Brussels in 2003 to carry out research on 'employment related policy challenges and to identify practical reform measures that can have the most direct and immediate impact on the ability of Member States to implement the revised European Employment Strategy'

(European Employment Task Force 2003). In order to raise efficiency of investment in human capital, all EU Member States' governments would be required to 'lay the foundations for lifelong learning for all. Employers must take on responsibility to build employees' skills throughout their career. Individual citizens must also invest in their own futures.

The European Employment Taskforce Report (2003) goes on to make specific recommendations for each player in this recommended tripartite configuration of forces. Governments 'must lay the foundations of lifelong learning systems that are accessible to all ... a number of Member States have implemented this approach on a voluntary, compulsory or mixed basis through sectoral or regional basis'. Employers are then described as having more efficient means to provide relevant training, but the Report states, employers often do not provide this, due to the threat of poaching from other companies. This throws light on a completely contradictory element of the employability campaign, for, if workers are expected to become employable through lifelong learning, should they not also take advantage of the choices for employment that presumably will naturally open up to them? This paradox is exacerbated by the rise in temporary contracts, and employees who are successful at becoming 'employable' are surely justified in limiting their loyalty to employers who will not offer guaranteed jobs. Nonetheless, employees are told that 'individuals will need to update their competences beyond initial education to maintain their employability and enhance their career prospects throughout a more diversified working life ... individuals should therefore be encouraged to take more responsibility and participate financially in the development of their own human capital' (ibid.). So, putting these EU recommendations under scrutiny reveals that it is workers, or potential workers, who are given the most responsibility in this division of labour, and their rights seem to stop at voluntary education schemes that require student fees.

Colonisation of the everyday lives of workers is clearly occurring in this scenario, as workers are expected to embrace their own alienation from work, are told that the project of self-employability generation must become a part of their subjectivities and self worth. The 2004 UK Pre-Budget Report states in its 'Skills in the Global Economy' that 'increasingly, job security relies upon employability rather than the classical notion of a job for life, and employability depends upon acquiring the skills that employers need. More widely, having skills can enable people to contribute to their communities and to aid personal fulfilment' (HM Treasury 2004: 2). As discussed here, elite reports on employability now include notions of citizenship, of subjectivity, and of self-fulfilment: of ideas that infiltrate increasing areas of life. It was also in this 2004 report that Sandy Leitch, Chairman of the National Employment Panel and formerly Chief Executive of Zurich Financial Services, was commissioned to conduct the independent review mentioned: the Leitch Review of Skills.

Leitch criticises the UK for its low skills base and claims that 'evidence shows that around one fifth of the UK's productivity gap with countries such as France and Germany results from the relatively poor skills of workers in the UK. If the UK had similar skills levels in these countries, its national income would be significantly higher' (Leitch Report: 29). Inevitably, there has been some dispute over the research findings in this Report, which emphatically suggest that companies need to become more involved in the training of their employees to basic skills levels, with actual penalties for businesses that refuse to comply to the 'skills pledge'. London First disputes the Report's claim of low productivity in comparison with France, saying that the average French worker does *not* produce 20 per cent more gross domestic product per hour than the average UK worker, and that French labour costs are higher than the British, as well as the typical situation of lower efficiency seen in French organisations. Gordon Brown pointed out that over 10 years, the UK rose from bottom to second in the measure of GDP in G7 nations 'so overall, we are not convinced that the UK actually has the productivity problem as described by Leitch' (Kingston 2007: 9). Nonetheless, this recent research demonstrates the urgency of restructuring of education to suit business demands, and the clear transformation of expectations on workers in the new world of work.

The LSC was quick to welcome Lord Leitch's ideas for how to integrate world-class skills into Britain's workforce. The Chair of the LSC, Chris Banks, remarked that 'This is a clear rallying call and Lord Leitch has set ambitious challenges to employers, learners and to those who work with them. The LSC is in full agreement that we need to seize this opportunity and ensure that the ambitions of being world-class in skills are met'. The Council acknowledged in

December 2006, directly after the Report was published, that they condoned the recognition of programmes and services operated through the Council, such as Train to Gain, Apprenticeships, Skills for Life, and the National Employer Service. The DIUS, which was previously part of the Department for Education and Skills (DfES), responded to Leitch in July 2007 with a 75-page report titled 'World Class Skills: Implementing the Leitch Review of Skills in England'. The report condoned Leitch's recommendations and pursued 'world class ambition' in the form of specific actions to be taken in the following few years. The Departments of HM Government set out this 'Plan for England', with the DIUS as its scribe. A shift in attitudes and aspiration was needed, the report claimed, 'not only in Government, but also within workplaces, schools, colleges, universities and society itself' (DIUS 2007: 3). The plan encourages employers and individuals to make a 'major new investment of time, effort and money that far exceeds the Government's direct contribution' (ibid.: 4) in a 'demand-led' approach (ibid.: 7).

On 2 August 2007, at the direction of the Minister for Employment Caroline Flint and Under Secretary of State for Skills David Lammy, the 'Employability Skills Programme' was released. The Programme was a group initiative by the DWP, Jobcentre Plus and the LSC, and the DIUS. The DIUS made a point of working on this particular project, in order to introduce a programme specifically designed to 'help people improve their skills, find a job and progress at work'. Lammy stated that

[I]t is important that low-skilled unemployed people have access to flexible training which gives them the skills that employers value, to help them get jobs, and progress in work. The Employability Skills programme will provide this access and will be hugely important for people trapped by a lack of skills between dead-end jobs and periods of unemployment. By assessing people's needs based on their skills levels they can be given structured learning programmes tailored to their needs that help them secure sustainable employment.

(Department for Work and Pensions press release 2007)

The Employability Skills programme has been designed as a 'package of learning' that provides basic skills, paired with employability qualifications. Jobcentre Plus customers have been promised chances to:

- Enhance their employability skills
- Improve their literacy, language and numeracy skills
- Secure and sustain employment
- Ensure that their *learning journey* continues and is supported once they gain employment [my emphasis].

(Ibid.)

Another parody that demonstrates the government's commitment to this sort of policy rhetoric is the 'World Skills' competition. This event is held every two years and invites participants from 48 countries to compete in a variety of skills, which 'range from Milinery to Mechatronics and Web Design to Welding'. The event gives young participants a chance to become 'intensively trained by skilled mentors, thanks to the work of UK Skills'. The competition is immediately aligned with publicity for the 'Our Future. It's in our Hands' skills campaign initiative introduced in August 2007 as another response to Leitch:

> *It's in Our Hands* is bringing the skills debate into front rooms and gyms, canteens and workplaces and really making people sit up and take notice. And it's a mark of the Government's commitment to one of the most important issues to face UK workers and businesses. But as we all know, the campaign will depend on many different partners all pulling together to achieve the same ambitions – increasing people's confidence, their skills base, their earning power and crucially, encouraging people and employers to engage in learning.

(Smith 2007)

So Liz Smith, the Director of Unionlearn, writes that 'we all know' that this campaign depends on all of us, and on our listening and 'taking notice', whether we are having this debate in our front room, at the gym, having lunch in the canteen, or in our very workplaces. The skills campaign is only going to work if it becomes part of 'our' day to day lives, and it is our responsibility as Marxist social scientists to think carefully and critically about the impact this will have in subsumption of our lives to capitalism.

Conclusion

Is this a story wreaked in ambivalence, and simply an obvious response to the process of overaccumulation in one developed, post-industrial nation? Or, is the employability campaign in the UK part of a rising tide of projects that accompany and define the managed expansion of neoliberal capitalism? Does the rhetoric associated with imposition of entrepreneurial lifelong learning personal projects demonstrate a return to the pre-industrial craft labourer for whom Marx felt nostalgia? Or, in the context of neoliberal globalisation, does it reveal national insecurities for the future of workplaces and the labour market, resulting in an emphasis of responsibilities onto workers for self management? Does the appropriation of the craft worker, seen in government- and employer-ordained projects of workers' required 'learning', result in increased colonisation of the everyday in a scenario that requires the blending of productive man/woman with the political man/woman; and indeed, does it demonstrate a relationship of renewed alienation? Is this campaign a characteristic intention towards increased colonisation of everyday lives?

An acute paradox is found within the reams of text available which informed education policy at the direction of the New Labour government whose policy uncritically embraced EU encumbrances, and aggressively recommended a particular set of practices and duties for workers' lifelong survival in the increasingly unstable world of work. Perhaps the current rhetoric of employability reflected the state's fear of mass resistance such as was seen in the 1980s in response to Margaret Thatcher's nearly complete destruction of manufacturing. Typically, management attempts to organise production in specific ways that is thought will minimise the chance for resistance. New Labour's employability campaign, in its rational and seemingly logical promotion of education and learning as intimately linked with work, and with the resultant blurring of productive with political man/woman, is a case of colonisation of the everyday for people who continue the struggle for survival in the neoliberal capitalist world. The implication is that those individuals who are fortunate enough to find employment in a rapidly flexibilising job market would then be held directly responsible for not only their own employability project, coupled with the drive towards 'lifelong learning', but also the prosperity of their nation on the globally competitive stage.

However, this is not just an event exclusive to Britain. It has become clear that employability is an idea that has become a matter of common sense to inform policymaking across different locations globally. Respective national skills revolutions have occurred at a similar pace, and over a similar period of time. This would not have surprised Meyer et al. (1997), who note that, despite distinct histories, organisations within varying nation states appear to converge in more ways than they diverge. The objective nature of a dominant and somehow benevolent world culture would inevitably emerge from a desert island if given the chance. These sociologists admit that this world culture is a Western invention, with a limited admission for locally specific ways of expressing what they interpret to be global norms, and which these authors believe will be ultimately beneficial to all states. This claim supports a blind liberal internationalism.

Meyer is therefore not critical of related policy on the day-to-day lives of people who are most immediately impacted by any emerging convergence project. It is clear that Meyer and his colleagues celebrate convergence and assume that it will be a Western-led project, whereas more recent research demonstrates the problems of this assumption. Different nations demonstrate different approaches to projects of capitalist development, but the impact upon the most vulnerable, or workers, seems to remain the same. Harvey and Bowers-Brown (2004) have shown that while expectations placed on graduates may be similar across the world, various methods are attempted to ensure employability expectations will be met.

The implications of continued private involvement in the public sector supports a view towards continued retrenchment of a welfare state and in turn holds implications for workers and their own employment security in a country that has over time embraced a liberalisation and flexibilisation agenda with more gusto than any of its European neighbours. The SSCs in particular have been implemented with a specific intention to manage the 'failures' of education to prepare an adequate labour force to suit contemporary market demands, with direct implications for citizens/workers today. This discussion brings the research into the contemporary framework of the Leitch Report, which placed the UK in a global framework of skills development, and which challenged the government to invite the private sector to become more intimately involved with labour force preparation. What responses to the Leitch Report would mean for the development of business/education relations and for the construction of a demand-side economy is still to be seen, but the report is very critical of the perceived employability of a workforce that has been insufficiently serviced by an education system that is being dramatically and continuously restructured.

Lefebvre reminds us that the worker is a 'whole', but that 'modern industrial labour both encloses and conceals the social character of all the work done in any one firm and the total labour in society, the growing socialisation of labour and the relations of production' (1958/1991: 81). It has been claimed here that workers and the relations of production that affect their lives are most often overlooked and this must be addressed in order to give a complete picture of modernisation of institutions within the public sector in the UK and the corresponding worker preparation, 'employability' campaign. Policymakers, business figures, and union representatives in the developed West have discussed the transformation of what makes workers 'employable' after industrial revolutions have apparently given way to knowledge revolutions, and have externalised responsibility through reference to the 'global' as though space has also buried the remains of the local. At tripartite discussions between employers, unions, and government representatives, leaders have attempted to shift responsibility for workers' security in a number of ways, as is demonstrated in unprecedented training initiatives. The insecurity and limited measurability of the globalised playing field have inspired governments to shift responsibility for workers' welfare to workers themselves, by way of the explicit creation of educational environments aimed to train workers towards a new genre of individual employability or entrepreneurialism of the self, which in effect allows ongoing retrenchment of the welfare state. The danger is, as well, that this kind of state activity can been aligned with other forms of repression and the constant expansion of everyday surveillance and intrusions into everyday life such as anti-terrorism measures that begin to increasingly invade into such activities as peaceful protest.

However, Lefebvre also conjures everyday life in a depiction of 'fertile soil'. He notes that a 'landscape without flowers or magnificent woods may be depressing for the passer-by'; the landscape being a metaphor for the generally perceived view of everyday life. 'Flowers and trees should not make us forget the earth beneath, which has a secret life and a richness of its own' (ibid.: 87). This optimism may allude to the richness of possibilities for resistance to such campaigns that gradually appear to dominate the micro-regularities of workers' everyday lives and to become a hegemony of necessary subjectivities. The next chapter looks at the case studies of East Asian hegemonic projects that take a similar form: government policy towards the inculcation of particular norms and behaviour, that is being done in the context of passive revolution rather than hegemony, and will continue to create patterns of *trasformismo* unless people become aware and resistant to the employability and skills 'revolutions' I indicate.

4
Skills Revolutions in the 'East'

South Korea and Singapore are two so-called Asian Tigers, and from the 1960s to the 1990s business speculators marvelled with awe at these countries' rapid rates of economic expansion. While the late-industrialisers attracted international speculation in the 1960s and 1970s, most of the 'Third World' lagged behind and experienced stagflation after the 1980s. Yet, during the 1980s, classical economists became baffled by the continued dramatic developments of a select grouping of nations, including South Korea. Orthodox economists viewed this period of East Asian development as a vindication of free-market principles and export-led growth as a reflection of comparative advantage (Wade 1993), while other economists were wary of the free-market explanation (Amsden 1994) and took into account the high levels of government intervention in development in the region. Even *dependencia* theorists could not explain why the semi-periphery rapidly began to challenge the model of reliance across a hierarchy of states (see Worth and Moore 2009).

But the Tigers' halcyon days came to an end in 1997 when the Asia Pacific economic crisis hit. In the International Labour Organisation's 1998–9 World Employment Report (ILO WER), under- and unemployment were portrayed as the most urgent problems that the crisis triggered. Responses to the instability of the Report's years 1998–9 across East Asia were varied, but the first category of stakeholders to be targeted in episodes of economic and social crisis tends to be the workforce. Highlights of the Report indicate:

1. Some one billion workers – one third of the world's labour force – remain *un*employed or *under*employed, a figure that is

71

largely unchanged from ILO estimates contained in its 'World Employment Report 1996–7';

2. Of the one billion total, some 150 million workers are actually *unemployed*, or seeking or available for work. Of these 150 million, 10 million unemployed have been generated this year due to the financial crisis in Asia alone;

3. In addition, 25 to 30 per cent of the world's workers – or between 750 million and 900 million people – are *under*employed, i.e., either working substantially less than full-time, but wanting to work longer or earning less than a living wage;

4. The ILO estimates some 60 million young people, between the ages of 15 and 24, are in search of work but cannot find it;

5. The global unemployment and underemployment picture contained in the 1998–9 report contrasts sharply with developments expected since the last 'World Employment Report' was issued in 1996, when the ILO said that a number of encouraging signs heralded a global economic revival and would cut unemployment and underemployment worldwide.

(ILO WER 1998–9)

The case studies presented in this chapter, South Korea and Singapore, undertook both the nationally specific and the external regime responsibility routes to deal with the economic and social turmoil of the crisis. To address increased unemployment, policy and public expenditure were accompanied by internationalised links. This is a scenario in which governments have begun to pursue a demand side set of policies that are analogous to the policies in the UK discussed in the previous chapter. Governments are promoting tighter links between education and industry by creating new categories in qualifications systems; building links in the region and internationally for policy transfer and convergence as well as project cooperation and leadership. Through these activities, governments are establishing an idealised subjectivity that could be apparently embraced by people who intend to remain employable in the face of rising unemployment. This idealised picture of the employable subject would create a hegemonic force of ideas towards what this means, in an Eastern context, which demonstrates comparable characteristics to the hegemonic project I identified within the UK.

A hegemonic leadership can be defined by identifying which individuals possess the dominant, connecting ideology that binds states to societies (Gramsci 1971: 376). Ideological hegemony cannot be assumed, and should not be seen as an immutable condition, but while negative ideologies support the interests of one group in society, positive ideologies can support universal interests (Ransome 1992: 118). Gramsci holds, in contrast to Marx, that 'positive organic ideologies are legitimate' (ibid.: 129). However, Gramsci stated that 'one must distinguish between historically organic ideologies [positive], that is, which are necessary to a given structure, and ideologies that are arbitrary, rationalistic, or willed [negative]' (Gramsci 1971: 377). So in this chapter, I identify the international employability project as one that is an attempt to formulate organic citizens in the negative sense, that is, that subjects are not, unfortunately, *emancipated* by the drive towards lifelong learning, but are homogenised and integrated into a hegemonic understanding of competencies. The hegemonic project discussed here is a policy-driven discourse that merges skills with competencies and requires lifelong learning from mobile and capable subjects. People who are not capable of surviving the skills revolution are, essentially, not 'employable' in the current era of globalising capitalism.

Han (2007) states that *lifelong learning* education and training systems in Korea, Japan, Singapore, Hong Kong, Thailand, and the Philippines were propelled forward by the 1997 economic crisis and 'were geared to function as a stabiliser, if in part, for the massive structural adjustment' (ibid.: 478). Han writes that 'lifelong discourse and its implementation into real policies seem to take its shape from such chaotic contexts' (ibid.: 479). Education of the self towards a specific type of subjectivity through lifelong learning is implicated with the idea of a 'self-woven safety net' (Moore 2006) that, even so, does not appear to have a great impact on employment figures or employability.

While the employability project is an international one, it is unhelpful to claim that less developed nations or newly industrialised countries (NICs) are simply following orders from developed/advanced countries. Over time, Korea has become a remarkable mentor for lifelong learning training programmes across East and Southeast Asia. As a leader in the region, and with a unique system of managing the shift from expected lifelong employment to lifelong learning, Korea is perhaps the best candidate for the comparative case study.

Singapore is the other case study investigated here to understand how the varying models of capitalism apply similar approaches to managing workers in times of crisis. This city state has a fascinating history of external links for labour market preparation and skills development that identifies it as a leader in relevant policy in this region. The Skills Development Fund (SDF) introduced in 1984 is an explicit gesture towards subjectivity invention and attempted inculcation and reflects the 'Asian Values' recipe nicely as well. So this chapter provides case studies of education and training policy as integrated with labour policy in South Korea and Singapore, perhaps most significant in times of crisis 1997 and 2008, both of which had a fast and significant impact on the security of work forces.

Neo-Gramscian concepts allow for the analysis of the expansion of particular ideal types for relations of production through educative means and allow theorists to make the links between the concrete evidences of the transfer and power of certain ideas, as well as allowing for the significance of ongoing struggle led by social forces. In order to claim that education and training projects and specific globalising 'cultural' transformations are a form of *trasformismo*, which most often occurs within the context of passive revolution, this chapter reminds the reader that 'employability' has been explicitly transformed by a globalising class of managers and politicians.[1] I look at specific projects that Korea and Singapore have adopted towards 'skills revolutions', in which leaders attempt to restructure knowledge through an imposed cultural shift. The case studies contextualise transnational relations between VET specialists through looking at internationalised educative strategies. Employability has become based on workers' proposed competencies as well as specific and newly introduced skills that are apparently specific to the present era that relies on the transition from manufacturing economies, to knowledge and information based economies. The exact skills for learning and work have become seen as employable in the culture of the changing job market in East Asia, as employment has become increasing unstable.

While the models of capitalism that are contrasted by the cultural characteristics across these countries differ and have themselves changed over time such as South Korea's moving away from the developmental state status, Coates points out that their foundations remain the same. The trust-based and the free market liberal models contain a range of idiosyncrasies, but they are, nonetheless, both *capitalist*.

Embrace of the education/industry model in capitalist economies is seen in several locations, and as Coates observes:

> The adoption of educational solutions to economic problems ... tells us less about economic realities than political ones. For the enthusiasm for training as the solution to economic under-performance appears to be part of a general retreat ... from any attempt to control capital, or to offer a qualitatively different analysis of the sources of economic difficulties from that canvassed by neoliberal intellectuals.
>
> (Coates 2000: 120)

The time has come in IPE research to look more closely at the similarities rather than the differences between governments' approaches to crisis across the models of capitalism. The series of programmes that focus on people's employability and subjectivities through educative means are portrayed as part of a global skills revolution that is more accurately identified as part of a global passive revolution in the Gramscian sense. While it is difficult to challenge education as an answer to a crisis, it is *only one* answer and, as Coates points out, this strategy is more about political 'problems' (ibid.) than proven solutions.

This study claims that the crisis recovery period following 1997 marks decisions to enter the 'knowledge economy' with implications for the emancipation of workers. However the most evident characteristics of the Korean and Singaporean labour cultures in the decade following the 1997 crisis and into the present era demonstrate a culture wherein workers are increasingly expected to take responsibility for their own employability according to a pre-designated series of competencies and skills. In this chapter, I look at skills and employment policy in two locations in East Asia to take note of the similarities in logic for what is occurring in the 'West' as outlined in the previous chapter. Governments in South Korea and Singapore are introducing a range of employability policy measures that appear not only to appeal to people's self-understanding and subjectivities, but are also part of an attempt to manage and prevent worker unrest in times of trouble. As a case of passive revolution in both instances, it is clear that the policies are only addressing part of the issues that mass unemployment and restructuring raise in times of social unrest. This chapter looks at how two countries have worked to prepare their labour markets for the shift from industrial development to post-industrial economic growth in the case of Korea, and ongoing high value-added technological progress in the case of Singapore.

South Korea's skills revolution

As an academic researcher, I have travelled to and within South Korea several times between 1997 and 2009. My first experience of Korea was during the 1997 Asian economic crisis, and seeing the immediate social responses to this crisis impacted me enormously and inspired me to begin a career in academia within which I could write about Korea and workers and the impact of the expansion of global capitalism (see Moore 2005, 2006, 2007). Over these years, I met and spoke with Ministers of Labour, union leaders, workers affected by the crisis, researchers, factory owners and managers, and civil servants, and I was able to get very real sense of the situation faced by workers and the unemployed alike in the context of economic changes and what has often resulted in social unrest.

In 2009 I returned to Korea in July and August to update material associated with employment, education, and training policy in Korea and to gather primary data that would fill in some of the gaps in my own research since visiting in 2005 as a postdoctoral researcher funded by the Economic and Social Research Council (ESRC). In 2009, the European Studies Research Institute (ESRI) of University of Salford funded me to take a field research trip to Korea. I spent a great deal of time at the Korea Research Institute for Vocational Education and Training (KRIVET) in Seoul and interviewed several researchers there. The Korea Labour Institute (KLI) has also proven to be an excellent resource as it houses dozens of industrial relations journals as well as texts on Korean as well as many other countries' labour relations. I was also able to visit the Korea Labour Foundation (KLF) to witness recently instituted training programmes, and the

Korea International Labour Foundation (KOILAF), which is technically under the umbrella of the KLF.

KOILAF was established in 1997 by labour, management, and the government to secure national labour engagement and to build exchanges and cooperation between Korea and the international community. KOILAF publishes the *Korea Labour Review* (KLR), which is a bi-monthly periodical covering a wide range of labour issues. KOILAF was established specifically to create a dialogue between management and labour, eliminating the government's role in an unprecedented formula. In 2007, the Federation of Korean Trade Unions (FKTU) and the Korean Employers Federation launched the Foundation and since then the attempt has been to 'support labour welfare, execute joint research and survey' and so on (Jung 2009: 7).

Labour struggle has an obvious component within the research I conducted, and the background of this struggle is covered in a previous monograph (Moore 2007). During my first visit to Korea in 1997, strikes were visible nearly every day on the streets of Seoul and, interestingly, during my 2009 trip to Korea, workers declared a strike against Ssangyong Motor employers in Pyeongtaek, Gyeonggi Province. Since February 2000 the automaker, which is the smallest in Korea, had been on bankruptcy protection, and had stated that it would cut 2626 jobs, which comprised 36 per cent of the total workforce. It was also searching for a KW250 billion loan to recover. Korean law requires companies to get Union approval before laying off workers, and managers asked the Union leaders for this permission in May 2009. Several demonstrations and strikes followed. The Executive Director of KOILAF told me in an interview on 28 July 2009 at the office in Seoul that this strike would be a pivotal moment in the history of Korean labour relations, as union leaders were actually offering to hold negotiations and were not simply taking a militant approach. Nonetheless, on several occasions union members occupied the Ssonyang factory and clashed with the riot police who were deployed to deal with the situation.

History of Korean skills policy

A historical South Korea was known for having a labour surplus, limited natural resources, and a small domestic market, and this surplus of labour supply is partially acknowledged for Korea's rapid economic development. In the 1960s, vocational training was 'born' when the Vocational Training Law was enacted in 1967. Korea had decided on an 'economic development plan', and planned the formal technical and vocational education that would accompany this plan, which focussed on labour intensive light industries (Lee 2007: 24). The government created a Central Vocational Training Institute (now Incheon Polytechnic College), the Korea-Germany Busan Vocational Training Institute, and other training institutes in rural areas were established to train workers into skilled positions. These vocational programmes included apprenticeship training, apprenticeship communication training, superintendent training, and a short term programme for foreign workers. Korea's government had decided to pursue a manufacturing based economy and the heavy and chemical industries needed manpower. A law requiring companies with 500 or more employers to offer in-house training over six industries was implemented. In 1976, a Basic Act on Vocational Training was introduced when it was noted that employers often did not provide training, in spite of the law, and in the same year the Vocational Training Promotion Fund Act went into force to provide more incentives for employers. This fund was to provide a training fee and vocational training subsidies for public and private training; to support research and promotion related to vocational training and education; and to make a contribution to the Korea Vocational Training and Management Agency (Kim and Chung 2005).

Largely, the 1970s saw a restructure of South Korea's economic development model and the government decided to advocate heavy chemical industries, meaning that once again vocational and technical training was needed. In particular this was strengthened at the secondary level. Five year junior technical colleges were transformed into two year junior vocational college with the goal to offer technicians and engineers to the heavy chemical and industrial fields. This was part of the supply side, paternalist developmental state, showing a model wherein the government chose the pattern of economic development and the workforce was predominantly controlled rather than negotiated. This is evident in the education systems that were established at this time.

Over the next decade, in-house vocational training requirements declined and in 1987 standards were simplified to cut the cost to employers. Also in the 1980s, the government busily liberalised the Korean economy and put an emphasis on technology-intensive goods and lowered the requirements for tertiary education, introducing the nationwide Preliminary Examination for College Entrance. However, for 'political reasons', the government began to emphasise junior college education, higher education (HE), and created Open Universities that provide degrees for the employed. Vocational junior and secondary schools as well as in-plant trainee systems began to decline, leading to a shortage of production-based trained workers in particular in the SMEs (Lee 2007: 25). Kyonggi Technical Open College was established in 1982 and 19 polytechnic institutes were opened over time. These institutions tend to offer evening classes for employed people who want to enhance their skills levels. Corporate Universities were established later; the first was at Samsung Electronics in 2001 and allows lifelong learning for workers, as specified in the Article 21 of the Lifelong Education Law. But in the 1990s policies, such as the Two-Plus-One Programme introduced in 1994, which resembles the German dual system, were implemented to raise vocational senior secondary school enrolments and policies to generally encourage schools' links with industry. To complete the programme, students take two years of vocational education in a school and go on to do hands-on training in industry. This programme was not a success due to a lack of infrastructure but, nonetheless, 'globalisation of trade and labour markets, rapid technological development, and heightened competition' (ibid.) led to an intricate review of Korea's vocational and training systems to determine how they could supply appropriate workers for the economic situations faced.

The Employment Insurance Act was introduced in 1993 and employers with more than 70 employees were required to provide what was known as 'vocational competency development' activities for workers. The Workers Vocational Competency Development Act was signed as a direct attempt to 'secure the employment of workers, raise their social and economic status, and improve the productivity of enterprises, thus contributing to social and economic development by promoting and supporting workers' vocational competency development through their lives' (Kim and Chung 2005: 82). Kim and Chung, researchers for KRIVET, state 'the purpose of vocational training is to enhance vocational competency (knowledge, skills and attitudes) of employees or prospective employees in order to increase labour productivity' (2005: 79). It can be provided in the workplace, school, and organisations specifically designed for training, and will enhance employability of workers, raise the productivity of the company, and contribute to development of society in an economic and social manner (ibid.).

Kim and Chung note that vocational competency development training should:

1. be conducted in a systematic way throughout a worker's life taking into account the hopes, aptitude, and abilities of the individual worker;
2. be conducted in a way to respect the autonomy and creativity of the private sector and based on labour management participation and cooperation;
3. be conducted in a way to guarantee equal opportunities for workers;
4. be considered important, especially for people like the aged, the disabled, women, discharged military service personnel, the recipients under the National Basic Livelihood security act, workers in small and medium-sized enterprises, daily workers, part time workers, and dispatched workers;
5. be conducted in a way to ensure a close connection between school education prescribed by education related laws and industrial sites.

(Kim and Chung 2005: 79–82)

In 1996, the Second Educational Reform Programme was introduced, that promoted the reform of vocational education, and the 'Lifelong Vocational Education System' was born. This was designed explicitly to realise the 'Lifelong Learning Society', and it was intended to allow each individual to pursue their own talents and nurture a high level of human resources development. This meant that junior college education was expanded, and enrolment increased 11 times between 1979 and 1997. The Polytechnic College Law was implemented so that polytechnic colleges were allowed to grant Industrial Associate Degrees, and thus the Korea Foundation for Polytechnic Colleges came to be (Lee 2007: 27).

School/industry links have been encouraged since the very first moment 'vocational training' was introduced as a concept, and the juggle between HE institutions and other training colleges with industry has been ongoing and fraught. Lee notes that 'industry generally tends to be disinterested in any agenda that is not related to immediate business benefits, which effectively limits the extent of their willingness to cooperate with schools' (Lee 2007: 41). Expectations for who is going to prepare workers for the world of work continue to be pointed away from corporate responsibility as well as government except in policy terms, leading the proverbial finger to rest once again on the worker him/herself.

Korean people suffered a dramatic rise in unemployment around the time of what was to become the East Asia-wide crisis of 1997. Unemployment rose from 2.0 per cent in 1996 to 7.7 per cent in 1998 and up to 8.1 per cent in the fourth quarter of 1998 (UNDP 1999: 40). More than 3 million Korean people were unemployed in 1998 (Amnesty International 1998), which is a significant number in a country of 48 million (Deen 2003). While layoffs have not been scarce in the Korean labour force over time, the *reason* for layoffs changed as a result of the crisis. Prior to the crisis, job loss was usually attributed to national economic conditions but, following the crisis, individual workers were also blamed for not having the necessary skills and attitudes required in the new global economic landscape to either retain, or regain employment in what the government named a New Labour Culture.

President Kim De Jung, though hesitant for the first three weeks of the crisis, welcomed the IMF bailout package, complete with its requirements for restructuring labour market flexibilisation, as a strategy in part to shift focus from his government, with the complicit understanding of the IMF as an all-powerful entity. Soon Kim also agreed to locate the regional headquarters of UNESCO's International Programme on Technical and Vocational Education and Training in Seoul and set up the KRIVET in 1997. In 2000, KRIVET joined forces with UNESCO/UNEVOC to become the regional centre for curricula development in a quest for VET policy convergence across the region and with links to other 'varieties of capitalism' (Hall and Soskice 2001), which, after the crisis in particular, were quickly seen to have more advanced recipes for sustainable development than the East Asian state-led model. The government looked to education and training and investigated renewed invest-ment for rising unemployment after the 1997 crisis, and put the focus on this relationship again in 2009 as the global economic crisis advanced internationally.

The 'New Labour Culture' introduced by the Ministry of Labour (MOL) at the introduction of the Tripartite Commission was a strategy to manage industrial relations after the crisis, to get workers, the government, and management to cooperate more effectively, but after research and an interview with the Vice Director of the Korean Labour Management Co-operation Division that I held in 1999[2] I noted that this project instructed unions and management to explicitly conduct a cultural restructure and to internationalise in a way that incorrectly fetishises industrial relations in other countries. The New Labour Culture in essence required workers' strict cooperation with the government and with management, simply dressed in new clothes. 'The government's rewriting of culture demonstrates a project of leadership that aims to potentially converge a multitude of voices, and to provide limited concessions within an age of uncertainty, but ultimately is designed to circumvent workers' upheavals' (Moore 2006).

Nonetheless, the crisis marks the origins for lifelong learning policy, as 'it was not until the 1997 financial crisis that lifelong learning and national human resource development was seen in government policy demands' (Han 2007: 480). Soon after the worst impact of the crisis had been felt, in 1999 the Lifelong Education Law was introduced, and the Bureau of Lifelong Learning Promotion was set up by the MOL. The Ministry of Education (MOE) became the Ministry of Education and Human Resource Development (MOEHRD). In some ways, these changes created confusion rather than solutions because the changes were not founded in specific policy directives (interview with KRIVET researcher Dr Kwon, Young Soo, 23 July 2009). The neoliberal structural adjustments in Korea 'fundamentally changed the way in which education and the business sector were put together' (Han 2007: 480). Developmentalism and the human capital approach were abandoned, with the government intention to adopt a marketised version of human resource development that has been seen in many Asian countries, as a symbolic representation for lifelong learning to compete in the knowledge-based economy. Lifelong learning was the 'global model for education reform [that] suddenly became an important initiative for national education strategies' (ibid.).

Lifelong learning accompanies the neoliberal development of South Korea, as this model of learning is both a skill and a competency and requires self-managed and motivated competencies, according to an often unwritten set of rules. To provide people with the ability to manage one's own learning trajectories over time, schools and HE institutions alike have been trying to integrate industry into curricula for decades. In Korea, one practice of school/industry collaboration is seen in Sudo Technical High School, which requires students to study theory and 'basic practice' courses in the first two years (Lee 2007: 47). In their final year, students learn the exact practical skills they will need for a technical job, working at the job site itself. The Two-Plus-One model is the most explicitly business-facing education model, and is perhaps on the extreme side of the spectrum in this regard. Teachers take a lot of responsibility for their students' progress and visit them once a month during their practical experience year. The problems with this programme have to do with finding willing industry participants, because to complete the programme students must conduct practical training, and industries must be willing to accommodate by way of creating an educational infrastructure. Often, parents are not willing to let their children work on industrial sites and would prefer their children took classical scholarship routes. The Yonam Junior College is a post-secondary school that encourages information and telecommunications work, and its Advisory Committee for School-Industry Collaboration sends lecturers to the surrounding industries to ask specifically what their needs are and to try to collaborate as such. LG provided the equipment needed for specific training programmes in computer and electronics at this school and sometimes provides specialists actually to teach in the school.

These practices are designed to encourage students to have a founding in theory and basic knowledge about performance expectations and competencies, and then to have practical experience in their final year, and to encourage lifelong learning aptitudes from this point onward. The Lifelong Learning Company Programme is seen as good human resource development (HRD) practice, and companies who wish to hold this title must have 'achieved greater productivity, created jobs, and improved the capacity to learn, all at the same time' (Lee 2007: 78). If companies can adopt this model, then the government hopes it will not need to invest as much in

HRD and can rely on a 'people-centred business management' style (ibid.). Teaching people to deal with 'real life problems' is one of the key objectives of this programme, and the Yuhan-Kimberly model is the one that is upheld as the best. The goal of this model is to 'develop workers into knowledge workers with hands, a head and a heart'. To develop workers in this way, the household and hygiene product company Yuhan-Kimberly helps employees to become knowledge workers through paid lifelong learning training. Workers are offered a wide range of subjects, including reading, leadership, music, and English language, and the subjects are intended to help workers develop problem solving abilities. POSCO, for example, is classified as a Lifelong Learning Company, in that it offers training to help workers develop their own individual goals and to look for learning opportunities all throughout life. Training programmes are not directly related to the exact activities in the workplace and emphasise the balance between work, life, learning, and performance (Lee 2007: 97–103).

The inculcation of industry into education is now advancing in Korea in a way that will overturn any attempt to romanticise the function of education and essentially thrusts it into the invisible hand of the market. The assumption that industry will *want* to be involved is of course challenged at all stages of this project and the question of 'who is responsible' for training workers in this previous hermit kingdom continues. The Lifelong Learning Company title is just one example of how leaders are attempting to make the 'lifelong learning' idea one that is hegemonic, through teaching life skills, problem solving, cultural and artistic and other unrelated activities to apparently motivate people to feel comfortable as individuals and perhaps, realistically, unemployed individuals who will be required to go into training at all ages of life.

There has been a sharp increase in the rate of enrolment in HE since the early 1980s. In 2009, 80 per cent of upper secondary school graduates entered HE, and the number of students enrolled in colleges and universities is about 2.7 million, four times more than that of early 1980s. This situation can be interpreted as reflecting the growing demand for highly skilled workers due to the expansion of so-called knowledge intensive industries (interview with senior researcher on 20 August 2009 at KRIVET, Seoul). HE increased from

15.9 per cent enrolment in 1980 to 33.2 per cent 1990, 68.8 per cent in 1997, and 80.5 per cent in 2000.

Recent training projects are actively preparing industry employees to have what is seen to be a balanced understanding of work and life, and the Credit Bank System actually awards people for Important Intangible Cultural Skills (Chung 2003: 7). This system is directly linked with the Lifelong Learning Law of 2000. Article 2 of this Law states that 'lifelong learning refers to all forms of organised educational activities outside of formal school education; lifelong learning organisations are the corporations and parties, of which lifelong learning is the main purpose' (ibid.: 3). Formal education does not reach every citizen in Korea, despite high levels of entrance into HE, so the Credit Bank System allows people to gain credits for other types of learning, based on the following categories:

1. completing programmes and coursework accredited at education training institutions
   - national technology qualifications are introduced in this category for those who can gain credits in relevant fields;
2. self study as an alternative to a Bachelor's degree
   - accreditation of certificates of qualification
   - self-study, which is limited to those who passed level examinations or to subjects that the learner has already completed, is accepted;
3. part time registration in colleges
   - Credit Bank system allows for part time study;
4. Important Intangible Cultural Skills
   - specialists with important intangible cultural skills and apprenticeships can have their skills approved as credits, through submitting copies of certificates of their particular cultural skills or relevant certificates issued by the cultural property office. Generally students should submit a copy of the official certificates at the beginning of their application process and submit a copy of their previous educational degrees.

(Ibid.: 7–8)

Activities conducted that meet the standards of this list can be aggregated to result in a participant's obtaining of a degree. For an Associate Bachelor's Degree, one should gain 80 credits, and for a diploma 140 are required. For a three-year college degree, 120 credits must be obtained. In 1995, the Presidential Commission on Education Reform developed this idea and it was approved and launched in January 1997. The system is designed to accommodate older people and students who have left post-secondary formal education. The theory behind the Credit Bank System is that formal education was becoming increasingly exclusive and created an atmosphere of crude competition for an increasingly marginalised set of people.

While this kind of flexible credit system works well for some industries, it is questionable whether it will fully meet all aspects of industry, which was the logic for its introduction. Chung, at the International Policy Seminar on Making Lifelong Learning a Reality in 2003 presented the Credit Bank System as a system specifically oriented towards creating a workforce that can thrive in the service/ technology-based economy. Employment in manufacturing and primary sector decreased by 3.4 per cent and 24.9 per cent respectively, from 1979 to 2000, whereas the service sector employment percentage rose by 28.3 per cent in this period. The Ministry of Information and Communication (MIC) reported in 2000 that the IT industry had increased its share of the GDP by 7.2 per cent in 1991, to 22 per cent in 1999 (MIC 2001, quoted in Chung 2003: 6). Goods, services, and ideas are now the marketable commodities, and the response to this seeming fact was to once again push education and industry into a reluctant marriage. The knowledge-based economy 'requires an education system which not only permits learning throughout the lifetime of its citizens and encourages their creativity, but more importantly, is sufficiently flexible to adapt to the changing demands of a knowledge-based economy ... should take place in multiple environments: at home, at school and at work ... above all, in a continuous upgrading of skills' (Merrill Lynch and Co. 1999, quoted in Chung 2003).

Recent policy

During a series of interviews in July and August 2009, researchers at KRIVET met with me to discuss vocational training policy in Korea. I organised these meetings so that I could more fully understand the cognitive scaffolding that is being built in this nation. The semi-structured interviews held with MOL-affiliated civil servants involved tailoring my questions around each researcher's specialism and strengths in vocational and training policy research.

In this section, interviews are summarised to give the 'insider' view on training policy. Overall, my interest is in what has been done in the contemporary and predominantly post-industrial era to reform training curricula to meet workplace demands. Dr Kwon, Young Soo has a background in labour economics and researches vocational training and education policy. During our interview in July 2009 at KRIVET headquarters in Seoul, I asked Dr Kwon what should be done to reform training curricula to meet workplace demands (as this is the direction that the government has been taking, as outlined in the previous section), and I asked from his perspective what the government has done to address this issue. Dr Kwon said that there have been no systemic efforts from the government to reform training curricula for already-employed people until very recently, because principal training providers were themselves expected to take charge of preparing and developing training curricula based on the belief that the market forces will make required adjustments.

As for training curricula for the unemployed, the Korean government has funded the development of training guidelines and training standards, which can be applied to initial training, especially special training programmes for the young and college-aged unemployed, who were badly affected by the 2008 crisis. In particular, occupational training has become compulsory for unemployed youth. The Preferred Selection Occupation Training, developed in 2001–2, is a project wherein the government chooses a particular occupation and favours it by identifying compulsory training programmes. The training is mainly for unemployed youth (ages 15–29), non-higher education students, and adults. This is an initial training programme that is required of any individual wishing to enter into the 'preferred' occupation, and is an indication of the way the government has pursued a supply-side strategy. There are 209 guidelines mainly for the training programmes of manufacturing sectors/occupations.

The government has also introduced completely subsidised training programmes held over the weekends and evenings that train non-standard workers in small and medium enterprises (SMEs) into 'short term job skills' (Si 2009: 21). These courses aid with marketing, financial accounting, personnel organisation, and production management, and include foreign trade, sales, purchasing, general affairs, and quality control. This 'programme to upgrade short term job skills of SME and non-regular workers' is a concrete strategy to allow workers to remain employable, and the 'programme to support paid leave for training and hiring of substitute workers' promotes the growth potential of SMEs and encourages employers in the smaller businesses to allow workers to go on paid leave for training, and to hire substitute workers during these periods.

While the government is targeting non-standard workers and SME vocational skill development, it is still not investing as much public money into these types of programmes as 'other advanced nations' (ibid.), and the recession will probably result in a further decrease in spending. Furthermore, it is increasingly difficult to locate international agency support for training projects. The World Bank reported in 1984 that 25 per cent of its education spending was spent on VET, in 1996 3 per cent was spent this way, and in 1999 11 per cent. The World Bank supported 24 projects that either completed or began in VET since 1990, and funding that was devoted to secondary vocational schooling dropped off, but dramatic increases in informal sector training were noted. Across the board, international agencies began to recommend the movement away from the public VET to 'centre' based training and consistent use of labour market information systems. The IADB reported that in 1990 100 per cent of its loans were for education and VET, but this was for one sole loan. From 1970 to 1990 the Asia Development Bank focussed 48 per cent of its education spending on VET, and from 1991 to 2001 lending was at 14 per cent for VET. Since 1997 11 loans were made under the ADB in the broad area of VET, and this includes traditional support for VET at secondary level. Emphasis has been placed on issues such as systems building, skills development for unemployed or highly skilled workers, and the informal sector and SMEs (KRIVET 2008: 191).

At an FKTU- and KOILAF-hosted International Seminar on 'Decent Work Strategy in Employment Crisis: from Global and Local Perspectives' on 23 April 2009 in Seoul, ILO Economics Specialist Mohammed Mwamadzingo stated that:

> Although countries are making efforts to overcome the crisis through policy responses such as financial rescue measures to avoid collapse of financial system, monetary easing, fiscal stimulus packages, and currency depreciation in some countries,

analysis of 42 rescue and stimulus plans shows that countries are only focusing on infrastructure spending, tax cuts and assistance to businesses rather than employment ... unions must counter monopoly capital's desperate attempt to shift the burden of the crisis onto the people and call for a new sustainable paradigm that favours the working men and women throughout the world.

(KOILAF 2009: 22)

However, Dr Lee, Kyung Hee, also a researcher at KRIVET, told me that over the decade from 1999 to 2009 the government concentrated on investment in the information and communications technology (ICT) industry, which led to an increased demand for qualified ICT workers. The government established a graduate school for ICT workers to train the unemployed who had lost their jobs in 1998.

Dr Lee also informed me there has been significant underprovision for youths. Employment for those aged 15–29 decreased dramatically from 2004 and was less than 40 per cent in April 2009. Of course, the decrease probably also reflects growing enrolment rates for HE. There is a huge amount of so-called NEET youths, that is, 15–29 year old people who are called 'NEET' because they are not engaged in employment, education, training or caregiving. There are an estimated 230 thousand NEET youths who are inactive because they 'are just relaxing' (definition 1); and 780 thousand inactive youths those who answered 'housekeeping and/but unmarried' (definition 2). The share of NEET has increased from 2.2 per cent in 2003 to 2.6 per cent in 2007 (definition 1), and maintained around 3.0 per cent from 2003 to 2007.

To address this situation, the Korean government had applied two kinds of policies, Brain Korea 21 (BK21), and the New University for Regional Innovation (NURI) initiatives, who joined hands in 2006 with the specific intention of raising research and development competitiveness in selected universities and in selected research projects and educational fields. Han Min Gu, Chairman of the BK21/NURI states on the policy website:

In a knowledge-based society, the efficient training and management of human resources is an important issue not only directly related to, but critical to the survival of our country and people. The BK21 Project and the NURI Project are crucial players in the planning of the advancement of national power through nurturing a highly skilled workforce, as well as through the improvement of national developmental equilibrium, which are both high-priority objectives within our society, and so are national projects that are charged with the hopes and future of the Republic of Korea.

(KRF 2009)

All these initiatives are for selected universities and colleges and urge them to change their curricula to afford the industrial demand assuming that the other HE institutions may follow successful examples of those selected colleges and universities. Despite these ambitious government initiatives, Dr Lee confided in me that the direct results of these initiatives are unsatisfactory, especially with regard to the upgrading of quality in HE. There exist, of course, some cases of success, but many people are worried about the possibility of inefficient use or misuse of public money due to the lack of sophisticated monitoring systems on the activities of HE sector. Furthermore, there are concerns about bureaucratic control over the HE sector.

About 90 per cent of Vocational Colleges outside of the HE sector are private. These schools are managed by the principle of competitive market rather than public interests. Therefore, vocational colleges have insufficient information about the demand for manpower, and the type or level of skill that industry needs. There is little forecasting of the required skills that are targeted from Vocational College graduates. College curricula should be more linked with the changes to industry and the government has to build a network among stake holders such as firms, vocational school and colleges, regional government, and labour unions.

I asked Dr Kwon of KRIVET during our interview on 23 July 2009 to tell me about any moves that have been made to update and upgrade the quality of education and training systems and curricula based on skills demanded by the workplace. I asked, are companies interested in providing training, or do they expect workers to be prepared before entrance to companies? Dr Kwon's reply referred to a variety of government attempts to make colleges and universities become responsive to the demands of industry. Such policies include colleges and universities and involve specialisation policy and industrial-academic cooperation policy. They are mainly focused on the further and HE sectors and reflect a high enrolment rate for tertiary education in Korea, which was more than 80 per cent in 2009. Concerning training provided by employers, large companies were providing many and various kinds of training to their employees. In companies with more than 300 employees, 92.2 per cent were required to provide training programs in 2007, but only 32.1 per cent of the companies with 10–29 employees went on to provide training programmes. Companies with more than 1000 employees in 2009 spent about USD800 for employee training, but small and medium enterprises (SMEs), or in this case, companies with 10–29 employees spent around USD300. So, at first glance, large companies seem to be quite interested in training, whereas SMEs do not. Perhaps the main reason for such a difference in expenditure levels is not that the SMEs lack interest in training, but that SMEs are experiencing severe labour shortages due to the increasingly large wage differentials between large companies and SMEs. The differences between large companies and SMEs have increased particularly since the 1990s, and the result has been a labour market divided into small versus large companies. For example, if people work for bigger companies, and are laid off, it is very difficult to find further work.

In the late 1980s, trade unions were legalised, and Korea saw a huge explosion of organisations. At this time, automation policy was enforced, which meant that employers tended to want to employ capital over labour, and large companies were able to automate more rapidly than SMEs. Trade unions tried to defend workers in this context but negotiations often ended in struggle. As for employers' expectations of the education and training sector, almost every Korean employer complains, Dr Kwon told me, about the quality of new entrants to the labour market. For some time, they have demanded better new graduates who are prepared for the real labour market, but without any substantial contributions to address the 'mismatch' between industry and academic side. Only recently have the sectoral level round tables (sector councils) started to exchange thoughts and look for common solutions between representatives of companies and education and training sectors. Since the last economic crisis of 1997, the rise in the share of employees with previous work experience can be contrasted with the reduction in hires of completely new employees, who would in the past have been trained within financial as well as public sector companies. This reflects the fact that large companies are starting to prefer to 'buy' than to 'make', that is, they prefer to recruit experienced workers from the wider labour market than to train novice workers within the internal labour market.

I then asked, generally speaking, what are the skills most amenable for workers to survive in the current labour market? My colleague answered that the most important skill now is English proficiency. Almost every company requires test results of English skills like TOEIC, TOEFL, and so on. The other primary skill is in information technology. Finally, I asked, has the Korean government changed the way that employability and un-employability are viewed over time as a result of any market changes? My colleague confirmed my impression from other sources, that there is no clear definition of 'employability' in Korea, but that the shift from lifelong employment within a single company is being overtaken by the lifelong career or occupation that should be developed in several companies. This reflects the fact that 'the opportunity for maintaining a job within a single company until retirement' is waning, and 'it becomes inevitable to change companies just to maintain their jobs' (interview 23 July 2009, KRIVET).

In South Korea, the Lifelong Education Act in 2000 provided the basis for the employability campaign and several Lifelong Education Centres were implemented in this respect. Between 1997 and 2001, several policies reflected the government's commitment to promote higher standards of VET, including the Promotion Act of Vocational Education and Training, the Basic Qualification Act, and the Act for the Establishment of the KRIVET as discussed previously. However this has not been enough and five suggestions were given to strengthen this commitment, as follows:

1. Provision of various opportunities for lifelong learning;
2. Construction of a more flexible learning path;
3. Strengthening of transition from learning to work;
4. Active use of information and communication technology;
5. More efficient system via distribution of role for private sector.

(Ibid.)

These suggestions in effect demonstrate the role of the government as manager for workers' experience with rapid economic changes, in particular, after economic crisis.

Technical qualifications and skills

Dr Chang Uk Park, Senior Researcher at KRIVET, spoke with me at length about the technical and vocation qualifications policy over time in Korea, as he has played a major role in his capacity as advisor for the MOL. The first Three Year principle plan for reforming technical qualification was implemented in 2006 and, when preparing the plan, the MOL were very ambitious but were probably trying to do too much at once, which meant that the outcome was not as comprehensive as had been hoped. As a result, the second Three Year Plan has been organised with several suggestions for reform. In 2003, the government had tried to introduce a national qualification framework, but this project was still being organised in terms of establishing national competency standards and a although a national qualification framework (NQF) would ideally be linked to existing vocational training several changes were still needed.

Dr Park was very thorough in his description of what should be done. First, the conflicts between the MOE and the MOL should be addressed. These two bodies have several important roles in the formation of policy that is then implemented by the HRD office as well as the Korean Chamber of Commerce and Industry (KCCI). The first agency is a testing organisation funded to deal with any manpower issues, and the KCCI is a private association supported by the MOL and is responsible for giving authority to any qualification systems. A total of 19 Ministries exist in relation to creating qualifications systems, but there is confusion about what should be done and by whom.

The vocational qualification levels are set as follows:

1. Professional engineer level;
2. Engineer;
3. Technician;
4. Craftsman.

There have been battles regarding MOE and the Ministry of Science and Technology (MOST) regarding who would 'possess' the professional engineer qualification. In the 1980s, the Ministry of Science 'possessed' this top professional grade, but it has now been given to the MOE. This reflects the changes in industry from a manufacturing base to service, and it was gradually decided that since the policy of advanced countries separates professional grades from other qualifications, a professional engineer is expected to hold unique characteristics. So to get this in place, and also to address the weakness in the system for its ability to recognise prior study and learning, the professional qualification system should be changed in the following ways:

1. The qualification framework should be separated into two tracks, one that allows for students who have degrees to apply for the qualification, and one for workers based on experience.
2. Students who have been based in Vocational Training Centres should be tested for the actual experience they have. On the other hand, workers who are applying based on experience should be tested specifically within the remit of the role they had within the company.
3. The track for students should be linked to the same track followed by workers and based on a lifelong learning system, and so linked to what students are studying.

KRIVET also suggested that the MOL should change the name 'craftsman', which in particular in Korea holds a significant stigma. The term is used in a discriminating way and this should be considered seriously. Perhaps the last level of qualification should be changed to 'technician'.

Another suggestion was that the MOL should establish a far more sophisticated information system, to represent the refinement of a qualification information system. Better software and accumulation of comprehensive data would make it easier to analyse the trends seen in Qualifications, with a focus for research on practicability, applicability, and transferability. In the first half of 2009, the MOL spent USD2 million to compile data regarding how technical qualification certificates are viewed and applied by employers. This demand-driven approach is the kind of investment that Dr Park argued should happen to advance the Technical Qualification System, since there has hitherto been a lack of research data from a demand-driven perspective. The MOL has been active in encouraging the private sector to become more involved in training and has delegated authority to the Professionals Association and the Professional Testing Organisation. The reform of professional engineer systems in Korea has been approached in terms of international standards. Across the world, in the US, Canada, Germany, and so on, there are standards to become a professional engineer, creating an international forum to secure equivalence. The Korean Professional Engineers Association has a close relationship with the United States' Professional Engineering Association and they meet annually for a conference and have discussed how to recognise two countries' qualifications. The European Qualifications Framework sets good benchmarks for Korea's approach, but each country's framework should recognise nationally specific culture and history, as well as specific industries. In particular, in the context of a much-discussed Free Trade Agreement between the US and Korea, which would increase exchanges between international and Korean engineers, the MOL wants to secure the fact that testing systems are internationally comparable. The main changes would be that interview testing has not been well organised and reform would be needed. A structured interview document to comprehend better the capabilities of candidates is needed: candidates' *experience* should be tested in the interview format. In this way, candidates can be given a chance to explain their backgrounds. For two years, Dr Park assisted the Kazakhstan government in establishing a vocational system. Kazakhstan has a strong will to establish this type of system, but their approach and their philosophy towards testing is very different from Korea's. Dr Park was also involved in several other regional projects that demonstrate Korea's role as consultant and guide for neighbouring countries' skills development, giving similar types of advice to the discussions with the MOL.

Dr Sung Won met me on 27 July 2009, also at KRIVET. He told me that recently the MOL had created an in-depth report to the government with recommendations for how the government should address the 2009 crisis, titled 'Strategy for Employment and Labour Relations Key Action Plan' and presented on 24 December 2008. Since unemployment was at a four year high of 3 per cent in February 2009, the MOL put forward recommendations that were predominantly designed to provide an investment to secure employment and to support the unemployed, youth and disadvantaged groups. The self-employed running small businesses, non-regular workers, and youth (ages 15–29) were the worst hit by the 2008 global crisis. On average, 147,000 people lost their jobs per month in the first three months of

2009. It was recommended that companies across sectors should be provided a subsidy to keep workers in jobs and to provide possibilities for retraining with some kind of living stipend. The MOL also provided a career transition support service so people could potentially change careers. For the most part, however, SMEs are the benefactor of these policies, unfortunately, since the examples of layoffs in the bigger companies such as Ssangyong made it clear that restructuring and resulting unemployment as was seen in the previous crisis of 1997 was not ruled out. However an apprenticeship system has been introduced for university students who have the opportunity to go abroad and participate in these programmes. Another action that the government supports is the replacing of foreign workers with Korean workers. This action has not been politically challenged in the way that similar activities in the UK have been.

For these policies to be implemented, employment service agencies were needed, and 626 people were hired to introduce the UK model of the Individualised Action Plan method, which is a customised employment service plan for jobseekers. The Plan specifically targets disadvantaged groups such as those with lower educational attainment and lower skills or the long term unemployed. One problem with the counselling that is required for this programme to work is that there is approximately one counsellor for every 8000 unemployed/disenfranchised, whereas in the UK there is one counsellor per 384. Another programme geared towards young adults is the New Start Programme, which is a benchmark project inspired by the New Deal in the UK.

After the 1997 crisis, the government reformed and expanded its employment services, and did so again in 2005, although the crisis at that time was internal, when the MOL was told that it would potentially be absorbed into the MOE. In 2009, restructuring and expansion of employment agencies was a response to the impending crisis. The Employment Zone is another policy that specifies local areas that lack employment opportunities, or on the other hand need more employable individuals. I asked Dr Won 'has the government changed its perception of what makes workers employable, over time, and if so, how? What is the impact on education and work policy?'. Dr Won referred me to Human Resources Development, which is a consulting firm involved in international development projects since 1982 when it was established. Human Resources

Development has sent delegates to Uzbekistan, Indonesia, Sri Lanka, Bhutan, Egypt, and Sudan and led the way in helping these countries advance in terms of training policy and vocational education and training. In terms of poverty alleviation and aid for economic growth, the Korea HRD Consulting International firm set up a consortium with the Human Resources Development Service of Korea (HRDSK), formerly Korea Manpower, and has worked very closely with developing countries. Specifically, this consultancy has worked with HRDSK on the Mobile Training Unit Development Project (MTU) of Indonesia (1994–8), a project to aid disadvantaged groups in 111 isolated and rural areas in Indonesia; Institutional Development of the National Technical Training Authority (2001); and the Capacity Expansion Project of Special Professional Education of Uzbekistan (2000–1), whose objective was to develop and strengthen technical manpower training in Uzbekistan.

However, HRDSK is in charge of the development and management of training guidelines. HRDSK was originally the Korea Vocational Training and Management Agency (KOVTMA), which was an agency that was merged from different ministries' functions. In 1991, KOVTMA became the Korea Manpower Agency (KOMA), and proceeded to develop vocational training schemes into 10 Polytechnic Colleges and 22 Vocational Training Institutes. In 1998, KOMA became the HRDSK, and under this guise became the leader for lifelong learning support, and the combination of polytechnic colleges with vocational training institutes. Serving directly under the MOL, the organisation has the following functions: lifelong competency development, national qualification management, global employment services, and international cooperation. In the context of lifelong competency development, HRDSK has been involved with the support of SMEs, methods of certifying 'excellent' enterprises with regard to HRD practices, and support for a vocational training consortium for SMEs. This agency is also involved in supporting training programmes to upgrade core vocational competencies, subsidising employees' expenses throughout training, supporting vocational training for the elderly, and e-learning enhancement. Furthermore, the support for 'skills development in priority industries essential to the national economy' is directed by this agency, as well as 'support for fostering middle-class technical

manpower in the field of national growth in the engine industry'
(HRDSK 2009).

The associated technical qualifications changes, agencies and relevant policies discussed here are part of South Korea's employability
campaign. This is less of an establishment of equality for tripartite
members than a reminder to workers and management regarding
who is still in control: the Korean government and the leading
managerial class and, with strategies of *trasformismo* in place, workers are excluded from development dialogue. The next section looks
into leaders' partnerships with international forces, showing that
extensive reconsideration of Korea's VET programmes has contributed ideas for employability that are being communicated to workers within the context of an emerging knowledge-based economy.
In particular, the New Labour Culture actually requires *workers* to
change their 'culture' more so than the other players, requiring workers' commitment to a new method of learning and unprecedented
requirements for skills and abilities. The following section discusses
how international partnerships in the emerging knowledge-based
economy have affected the restructuring of ideas regarding work and
employability to incorporate skills and competencies, within the
imposed cultural shift discussed above.

Education, skills and competencies and the convergence club

In the mid-1990s, in order to accommodate the state's objectives
for globalisation, the Korean MOL began accelerating relations
with international organisations with a goal to model Korean VET
programmes to those seen within the culture of the 'convergence
club'[3] (Magariños 2001). Korean President Kim, Dae Jung (1997–2001)
reasoned that 'the ideas and the modus operandi of the industrial
society of the past will not prepare us for adaptation and
adjustment ... the time has come for us to positively transform our
consciousness to fit the coming century' (Kim, D. J. 1997: 205).
As Korean management and the government sought to mould
society to accommodate knowledge-based development, it invited
increased participation to fuse responsibility for this process.

> The knowledge society comes about through becoming a 'learning
> society'. *Everybody* (researchers, managers, workers) contributes

to that process through sharing their distinctive insights and know-how in building institutions and social systems capable of holding/memorising, mediating and continuously building new knowledge.

(Nyhan 2002: 20)

With this in mind, the Korean government also strengthened international partnerships; relations that have become to some extent stronger than international partnerships between revolutionary groups that could emerge from the network of Unions (O'Brien 2000). The strength of the increasingly established dialogue lent credibility to the Korean governments' relatively new expansion of networks with UNESCO's International Project for Technical and Vocational Education (UNEVOC). In partnership with UNEVOC and other international organisations, the MOL aimed to standardise and reform VET programmes to give them a more globally competitive edge (ROK 2001: 61–2).

UNEVOC's secretariat (2002) states that the *shifts in job knowledge and skill* open a need for vocational educators to collaborate on projects across national and regional spaces. Korea's greatest resource for development is human power, according to experts at UNESCO, but it is unrefined in its potential. The Asia Pacific coalition of UNEVOC emphasises 'innovativeness, creativity, adaptability, and self-learning' (ibid.) as the most attractive performance indicators for workers in the Knowledge Economy, and holds meetings for educators to discuss implementation. The principal strategy for training is 'entrepreneur-ship skills development' (ibid.), one of the primary components of neoliberal economic growth as entrepreneurs are often the strongest negotiators of capital and the 'brains' behind the system.

The OECD emphasises that knowledge and information as 'assets' are becoming increasingly valuable for nations to position themselves as competitive players in the global Knowledge Economy (OECD 2000: 12–13). As the value of assets has shifted from tangible to intangible, workers' supposed 'lag' in adjustment to expectations of what knowledge *is*, appears to require government led strategies to provide training that can hone capability quickly and efficiently (Leadbeater 1999: iv). The implications of a knowledge-based economy or the 'new capitalism' (ibid. 1999: 384) are that very specific types of worker knowledge and behaviour are expected for the effective utilisation of human capital for development, and that these will enhance national economies' competitiveness.

> The new capitalism, that of the Knowledge Economy, will be driven by the discovery and distribution of rival intangible goods – information and knowledge – created by largely intangible assets – human and social capital. These knowledge-intensive goods are best produced through collaboration and competition, partnerships and networks, which bring together public and private.
>
> (Ibid.: 384)

In this context, the Korean government has adjusted investment strategies, and has restructured VET programmes, requesting that workers and civil society co-operate with its incentives (ROK 2001: 12, 13).

Industry in South Korea has been changing, the 'Republic of Korea' states in one government booklet and, therefore, the government is changing investment strategies to prioritise research and development surrounding this issue. 'Until now', the booklet states, Korea has 'focused on research and development in medium-high tech industries, such as electronics, automobile, machinery and shipbuilding, in which it retains relatively high competitiveness' (ibid.: 7). 'Recently', however, the government has changed its strategic investment into 'fields of new technology, such as IT'. When the share percentage of ownership of the total market by 'foreigners', or non-Korean investors, rose from 2.24 in 1983 to at 9.11 in 1997, jumping to 18.6 per cent by late 1998 (the highest percentage since 1983)[4] the 'market' required a critical overview of the work force. This influx of foreign capital is located in the knowledge industry more predominantly than any other industry and this has created an increase in demand for skilled 'knowledge workers' (ROK 2001; Lee, K. 2001) thus changing the nature of what it means in Korea to be 'employable'.

In response to these changes in industry-specific investment, new demands have been made of the labour market, and the very concept of employability and what constituted re-employability has been quickly thrown into disarray. If workers could not keep jobs in the insecure post-crisis situation, they were expected to join VET programmes that would make them 'employable'. If workers were privileged to remain in positions of employment, they were expected to attend developmental VET programmes that would aid in their retention of 'employability'. The government's hegemonic project intended to involve workers by providing the means for workers to 'help themselves'. Yet it corresponded directly with the labour power needed to accommodate its emerging industry investment strategies.

In an interview that I held with a Senior Researcher at KRIVET in 2002, our discussions focussed on workers' situations with regard to training. We talked about how she, in her elite position as a government-funded researcher, understood the idea of 'employability'. Dr He Mi Ran stated that management had developed different expectations and needs for training than workers in the post-crisis period. Workers were expected to seek qualifications and training for lifelong learning, which would increase their mobility for job transfers and changes. Management in the restructuring scenario sought workers who could prove they had gained training in what were called 'international skills'. Dr Ran reflected on a July 2002 newspaper article about the end of the contract system for labour, which stated that the average age to leave a job had become 38. Thus workers may want to gain new skills in order to keep up with changing expectations occurring in the increasingly flexible labour market and the high rate of worker turnover.

The KRIVET researcher mentioned that people in the automobile and the computer industries were more likely to keep their jobs. However, the reasons for layoffs had changed, she stressed. During the economic crisis of 1997 many educated people lost their jobs due to external forces. Unemployment became the result of the actual *unemployability* of individuals. Unemployed workers after the economic crisis were forced to accept their own 'unemployability' in the face of new skills requirements, and enter VET programmes that teach internationally accepted knowledge and ideas for self-improvement and skills development. Cox categorises 'ideas' twofold: firstly, habits and expectations are formed by 'intersubjective meanings' and secondly, 'collective images of social order held by different groups of people' which are less inclusive than the first type (Cox 1981). Shared ideational interpretations of *employability* are neither immutable nor inevitable, and conflicting 'images of social order' can lead to a crisis of leadership. This demonstrates one of the contradictions of capitalism. While development economists claim that economic change opens up opportunities for the self-development of workers through lifelong learning, it is soon clear that only a particular type of 'learning' and thus ideational structures are advantageous in changing job markets.

Post-crisis Korean VET programmes were designed to prepare workers to take an active role in integration into certain fields of technology that are seen to require flexible workers who commit to a lifelong plan of learning in order to remain employable. Knowledge itself has thus become a commodified asset. The major changes introduced by VET programmes are in the areas of performance appraisal and payments systems, lifelong learning, and the individualisation of work. These cultural shifts are reflective of the post-Fordist age wherein modes of control over the process of work have been rewritten. In the post-Fordist production age, the stipulation for manual skills has become nearly *completely replaced* by the demand for individuals' 'knowledge' (Aronowitz and DiFazio 1994: 83). The new systems have eliminated the core methods for climbing the corporate ladder, making the process more *individually* motivated. New work styles have changed promotion and compensation techniques to fit individual performance, which was to be appraised by managers who were equally inexperienced in the new standards (Kim and Briscoe 1997).

Perhaps the two most difficult requests made by the government for labour discussed by the first Tripartite Commission in negotiation for restructuring of culture were labour flexibility, and changes to the traditional payment system towards a *performance*-based system.

> Manpower with intelligence, skills, creativity and willingness, and the knowledgeable are critical for sharpening competitive edge in the era of infinite competition. ... It is becoming increasingly important to lay a solid ground for economic recovery through remodelling corporate infrastructure and creating an atmosphere where workers of ability are valued.
>
> (KOILAF 1999b: 11)

In November 1997, just as the economy began its dangerous slide towards crisis status, the MOL took a renewed interest in vocational programmes designed to achieve the above points. The Vocational Training Promotion Act No. 5474, of 24 December 1997, began a trend by changing the titles of the VET facilities to vocational *ability development* training facilities, and the term 'vocational training' became vocational *ability development* training (MOL 1999, 2005). 'Ability', a relatively ambiguous term used repeatedly in the emerging training institutions, refers to a particular work ethic included as part of training procedures, a new priority towards a less tangible worker power than tangible skills alone. Workers were increasingly expected to assume new responsibilities and skills for the international work standard regardless of their incongruence with the past work culture in Korean corporations and businesses.

1997 marked perhaps the inaugural moment of Korea's entrance to the neoliberal global knowledge-based economy with the establishment of the UNEVOC Regional Centre in Seoul in partnership with KRIVET. At its inauguration it was declared that KRIVET/ UNEVOC is:

> ... dedicated to research on technical and vocational education and training (TVET) and human resources development (HRD), and supporting government policies to develop the vocational capacity of its citizens through TVET as part of lifelong learning.
>
> (KRIVET 2008)

At the International Conference in Seoul in 1999, UNESCO declared that it intended to strengthen the UNEVOC Network across the region and:

1. Challenge existing education and training programmes to meet the changing demands of the world of work;
2. Improve systems for education and training throughout life;
3. Reform the education and training process;
4. Promote access of special groups to technical and vocational education and training;
5. Change the role of government and social partners in technical and vocational education and training;
6. Enhance international cooperation in technical and vocational education and training.

> (KRIVET 1999)

One KOILAF publication recommends some 'basic directions' for the implementation of a performance-based wage system. Guidelines are as follows:

1. Help workers and employers to find common ground on the introduction and operation of a performance-based system;
2. Ensure that the procedures for adopting a new wage system comply with the law and any counterproductive effect is averted;
3. Induce a simplified wage system.

(KOILAF 2002: 11)

Employers and workers were encouraged to introduce a profit-sharing system wherein profits exceeding targets could be shared equally. Management was requested to run business openly and with transparency, so workers could easily identify what types of performance would be expected of them. These suggestions aimed to democratise the performance-based system that required an entirely new set of performance requirements that required individuals to take responsibility for their work and performance in the restructured economy.

Employability, competencies, and the skills revolution

After the 1997 crisis, and again in the 2009 recession, individualism and lifelong learning became seen as crucial worker qualities that are sought in the knowledge economy, and workers were expected to prepare to demonstrate those skills. Korean workers have historically not been judged according to individual performance evaluations but, as suggested above, these have become a new requirement imposed on workers in many restructured companies. Traditional Korean culture is said to be more community-oriented than individual. However, workers were expected to adopt individualistic attitudes. Korea has no time to account for cultural work styles, or for its Korean 'spirit'. Koreans will have no choice in the matter, because of 'unlimited competition around the world'.[5]

While this set-up appears to benefit education institutions and uses positive terminology, what is actually occurring in Korea does not exactly match the humanitarian initiatives and the social safety net objectives of these changes. The provision of education of particular skills capabilities that support a particular type of shared meaning reduces the risk of social instability. If this 'provision', however, is the only option for basic survival, then it is a concession, or part of a forced programme for modernisation, and thus a method of *trasformismo*.

The concept of 'skill' has begun to include not just competencies, but includes 'knowledge, thinking, understanding and motivation' (Wellington 1987: 30). Wellington writes that the term 'skill' also refers to 'social and life skills, employability skills, communication skills, attitudes to work, and preparation for life skills' (ibid.). This phenomenon has occurred to facilitate expansive neoliberal ideology. 'Understanding' and 'knowing' could become skills on a par with reading or mathematical skills, demonstrating a reformation of what would be seen as employable abilities. Workers' skills were traditionally connected to craft-based work. Mental and physical abilities were associated with direct production. Now, however, low-skilled jobs are increasingly exported to developing nations, so the answer must be to 'give' unskilled workers the skills they require, competing for a pool of skilled positions; but the definition and understanding of skill is also a moving target.

A series of skills and competencies were soon to be emphasised in the workplace. The 'X' and the 'N' generations are very individual, and a higher quality of education would be offered to the younger generation, and this was intended to distinguish the workforce of the future. Employees increasingly need to be 'creative, and they will also need to be able to adapt to rapid changes in society ... employees should be given various opportunities to study continuously in order to adopt self-directed learning methods for absorbing new information' (Lee, K. 2001: 4).

Twenty experts and officials at the KLI were brought together in 2003 to form a research team under the Qualification System Reforms Task Force (KLI 2003). The research team intended to come up with visions and innovations for the qualification system and to review changes to VET since the restructuring of 1997 and onward. The study notes the shift towards learning for life and work, which is centred on the individual and states that 'decent work underpins individuals' independence, self-respect and well-being, and, therefore, is a key to their overall quality of life' (ILO 2002: 5). The study notes that every individual has a right to VET and compares Korea to several other nations including Argentina, Bolivia, Brazil, Chile,

Germany, Guatemala, Italy, Mexico and Spain, whose national constitutions accommodate for this. This right is also acknowledged at the international level, for example in the Universal Declaration of Human Rights (1948) and the American Declaration of Human Rights and Duties of Man (1948). In the most recent phase of VET in South Korea, researchers at the KLI have decided that education is the right of citizens and is a crucial way to find access to employment, reduced likelihood of unemployment, and significant increases in life-cycle earnings.

The KLI 2003 study claims that economic, social, and technological factors cumulatively account for the growing emphasis on the individual in Korean VET, and also that production of goods and services in *any* contemporary economy has begun to rely on human, rather than physical, capital, or 'on its workers' individual and collective endowment of knowledge and skills'. The 'individual' is the new citizen of society and has been granted the central place in statements of education learning, and training objectives. So the process of formal education and training in 2003 was no longer isolated to the passing on of information but envisions a society that prioritises a scenario of 'individuals learning to learn so that they can find out for themselves' (KLI 2003). Factual knowledge itself is no longer enough, but individuals are encouraged to learn how to analyse, access, and exploit information and in turn to devise and create new knowledge. Taking charge of one's own learning and ability to learn is the only way to survive or to 'live and work in the knowledge and information society' (ibid.). VET makes individuals employable and productive and helps them escape poverty through mobility and choice. These statements, perhaps, do not sound controversial at first reading. But who decides the VET provided, and to whom? Who decided that 'individuals' were to become the primary producers in Korea?

'Individuality' was not only part of a new concept of the culture of employability, but was concretely associated with 'citizenship'. According to the EU Memorandum on Lifelong Learning, active citizenship refers to how 'people participate in all spheres of economic and social life, the chances and risks they face in trying to do so, and the extent to which they feel that they belong to, and have a fair say in, the society in which they live' (EU 2003). This incorporates ideas of participation as well as replacing ownership, similar to the ownership that is increasingly expected of nations' development (see Cammack 2001, 2002a, 2002b). *Trasformismo* as the re-articulation of workers' needs has, in the knowledge economy, renewed emphasis on individuals and ownership of work and production, but ultimately, until workers are given a say in industry investment and human resources management, the process will probably remain undemocratic.

So individuals are now expected to take responsibility for their own employability and the government has declared that VET is an important factor in this process. 'Lifelong learning' is the way in which workers can adapt to rapidly changing economies over time, and the government (ROK 2001: 42) suggested a widespread series of facilities to support and incorporate lifelong learning into the very core of Korean culture. National and regional lifelong education centres lifelong learning halls were to be developed. Libraries, self-governance centres, social welfare halls, human resources of women's halls, and citizens' centres were to be strengthened. A pilot project titled 'learning clubs for tuning local culture into lifelong learning' (ibid.) was suggested. An information network was intended to spring from this campaign and a database to organise information on professors, lecturers, and education programmes of educational institutions in relation to lifelong learning. One booklet, 'Occupational World of the Future' was proposed to offer workers access to available VET and other forms of education so that they, as citizens, could prepare themselves for new employability requirements in the knowledge economy.

In late December 2004, the Korea Employer's Federation held a survey with 88 human resources management officers. This survey discussed the potential for stable labour-management relations in 2005 (KOILAF 2004a). 61 per cent of officials indicated that they expected industrial relations to be less stable in 2005, and only 11 per cent predicted improvements. The survey also showed that the primary difficulty in resolving ongoing labour-management strife was due to 'the struggle-oriented tendency of unions (28 per cent)', 'influence from higher-level labour organizations (25 per cent)' and 'irrational laws and systems (19 per cent)'. From these most recent comments it seems as though the intentions of the new labour culture, have not been completely realised. In terms of unemployment, in October 2004, Korea suffered a three-year high, as farms and non-service industry sectors continue to dismiss workers (KOILAF 2004b).

Is this because workers have failed to become employable? Or have the issues reached new levels of magnitude?

While this supposedly new labour culture was implemented to encourage tripartite communication between involved parties, it does not appear to have promoted harmony of social dialogue within the Tripartite Commission. In 2001 at the meetings of the Third Tripartite Commission, which had been reformulated after a series of failed attempts to complete negotiations since its first meetings in 1998, leaders discussed the issue of vocational training. The government promised to 'look for ways of enhancing the efficiency of operation of systems including efforts made for stabilisation of insurance for projects of job skill development, [and] rationalisation of the system' (Tripartite Commission 2001). Management promised to cultivate an environment that would encourage workers' voluntary education and training, with the recognition that 'such education and training will form the basis of the nation's industrial competitiveness in the future' (2001). These statements demonstrate the ongoing impulse to call workers to the challenge of maintaining individual employability for the sake of their nation's sustained development. But while the government and management have been clearly represented at the Commission's meetings, unions have not enjoyed the same appearance. One of the two most prominent umbrella labour unions, the Korean Confederation of Trade Unions (KCTU), has not rejoined the Commission after withdrawal in 1999 due to members' disapproval of its decisions at the first meetings.

On Wednesday, 2 February 2005, the leader of the KCTU resigned after confrontations at a special meeting called to discuss whether this important organisation should rejoin the Tripartite Commission, despite its history of disappointment and paralysis of union representation. Mr Lee Soo-Ho sought 'agreement or disagreement' from union members but, in protest, some members poured flammable liquid on the floor. These members perhaps felt that the Union's membership of the Commission would bare a double-edged sword and will not promote worker representation, but will represent complacency towards the passive revolution of changes to the Korean 'Labour Culture'. The failure to include worker representation in restructuring and development plans, through the promotion of their employability but without inclusive and representative union involvement, demonstrates an ongoing hegemonic crisis. Several pressures have contributed to stymied relations, including the impulse to globalise and to become increasingly competitive within the knowledge economy. Nonetheless, without hegemonic resolution, attempts to locate an inclusive forum for negotiation of globalised development strategies will continue, and ideally may play a role in the formation of true democracy in this small but volatile nation.

Korean labour unions have been criticised for not addressing the issue of precariat and informal workers. As a result, unions began formally to recognise the risks involved in precarious and informal work and have become increasingly active in training projects through the newly established KLF, and the next chapter discusses how the government-led straightjacket of employability is not simply happening without union response. The FKTU and KCTU alike are participating in the projects to train unemployed, underemployed, and human resources workers across Korea, and give hope that specific social forces are responding in an explicit way to the rhetoric of employability.

Both the umbrella labour unions, the KCTU and the FKTU, declared a 'change in direction of the labour movement' (Jung 2009: 6). In 2007 the FKTU declared its Society-Reforming Labour Movement, and the KCTU declared a Social Solidarity Movement. Overall, the unions had been accused of failing to represent non-standard workers and to deal with the issues these workers face, and in the era of flexibilisation and deregulation of the labour market, the precariat and underemployed as well as informal and contracted workers represent the bulk of the workforce. The FKTU insisted in its Social Solidarity Movement that its ideology starts from the point of recognition that a labour movement for standard workers alone is simply not justifiable (Jung 2009: 9).

While infrastructure and material conditions can be restructured relatively easily according to both international and national pressures, it is not as immediately easy to 'restructure' people's skills, attitudes, and behaviour through education, or to ensure the cooperation of workers. Perhaps the remedy is a democratisation of the process of changes made to VET, through extensive consultations with workers; a much-needed area of analysis that requires exploration beyond the scope of this volume. Here, it is argued that Korean restructuring occurred within a historical period of passive revolution, within which consent from the perspective of workers was *not* evident. A lack of consent actually provides a clearing space for a rethinking of existing social relations. Power relations can only exist outside of a completely coercive relationship and, in the context of passive revolution, coercion as well as consent must be evident.

Leaders' passion to promote globalisation of this tiger knowledge economy began to alter the idea of employability itself, as though it were an immutable requirement for the transformation of an entire culture of relations. In fact, the culture of tripartite relations between management/government/worker has not actually been altered, but merely involves a worker mandate shift that places the responsibility of self-improvement into the hands of workers, saving the government from the need to fully advance a welfare-state role. In the latter case, leaders might recognise that the history of intimate state/*chaebol* relations that developed during Korea's period of dictatorship rule from 1948–92 has in essence allowed for certain sectors to develop most prominently and has thus affected the kinds of skills available from the workforce, and accommodated accordingly. Despite several active labour market policies already outlined it quickly became apparent that the levels of competency and skill did not meet market demands, and in particular the shift from a manufacturing to a post-industrial economy affected the way vocational training and industry/education links matured.

The DAC Poverty Reduction Network (POVNET) 2003–7 was a project that looked at the 'pace and pattern of growth that enhances the ability of poor people to anticipate in, contribute to and benefit from growth', and the idea that 'vocational training strengthens the qualification and functional flexibility of the workforce' (KRIVET 2008: 96–7). At the UNESCO Regional Centre Project, KRIVET International Workshop on 'Official Development Assistance and Technical Vocational Education and Training', 18 November 2008, several sessions were held to 'search for practical suggestions by donors and recipients of official development assistance (ODA); design recipient-specific action plans for improvement of the effectiveness of ODA in TVET programmes; and identify and discuss, from a global perspective, the common challenges and tasks in deploying donor-recipient collaborative networks' (ibid.: 2). At this meeting, during the presentation on POVNET, the speaker indicated that the main policy message on vocational training was 'the productivity and employability of the poor can be significantly increased with well tailored and recognised (certificated) vocational training, especially for workers in the informal economy, that builds on basic education and life skills' (ibid.: 99).

Vocational training should:

1. Address the informal economy and reach up to 95 per cent of the workers;
2. Be well tailored, that is, demand driven (stakeholder participation) and adapt to existing (informal) training;
3. Lead to recognised certificates; go beyond training events;
4. Build on basic education and life skills, which is a prerequisite for vocational training to be effective;
5. Promote entrepreneurial skills, wherein job-seekers become job-creators.

(Ibid.: 99)

However, competencies and skills are not the *same* thing, and they can be defined as follows:

Competence:
• The ability to perform activities within an occupation;
• The ability to transfer skills and knowledge to new situations within an occupational area (Fletcher 1991).

Competency:
• The specification of knowledge and skills and application of such knowledge and skills to the standards of performance required in the workplace (ANTA and DETYA 2003);
• Relevant knowledge and skills applied to the standards of performance expected in the workplace (ILO 2006).

Skills, on the other hand, can be defined as the evidences of competencies based on qualifications. Competency standards can be measured by looking at exactly what is required for effective performance in the workplace depending on the specific industry, and these standards are expressed in terms of outcomes.

'Key competencies' can be identified as follows:

1. Collecting, analysing, and organising information: the capacity to locate information, sift and sort information in order to select what is required and to present it in a useful way, and evaluate both the information itself and the sources and methods used to collect it;
2. Communication of ideas and information: the capacity to communicate effectively with others using the range of spoken, written, graphic and other non-verbal means of expression;
3. Planning and organising activities: the capacity to plan and organise one's own work activities, including making good use of time and resources, sorting out priorities, and monitoring one's own performance;
4. Working with others and in teams: the capacity to interact effectively with other people both on a one-to-one basis and in groups, including understanding and responding to the needs of a client and working effectively as a member of a team to achieve a shared goal;
5. Using mathematical ideas and techniques: the capacity to use mathematical ideas, such as number and space, and techniques such as estimation and approximation for practical purposes;
6. Solving problems: the capacity to apply problem solving strategies in purposeful ways both in situations where the problem and the solution are clearly evident and in situations requiring creative thinking and a creative approach to achieve an outcome;
7. Using technology: the capacity to apply technology, combining the physical and sensory skills needed to operate equipment with the understanding of scientific and technological principles needed to explore and adapt systems.

(Mayer Report 1992)

These competencies should allow subjects to transfer education, from the third grade in the case of South Korea, to apply the skills and knowledge acquired to the workplace, across industries and sectors.

'Key competences are competencies essential for effective participation in the emerging patterns of work and work organisation. They focus on the capacity to apply knowledge and skills in an integrated way in work situations. Key competencies are generic in that they apply to work generally rather than being specific to work in particular occupations or industries (ibid.: 5).

This idea complements the shift from repetitive tasks at low skills levels as were typical within the Fordist management structures, and 'applying key competencies encourages individuals to initiate creative insights, construct new meaning and to find new links and integrations within all workplaces and within adult life in general' (ANTA and DETYA 2005: 127). The industry shifts in worker expectation means that people are expected to:

1. Manage a broad range of activities;
2. Take greater responsibility for quality;
3. Solve problems;
4. Work with advanced technologies and work systems;
5. Develop new products;
6. Adapt products for new markets;
7. Deliver improved or new services.

(Ibid.)

Incentive structure

But in a nation with such a tumultuous history of unrest, how would workers react to drastic changes to the employment structure and labour market in South Korea? The government has quickly honed in on aspects of employment that would prove to be the most volatile during moments of crisis, and has tried to create an incentive structure to circumvent uprisings in the atmosphere of rapid change and reform. Through framing the government-required training programmes as positive incentives for personal development (in a tone of *trasformismo*), and in the post-crisis era as a means to remain or to become 'employable' after the enormous number of lay-offs, the government applied a 'strategy on the part of the dominant power to gradually co-opt elements of the opposition forces – a strategy known in Italian politics as *trasformismo*' (Cox 1999: 25). '*Trasformismo* can serve as a strategy of assimilating and domesticating potentially dangerous ideas by adjusting them to the policies of the dominant coalition and can thereby obstruct the formation of class-based organised opposition' (Cox 1983: 166–7). The Korean government sidelined potentially dissident groups by providing a social safety net taking the face of VET programmes, to appease laid-off workers who are most likely to oppose elite-led accumulation strategies.

About half of the employers surveyed in 2001 (Park et al. 2001: 144–5) stated that the most difficult item for firms in the process of employment adjustment was to convince workers of the *necessity* for employment adjustment. The following items were ranked as the second, third, and fourth most difficult things in the implementation of employment adjustment: 'consultation about the criteria to select who are to lose their jobs', 'consultation about the compensatory package for workers to be adjusted', and 'consultation about the number to be adjusted'. These were not favourable signs for the application, ease, or effectiveness of 'adjustment'. Management realised that sudden layoffs do not tend to settle easily with workers, and sought ways to appease and help prevent backlash and resistance to what they had been told was a market-driven inevitability. Employment adjustment includes attrition, 'honourable' retirement, dismissal, and 'others', which refers to spin-offs or early retirement (ibid.: 128).

Management created regulations that introduced the idea of *voluntary* participation with incentives for involvement in training schemes, which in some cases provided a rare opportunity to secure employment in the midst of the crisis. New incentives were introduced under the Employment Insurance System (EIS), a system designed to reduce the risk of job loss after the Lifetime Employment laws had been revised (KOILAF 1999c: 112). The EIS 'purports to popularise vocational training and enhance firms' competitiveness ... provides incentives such as subsidies and financial assistance to encourage individual firms to invest in the internal labour force, thereby improving labour productivity, employment stability and the firms' competitive edge in international markets' (ibid.: 58).

But the 'hottest issue' was how to encourage workers to participate voluntarily in Vocational Competency Development Programme (ibid.: 110). To encourage voluntary participation, the government offered businesses two forms of support for implementation: the subsidisation of implementation costs to employers and paid leave for training (ibid.). One KRIVET report (2000) shows that workers who do not attend offered training programmes stated that they did not do so simply out of lack of desire, and out of a resistance to requirements for attendance. The study shows that 47.4 per cent of attendees of training went due to mandate, whereas 14.9 per cent attended training programmes voluntarily. The study 'Educational and Training Program Situation in Korea' (KRIVET 2000b), shows 15.9 per cent of companies have taken part in internationalisation strategies via vocational training programmes. There are 191 new types of pro-grammes being implemented and the number of companies who now require participation in these is increasing every year. Laid-off workers were opposed to forced training programmes because of unwillingness or because of a suspicion of the limited short-term ben-efits, thus demonstrating the lack of consensus for these initiatives.

Korea's VET reform has been managed by a government that was not immediately able to consolidate hegemonic consensus or com-mon sense but led a programme of passive revolution. The Govern-ment has demonstrated that it almost completely unswervingly took unilateral charge of crisis recovery at the guidance of the IMF in 1997 and with further cooperation with international and national indus-try from 2008 as demonstrated here, demonstrating an ongoing pas-sive revolution via a series of programmes of *trasformismo* by way of the introduction of the new labour culture. This process requires an explicit requirement for workers' cooperation with management and the government, and for an adaptation to the knowledge economy VET-taught employable skills.

Lines of force?

Arguably, Korean development has been an externally led activity with significant links to FDI and international advisors and partner-ships in major organisations and membership in the OECD since 1996. But over time Korea has taken a leading role in education and training regional assistance. The Korean MOL has led assistance activ-ities by way of Developing Countries Human Resources Development (DC HRD) funded by the Asia Development Bank and the Economic Development Cooperation fund (ECDF), which is a low interest rate long-term loan fund. The agencies that were set up to participate in these activities are the Korea Chamber of Commerce, the Korea Technology Education University, HRDSK and Korea PolyTech Universities. These institutions are the driving force for national human resource development in Korea, and not only are they the leading groups within Korea but they have begun to participate in multilateral projects with APEC. Korea has been involved in devel-oping training programmes in Sudan, Vietnam, Tunisia, Guatemala, Afghanistan, Iraq, Sri Lanka, Kazakhstan, and many other countries. ODA is therefore a major part of Korea's HRD activities, indicating a shift in the power balance that is often assumed in understanding periphery/core relationships. While Korea may have been identified as a semi-periphery country, it is now taking a core role in the region through these types of activities. Specialists working for the KRIVET in Seoul, which is the regional hub for UNEVOC, have become involved in projects providing consultancy and advice for developing countries' training policy across Southeast Asia and are taking a leading role in developing skills across the region. This nation has become very influential and challenges the West to East hierarchical policy transfer view. The next section indicates that Singapore has also taken a skills-led approach to the employability campaign.

Singapore

If Singapore is to be incorporated into the study, its divergent status as a city-state, as well as its elected but authoritarian People's Action Party (PAP), must be addressed. Currently, the PAP has played a wide-ranging role in the institutional environment surrounding the Singaporean economy, and 'subscribes to a philosophy of economic liberalism, with some state controls' (Lim and Fong 1986: 8). Historically, this economy has a similar experience to the previously colonised Korea, as it was a British colony from 1819–1942, a Japanese occupied territory between 1942 and 1945, and was returned to British rule in 1945. After 1959, Singapore had a flirtation with self-governance, became part of Malaysia in 1963, and finally became its own republic in 1965.

Anti-colonial and workers' struggles were prevalent during the periods of external rule, but the PAP worked hard to build links between the British and a Malaya-Singaporean federation and, after its accession to government, it consolidated the unions into one umbrella union called the National Trades Union Congress, which is similar to Korea's FKTU for its synergy with the state. Through this entity, the PAP controls any semblance of a labour movement (ibid.; Cheng and Chang 1996: 206). But education quickly became the nonpareil of social control for the regulation of struggle (Tremewan 1994: 75).

In the mid-1980s, the PAP found itself in a crisis of authority and legitimacy and tightened its control of education in response, shifting responsibility to seemingly immutable and incontestable markets as a kind of external regime, similar to Korea's activity. Its ongoing rigorous control of labour and education in the 1980s has enabled it to 'meet the labour requirements of a high-technology economy' (ibid.: 122), but social conflict simmers below the surface. In the late 1980s, the PAP introduced a 'Shared Values' campaign that intended to promote a shared civil society/state ideology (Quah 1990). Singapore has invested heavily in preventing dissent, and imposes stringent control on any dissident behaviour that is typically discussed in hesitant terms as a 'natural tendency among human beings in general and is not a phenomenon peculiar to our PAP leaders' (Tan 2000: 101). Because the 'PAP government has been extremely successful in providing for Singaporeans in a wide variety of areas ... [it] is generally impatient or at best uncomfortable with any form of organized dissent' (ibid.). Thus I can identify traits of *trasformismo* that give a unifying logic for my choices of case studies.

Singapore is a unique case when looking at the trajectory of ideas surrounding 'employability' in that it has been occupied by international forces in both tacit and explicit ways since 1819, and this colonial relationship continues to influence the government's association of development with foreign capital. One interesting thing to note about Singapore is that it became an internationally recognised entity purely based on internationalising capitalism. In 1819, the island of Singapore was populated by just over 100 people and was led by the Sultan of Johor and the Temenggong, who was the head of 'state'. That year, the East India Company (EIC) signed an agreement with the Sultan to found a British factory in Singapore. The island quickly became an ideal port for free trade between several countries who used its lack of tariffs to carry on commerce in the region, and in 1824 it was claimed by the British. The Treaty of Friendship and Alliance was agreed between the EIC and the Sultan of Johor and the Anglo-Dutch Treaty, which consolidated British ownership of Singapore, and many prosperous Chinese merchants quickly settled there. In 1826 the EIC formed the Straits Settlement, consisting of Penang, Malacca, and Singapore, and furthered the growing trade relationship between Britain and China.

The population of Singapore was predominantly Chinese to begin with, but the Chinese were an ethnically diverse mix. Ethnic groups predominantly governed themselves internally and the EIC had very little actual control of the island. The Straits merchants became devoted to the British for commercially strategic reasons even to the extent of turning against the 'rank and file of their own countrymen' (Turnbull 1989: 55, quoted in Tremewan 2000: 7). It was from this platform of loyalties that the PAP emerged. Lee Kwan Yew, an extremely intelligent and sometimes ruthless political leader, essentially shifted the PAP ideology from Chinese elitism and nationalism to a strategic reformist mentality that opened the doors to international investment and industrial policy. This rewriting of ideologies occurred in a manner that was designed to incorporate the subaltern in a limited fashion but ultimately aims to exploit their labour and productive capabilities: a classic case of *trasformismo* in the Gramscian sense.

Since Lee Kwan Yew became elected through relatively suspect means as prime minister in 1959, this party has used myriad methods to administer Singaporean society via education and housing projects. Over a series of phases discussed below, the government directed a programme of social control that grappled with the issues of a multi-racial society in a region that is normally infatuated with homogeneity. Tremewan argues that 'the relationship between the Singapore capital-ist class, represented by the PSP-state and foreign capital, constitutes the central political alliance which maintains the economic strategy and which thus underlies the system of social control' (1994: 4).

Tremewan (1994) analyses Singapore's political economy since 1959 in a series of phases, noting the government's strategies of social control. Categories include the phase of Import-Substitution Industrialisation, 1959–65, during which time several oil compa-nies set up refineries in Singapore; to what became Export-Oriented Industrialisation 1965–78; to Singapore's so-called Second Industrial Revolution, when the PAP decided to move to technological pro-duction of a capital-intensive, higher value-added manufacturing as opposed to the labour-intensive and low-waged manufacturing of the first periods of industrialisation. A low-waged labour market could only ever be a temporary attraction for foreign investment, particularly with the rise in automated processes and regional com-petition with the other tiger economies, so the government aimed to target the supply-side of its economy and to require an alignment between education and industry.

After Singapore broke from the merger with the Federation of Malaysia in 1965, the first period of import-substitution industri-alisation merged into an export-oriented and technologically driven phase of economic growth. Driven by foreign capital, and in the context of global economic expansion, this city state seemed to know no bounds in its growth and prosperity. However the 1970s revealed a significant labour shortage in Singapore, in the face of regional competition regarding the production of similar products and surrounding countries' similarly low-cost labour. This shortage raised market wages and posed a threat to the government's growth-focussed plans. In response, the PAP cut the ribbon for a 'Second Industrial Revolution' in 1979, a period that was to propel an era of high-tech and value-added production. Competition with the surrounding NICs inspired this strategy to pursue a modernised approach to development (Choy and Yeoh 1990: 89–90). But, from 1959, all phases of political economy in this state demonstrated that 'economic strategy has always been an expression of the PAP-state's political relationship with foreign capital' (Trevenan 1994: 43).

To encourage firms to upgrade their operations technologically during the Second Industrial Revolution, the PAP transformed policy in three crucial ways. First, efficiency of labour use was encouraged by the National Wage Council. By requiring a widespread incremental wage-increase, the government expected firms to pursue automation strategies using less labour. Transference of responsibility for workers' livelihoods was inherent to this policy as it prioritised profit and complicit welfare neglect. The second policy plan was centred on capital incentives for research and development (R&D) on technological advancement. The government offered tax holidays to high-tech firms, capital investment into firms' automation and mechanisation-related projects, and accelerated depreciation allowances for related operations. Third, an awareness of an oncoming need for newly skilled workers drove the creation of a Basic Education Skills Programme, a Secondary Education (WISE) programme, and the Core Skills for Effectiveness and Change (COSEC) programme. These projects would prepare workers to adapt to learning in the workplace to meet the requirements of high-tech industry. Workers were quickly expected to 'further themselves by learning improved methods so that they are kept up to date and can cope with new adjustments and changes in the technology of their specific fields' (Choy and Yeoh 1990: 91). So perhaps in the era of the Second Industrial Revolution we begin to see the signs that employability would soon divide workers into unprecedented formations of inequality: those who would be capable of survival in rapidly changing worlds somehow independently and assisted by limited educational provisions, and those who would not be.

Singapore has been explicit and direct in its skills preparation campaign and its Skills Development Fund (SDF), starting from 1984, as well as the launch of the Manpower 21 Plan that has encouraged business/education links. The PAP did not mask its strategy to build an internationally 'employable' workforce to accommodate its development programme around knowledge intensive industries after 1985, using education as an instrument for both this preparation process and a way to consolidate class divisions. Industrialisation had put people in their places (Tremewan 1994: 79).

Despite the PAP's expectations, international investment did not come pouring into the value-added industries of technology. In a 1986 PAP document the party noted the dearth of employable subjects within its economy to satiate this second revolution. Perhaps this was the catalyst for the introduction of supply-side policy towards welfare-like programmes as multinationals gradually took interest in this burgeoning economy.

Maximising regional role by opening its doors

The fourth period of development thus occurs after 1986, at which point the government emphasised its 'regional role' in Southeast Asia. Singapore had competitively low wages after 1985 in comparison to the high wage increases in other accelerated developing nations in the area such as South Korea and Taiwan, and the assumption was that a cheap and disciplined labour force would naturally adjust to the 'needs' of foreign capital. Chua notes that the Confucian mandate of heaven, was used to excuse the government from embracing democracy and permitted elite-led, paternalist-authoritarian social order. The PAP tended to manipulate understandings of Confucianism to suit its economic development strategies. For example in the 1990s, individualism, which the government had promoted as a competitive frame of mind, was discredited and replaced with the ideal type of community and collective purposes. Steinfels (1979), however, makes a comparison between this kind of reasoning and neo-conservative American intellectuals.

In 1996, the World Competitiveness Yearbook stated that 'Singapore has created a very successful model characterised by a highly effective government ... a sound structure in finance ... and a good performance in management' (IMD 1996: 18). Singapore ranked highly in the 'competitiveness index' also available in the Yearbook, particularly for the strength of its domestic economy. Out of the 61 economies analysed, Singapore scored first for 'internationalisation', fourth for 'management' and twelfth for 'industry and technology'. Internationalisation has come about as a direct result of government intervention in creating a penetrable and 'attractive ... domestic environment which is conducive to direct foreign investment' (Low 1998: 175). In fact, Low claims that Singapore is a completely 'government-made' country, defined as 'one in which the government designs and implements policies in all areas of public policy under a mnemonic framework of social, technology, economics and politics (STEP) to ensure economic and political viability and survival' (1998: 170).

Education and skills policy

The pace of Singapore's economic growth has meant that specific demands for a skills base have changed quickly and unpredictably. Similar to the other Asian Tigers, the government has been careful to cultivate institutions within education that may be able to ameliorate such transitions. Amsden (1994) challenges development specialists to look beyond typical analyses of newly industrialised nations' getting the prices 'right' strategies, and to identify state-created institutions that have aided what appeared to be three decades of miraculous growth. The High Performing Asian Economies (HPAEs) tended to invest heavily in education, and the leading development agencies began to applaud this behaviour as an excellent long-term investment. Authors from the Inter-American Development Bank, the Economics Department of Bryn Mawr College, and the Policy Research Department of the World Bank (Birdsall et al. 1995) uphold this strategy as *the* key to sustainable growth. Education, these authors stress, has a direct effect on productivity and reduces income inequality. However, this piece from the *World Bank Economic Review* was written before the 1997 economic crisis and was perhaps overly optimistic not only in its predictions for the future of these countries but in its measurement of equality.

Ashton et al. (2002) note that the World Bank tends to encourage investment in secondary rather than higher education, because the latter can only allow private return rather than national benefit.

The World Bank seems to leave training to the market and to multinational corporations (MNCs). Middleton et al. (1993) note that it is not always straightforward to measure the effect that worker training has on economic growth, although it benefits workers themselves in several ways. The dominant argument appears to be one that relies on external factors to provide the necessary skills for labour forces.

Singapore attained self-government in 1959 and independence from the Malaysia Federation in 1965, and it soon became evident that the commerce and service sectors on their own could not provide sufficient employment for school leavers, so technical industries were promoted and industrialisation became the hoped-for mantra for Singaporeans' hearts. During the years from 1960 to 1992, the vocational education system in Singapore was restructured three times in ways that had a significant impact on the way in which training was managed and represented. In 1960, the Adult Education Board (AEB) was established, but its language and academic programmes were soon seen to have less utility, as technical skill became a new priority agenda. The plan of the PAP was to accelerate economic growth and industrialisation from the 1960s and, in turn, to propel the momentum of vocational education and to restructure education in order to cultivate a labour force that would be appropriately prepared for industrial transformation. Lee Kwan Yew had been elected in 1959 after the UK made its final exit and his vision was to transform Singapore from an island dependent on colonial forces to a powerful trading entity in a region that was soon to become highly competitive in global markets. With this in mind, Lee placed emphasis on technical training throughout the 1960s and the first vocational institute was opened in 1964. By 1972, nine vocational institutes had unfurled. Apprenticeship schemes were moved from the MOL to the Technical Education Department (TED) of the MOE, and the number of graduates increased from 324 in 1968 to over 4000 in 1972.

By 1973, Singaporean vocational training became formally separate from education, when the TED joined hands with a new Training Board titled the Industrial Training Board (ITB), which was intended to coordinate and intensify centrally managed training. Soon, however, the ITB and AEB merged to make full use of their resources and to further expand education for workers and school leavers. The Vocational and Industrial Training Board formed as a Statutory Board in 1979 and, by 1989, full time enrolment in education programmes increased to more than 17,000. In 1992, the Institute of Technical Education (ITE) marked the upgrading of vocational training to post-secondary education. Perhaps the most important event during these 30 years was the introduction of this Institute, as it seems to mark Singapore's transformation to a nation that would meet the 'needs of the global economy in the 21st century' (Law 1996: 11).

To direct the process of what Low (1998) calls economic 'integration' with as little social unrest as possible, the PAP had to justify rapid and frequent changes to the education system while maintaining social control over a racially and linguistically complex society. Education policy has been tied to the PAP's economic development initiatives, and studies of this nature have usually presumed that policy is 'determined by the requirements of the economy' (Tremewan 1994), as though there were no alternative. However, until the late 1970s, the PAP directly exacerbated racial tensions through centrally controlling education and reproduction alike, and through taking measures to educate the children of upper-class women, while encouraging working-class women to stay at work rather than have children. In the 1980s, the schooling system as well as reproduction policy were geared towards consolidating the class divide. Upper-class women were encouraged to have children, while working-class families were not, which Tremewan sees as a method to keep the gene pool clean.

> The change in schooling pattern [in the 1980s] was primarily designed to obtain the labour power of working-class women in the workplace as well as in the home and to achieve this objective without increasing the costs of education and other welfare expenditure. It was a way to cut the overall costs of reproducing the working class.
>
> (Tremewan 1994: 116)

From the 1970s and into 1980s, a shift from individual to 'collective', 'community', using 'East Asian team spirit', Confucianism-type rhetoric was used to 'privatise education' (ibid.: 126). The 1978 Goh Report concluded that the 'Education for Living' course was insufficient to instil traditional values in the young.

> [T]he more intensive exploitation of their labour involved in upgrading the economy required an ideological basis for forcing

people to stay in their social places and not seek escape ... this initiative may have been related to a corresponding move in labour relations during the same period when Lee Kuan Yew called for greater 'team spirit' among workers and urged that the Japanese system of industrial relations be followed. Since there was a labour shortage, workers were able to change jobs ... since the PAP could not legislate to force workers to stay in their jobs without undermining the whole ideology of its wage labour system, it encouraged an 'East Asian' ethic of company loyalty along with Japanese methods of intensifying work practices by means of more 'collective' work methods such as quality control circles. The government also tried to instil a higher degree of selfless obedience in the next generation of workers through its ideological formation of school students.

(Ibid.: 117)

Skills development and multinationals

Singapore has counted on MNCs not just to ensure the introduction of technological know-how but also as a direct partner to privately and publicly run educational institutions. As an entrepot from its inception, this city state attracted chemical and oil industries and, later, those of electronics, which required a value-added production base. Singapore made moves to develop its banking and finance services during the 'Great Leap Forward' and worked to prepare its relatively small labour force around these initiatives.

Ashton et al. (2002: 13) explain the implications for the role of MNCs in Singapore in the provision of managerial expertise, capital and technology.

1. Singapore's education and training system had to deliver progressively higher skills across a narrow range of industries;
2. The use of MNCs aided in a process of firm embedding into the labour force of particular necessary skills;
3. However, particular corporatio ns may seek to hone particular skills that are seen to capture particular needs rather than fulfil needs for the economies' ongoing development needs;
4. Maximum use must be made of all workers due to the nature of the small labour force.

Perhaps as a result of the situation mentioned in number 3 above, the government began to invest in supply-side policy and to become involved in skills development for the long term. In 1979, the government imposed a tax on employers that amounted to 1 per cent of each employee's remuneration and was put towards what was eventually called the SDF. Over the years, the Skills Development Levy Act was renewed to suit development initiatives, but in 1996 the Act described the reasoning for the Fund, which included (a) the promotion, development and upgrading of skills and expertise of persons preparing to join the workforce, persons in the workforce and persons rejoining the workforce (b) the retraining of retrenched persons, and (c) the provision of financial assistance by grants, loans or otherwise for the purposes of the abovementioned objects. In 2001, the Lifelong Learning Endowment Fund (Chapter 162A) was established, which was perhaps the first time the word 'employability' was used in the language.

The SDF's Objects and Application for income was towards:

1. The acquisition of skills and expertise by persons, and the development and upgrading of skills and expertise of persons, to enhance their employability;
2. The promotion of the acquisition, development and upgrading of skills and expertise to enhance the *employability* [my italics] of persons.

The Skills Development Levy Act then states that the Fund may be authorised to assist:

1. The provision of financial assistance or incentives to persons to acquire, develop or upgrade, whether in Singapore or elsewhere, skills and expertise to enhance their *employability*;
2. The research or development, whether in Singapore or elsewhere, in or of learning methods and technology to enhance the acquisition, development or upgrading of such skills and expertise;
3. The promotion of the acquisition, development, or upgrading of such skills and expertise;
4. The provision of financial assistance or incentives to persons to carry out, whether in Singapore or elsewhere, activities or programmes which are consistent with the objects of the Fund;

5. The establishment, expansion, or maintenance of facilities, whether in Singapore or elsewhere, to be used for purposes consistent with the objects of the Fund;
6. Such other purposes consistent with the objects of the Fund, whether carried out in Singapore or elsewhere, as may be prescribed.

In 1999, Mr Goh Chok Tong declared in a speech titled 'Singapore: City of Excellence – A Vision for Singapore by 1999':

> More of us will develop our own way to compensate for the high-tech influence of the computer in our work and home environment ... we will have a greater need to compensate for technology by being out in nature more often ... In high-tech info work, where we use our brainpower instead of performing physical labour, as did the factory workers of the industrial era, we will want to use our hands and bodies more in our leisure activities to balance the constant use of mental energy at work.
>
> (Tong 1999)

Singapore employability skills system

Singapore has continuously upskilled its workforce over the past few decades and explicitly invited foreign involvement in worker training since the 1980s. This city-state tends directly to link training policy with economic development by way of the SDF, which provides incentives for investors to collaborate with the state in establishing training centres across the country, with a guaranteed right to hire graduates from the training centres. The SDF initiative began in 1984, and became quickly preoccupied with 'enhancing creativity among the youth and with developing entrepreneurial risk-taking behaviour' (Kuruvilla et al. 2002). The launch of the Manpower 21 Plan in 1999 was part of Singapore's vision to become a 'Talent Capital', and to promote 'continuous learning for lifelong employability and a country where the Government, employers, unions, community organisations work in unison to achieve the country's goals' (Launch of Manpower 21 Plan Press Release). The ongoing upgrading and explicit focus on skills sets Singapore apart from the other case studies, but its focus on a subjective aptitude for personality development in conjunction with education and training of the self in relation to government policy resonates with the earlier case studies presented.

Conclusion

'The 21st century', the Korean MOL website reads: 'is the era of knowledge and information! In this era, superior human resources are the basis of individual, corporate, and national competitiveness' (MOL 2005). Vocational 'ability development' is 'preparation for productivity increase, employment stability, and a prosperous future'. The new labour culture, a framework for tripartite relational changes, was intended to reverse a history of intense labour conflict and ultimately to achieve 'superior human resources'. Simultaneously, it introduced globalisation of expectations into the workplace, introduced through 'voluntary' training programmes that employees were required to attend, in order to maintain or to rediscover individual employability in the impending knowledge economy. Has this strategy been effective, ultimately? Has the government's strategy for implementation of *trasformismo*, in the discussed 'crisis of hegemony', resolved the issues of unemployment and labour struggles that it set out to address?

The rationale in examining why VET policy over time has not fully prepared Korea for industry transformations involves the insinuation that workers are at fault for their lack of preparedness for the future of the labour culture. Crisis reform-inspired restructuring of VET in 1997, and the reforms in 2005 and 2009, are part of a MOL project that this Ministry titled the 'new labour culture', which has come about in partnerships with international organisations that advocate Korea's globalised stance. New requirements for training and workplace norms were expected to give workers the tools to adopt new forms of learning for renewed employability. In this way, post-crisis VET, that is, training to adapt to the supposed 'new labour cultures' of Korea, and of Singapore, are conceptualised as a mechanism of the concept of *trasformismo* as defined within the neo-Gramscian literature.

The labour process in these countries, similar to the case study of the UK presented in the previous chapter, includes relations between management, government, and workers; and the relationship between the nation state or, in the case of Singapore, city state, and the relationship with the wider region in a way that encourages policy convergence of specific workers' programmes designed to assist in establishing workers' employability and re-employability.

Governments' management strategies, in particular in times of crisis, are based on a hegemony-seeking formula that defines how people are expected to behave and survive during the supposedly inevitable and ongoing instability of the labour market, and I associate this with the way in which subjectivities are expected to change. Education, being the obvious place for socialisation or even social engineering (explicitly so, in the case of Singapore), has been called upon to serve as an ally for governments' strategies. Links between education and industry in a supply-driven model were usually encouraged but the demand-side model is being investigated more fully over time in both countries, which is another indication of shifting expectations for workers' subjectivities.

The next and final chapter looks for solutions to the critique I have put forward, and attempts to understand how people might be able to overcome the policy precision of the case studies presented. I look at one social enterprise project formed by Chun Soonok, sister of the well-known activist Chun Tae Il who committed suicide in 1970 outside the textiles factory where he worked in protest of the treatment he received at work. Dr Chun worked in the same factory where her brother worked, and since his death has been active in organising training programmes for women who have worked in textiles sweatshops for 20 years or more, teaching them sophisticated dressmaking skills. With help from the KLF, she has opened a factory where her clothing of the Sooda (in Korean this means 'many hands') brand is produced with the use of all natural materials. This project is an inspired activity designed to promote women's skill in a way that is not simply postured towards the market, which is the manner in which the employability rhetoric defines the self. The next chapter also identifies an independently formed project led by people who do not intend to follow the skills and employability agenda but have become creators in their own right, emerging from the emerging social force of Open Source and peer-to-peer production. I argue that nationally formulated but globally minded skills revolutions are not going to provide the tools people actually need to become lifelong learners. Those learning for life are those who cooperate rather than compete and their subjectivities are not bound by government policy.

5
Employability as Renewed Subjectivity: Sooda Korea, and Peer Production

> *The central event of the 20th century is the overthrow of matter. In technology, economics and the politics of nations, wealth in the form of physical resources is steadily declining in value and significance. The powers of the mind are everywhere ascendant over the brute force of things. This change marks a great historic divide.*
> —*Gilder et al. 1989*

So far, this text has demonstrated that government policy since the 1980s has encouraged the incarnation of a particular subject who is seen to have a set of competencies to survive in the late capitalist world of neoliberal information-driven capitalism that were not needed during the era of industrial capitalism. People are expected to reformulate individual subjectivities around a series of ideal states that allow entrepreneurialism, forms of work and personal flexibility, and the ongoing willingness to reskill and to match any foreseen or unforeseen market demands. These ideal states, on the contrary, also call for teamwork and networking skills, as well as the 'freedom to manage' that is seen in much of the new public management literature (critiqued by Hood 1991). 'Subjectivity' and subjectivation are processes that are discussed in the literature of Lacan (who wrote about 'identifications'), Althusser (vis-a-vis 'interpellation'), and Foucault (with his work on governmentality and subjectivation), but these social theorists' views on how subjects are realised do not provide a modus operandi for radical transformation. These influential theorists do not consider the agency or will of the individual. Neither do their theses look at how specific institutional processes towards the creation of particular subjects can be paralleled and compared at an increasingly global level. Government and management policy is executed with the underlying assumption that people can, and will, attend diligently at a psychological and cognitive level to what they are being told. In the contemporary context this recognition involves the imperative that technology is decreasing the need for physical labour and, as a result, people must become mentally innovative and competitively creative and, in sense, must compete with capital itself.

Gramsci's ideas on *trasformismo* and passive revolution are useful for understanding how the potentially liberating discourse on self-management and personal ownership of labour time and lifelong learning has been reviewed and reinvented, and finally reincorporated by the capitalist class into the hegemonic discourse of workers' *employability*. Management and policymakers have effectively turned what looks in principle like a language of liberation for workers, via self-management and creative innovation and the new medias for production, into a technology of control, which would in practice allow elites to make the rules for performance despite the associated assumptions that workers will manage their own career development and production, not through taking ownership of the means of production or rewriting the labour theory of value of course, but simply through remaining employable and thus subject and subordinate to 'market forces'.

In Marxist International Political Economy, the World Systems theorists (Wallerstein, Gunder Frank, Chase-Dunn, Arrighi, etc.) were some of the first to portray the world system as a social formation that can subordinate as well as incorporate all social formations (Robinson 2004: 3), and we are now experiencing an epoch of neoliberalism and the era in which the system is becoming *global*, rather than the previously defined *world* system. Robinson writes about four epochs of the histories of world systems, referring to the First Epoch as one of European expansion and mercantile and primitive accumulation; and then the competitive and classical capitalism of the industrial revolution; followed with the Third Epoch of monopoly capitalism wherein a nation state system was coupled with a single world market. The Fourth Epoch is the globalised Information Age. With the introduction of the computer, this Epoch is defined 'politically, by the collapse of twentieth century attempts at socialism, and the failure of a whole generation of Third World national liberation movements to offer an alternative to world capitalism' (Robinson 2004: 5). The label 'cognitive capitalism' is relevant for this increasingly alienating period. While there are clearly problems with the 'epoch' as a reliable and fully accurate timescale, it is clear that in a manner unprecedented, capitalism is becoming increasingly relevant to people's awareness of themselves as subjects, and workers, and in this way, capitalism encroaches on everyday lives. The expansive process includes the arenas of education and work that have been discussed in my other research (2006, 2007, 2009). Influential labour process theorists Braverman and Burawoy, as well as Gorz, Thompson, and others have made similar arguments since the 1970s, albeit without the international dimension. In the post-industrial age, capitalism works to infiltrate every aspect of lives not only within geographical spaces, but also in the very minds and subjectivities of human beings.

So perhaps the primary question of this chapter is: what exactly has happened to workers, in the neoliberal capitalist era of information and technology, at both the institutional and cognitive levels? As seen in the employability rhetoric delineated in government policy in previous chapters, workers are now expected to compete directly with capital, as the means of production becomes increasingly powerful, while during the political economy of Fordism capital was seen as an independent entity that provided a competitive environment *around* itself. Capitalism has extended its power through the dematerialisation of productive forces by eliminating the boundaries between *explicit* and *tacit* work, and through the penetration of workers' subjectivities in conjunction with often immeasurable skills. Capital has 'overcome the crisis of the Fordist model' through detaching itself from lived realities and fixed capital (Gorz 1999: 6).

The way that labour has supposedly become dematerialised is through the elimination of skill as technically and tangibly measured, and it certainly cannot be perceived as a form of fixed capital. Proprietorship over abstract skill is not easily identified. Labour power is now located within the cognitive rather than physical dimension. Post-Fordist capitalism seems to have embodied Stalin's formula: 'man is the most precious capital'. The individual is now expected not only to work, but also to valorise his/her own work, and to become a competitive entity as capital itself through the incorporation of his/her own subjectivity and lived reality in the experience of life. In this way, capitalism has overcome its own anthropological significance. Knowledge workers are expected, as the cognitive capitalists suggest, to contribute endlessly to value creation by way of personally directed lifelong learning, and mass intellectuality. Virno (2002) and the advocates of *operaismo* note that work is not just alienated from the producer in the capitalist relationship of production but, in fact, life is completely subsumed by work. The Italian 'workerists' disagreed with Gramsci's thesis on the war of position, and instead advocated direct action: the 'multitude' is a movement that will enact radical transformation and change through a configuration of subjectivities. Berardi claims that 'Gramsci's notion of the organic intellectual is ... losing its concrete reference, since it is based on the intellectuals' attachment to an ideology, while nowadays what is important is the creation of a new social sphere ... representing the social subjectivity of the "general intellect"' (Berardi 2009: 35). While this movement has differences with Gramscian theories of power, the commitment to ideas and emancipatory possibilities located within the superstructure is shared. Neo-Gramscians have given Gramsci's theories an international dimension (i.e. Cox 1987; Bieler 2000; Bieler and Morton 2006), and their work provides analyses of how ideas are made concrete, and hegemonic, and continue to prevent revolution.

Work has not been abolished as the workerists desire, although *unpaid* work in many instances has been a real issue and at times has become a means to an end, and in the case of unemployed workers it is a means to re-enter job markets, such as the case of software developers in Open Source communities (Moore and Taylor 2009). A growing population of over-qualified, highly skilled individuals now works in the internal margins, or the internal ghettos that line the side streets of the market for knowledge workers resulting from a growing lack of stable employment. As a result of the emerging impermanence of work and as knowledge becomes the new land, several contradictions have emerged. This structural violence is accompanied by a still-hegemonic idea that full time, permanent work is desirable, which endures despite the rhetoric otherwise (particularly within the 'employability' discourse in policy). As a result, assumptions of the work-based society have not disappeared, and as full time, stable positions are increasingly scarce, they have become related to social status and can dramatically affect individuals' self worth. Assumptions extend into the realm of people's abilities and skills, despite the difficulties that knowledge work poses for traditional distinctions between the objective or technical skill needed for task related work and the subjective, social capabilities, that are now increasingly measured by employers in a 'war for talent' (Brown and Hesketh 2004: 65–88).

> [N]etwork technologies cannot be reduced to instruments of oppression and casualized labour that squeeze every last drop of genuine energy and creativity out of the worker. Cooperation-enhancing technologies are not by default networked assembly lines. The Treo is not the beast. Laptops are not merely locative Wall Street furniture. Cell phones are not the pervasive enemy. Groups of protesters at the Republican convention used them to escape police tactics. But at the same token networked technologies are also not inherently linked to a deviant life style or oppositional cultural practice. Technologies define us.
>
> (Scholz 2009)

This chapter investigates projects that intend to provide a preferred alternative to the struggle for hegemony over specific ideas towards what makes an employable worker, first through looking at an innovative project occurring in South Korea that attempts to explicitly promote work-related employability through training rather than the expectation of self-managed learning. Then I review, in the context of the digital age, how the multitude and the circuit of the common are seen in the networked commons as peer-to-peer (also referred to as P2P) producers. These ecologies of cooperation, I argue, pose the most resilient threat to globalised information capitalism, through contributors' value systems and material outputs. This is an alternative model; not a model of capitalism, but a model of post-capitalism that has yet to be addressed by the literature that creates these categories (Coates 2000; Hall and Soskice 2001; Bieler 2000; Bruff 2009b). In this sense, the global passive revolution I have identified may become challenged.

Korea Labour Foundation and training for skills

On Monday 3 August 2009, Sang-tae Yeo, employment and Human Resources Development Service of Korea (HRDSK) team leader, and Dr Kim Sung Jin, Executive Director of the Korea International Labour Foundation KOILAF, met with me in Seoul to discuss the establishment of the Korea Labour Foundation (KLF). KLF is associated with KOILAF and was established to pursue an unprecedented regime for labour/employer relations through building social enterprise networks. The training sessions were designed to provide training for both union leaders and workers, and were intended to support negotiations with employers, getting more people into work within specific areas of production, in specific regional niches.

KLF was founded in 2006 by the Chamber of Commerce and Industry, the Employers' Association and the Federation of Korean Trade Unions (FKTU), through the reorganisation of KOILAF, which has existed since 1997. This Foundation was set up with a view to 'promoting an institute that practices/expands the new paradigm of labour-management relationship, conducts projects in labour-management cooperation, and brings the spontaneous role of labour-management' (KLF 2009).

Building relationships across civil society groups, KLF, in conjunction with the Ministry of Labour (MOL), offers funding to projects that will fulfil a labour market shortage or promote enterprise depending on need. There are three predominant projects organised by KLF, one in Bucheon run for labour union or HRD delegates; one in Kwang Yang to train the unemployed into steel production jobs; and another in Seoul for textile workers and in particular seamstresses. These programmes act as a mediator between workers and employers and in the latter case do not always include a trade union. The point is actively to provide training in particular for the underemployed or unemployed, at sectoral and regional levels.

In the case of the Bucheon project, the FKTU, the Bucheon Chamber of Commerce, the Employment Security Office (akin to UK Job Centres), and specialists from the local PolyTech college created a committee to discuss the HRD training programme that would be offered to union representatives from the various industries. The FKTU sent out a memorandum to recruit people from 100 subsidiaries in Bucheon, to locate more than 50 HRD representatives from taxi companies, air circulator fan companies, and so on. The representatives who are trained from each sector or industry then return to their own companies prepared to suggest specific things that would be needed to improve each case. These projects are then funded through the KLF to provide again effective training programmes in each case. In the case of the Shin Hanil fan company, one trained labour union representative suggested providing a Japanese language programme for workers due to their high levels of export to Japan. This turned out to be a positive outcome and is just one example of the impact this project is having.

The Kwan Yang training project was established in 2006 in conjunction with the Korean Confederation of Trade Unions (KCTU), Kwan Yang Steel Plan, the Suncheon General Employment Centre and the KLF, and on-the-job trainers from the local PolyTech. This project was designed to train often completely inexperienced unemployed workers from the area in welding, soldering, plumbing, mechanical assembly, and computer aided design. The process was organised at the suggestion of a running committee with representatives from the aforementioned groups and USD250,000 was granted. In general, the programme benefits the unemployed and, more specifically, those laid off due to corporate restructuring, irregular workers, and workers whose small businesses have gone bankrupt. Semi-skilled workers who were earning KW80,000 a day are seeing their wages increase to KW120,000 a day. This is an unprecedented skill-specific training project that has resulted in almost-guaranteed jobs for participants at the Kwan Yang Steel/POSCO site. The role of the KLF is partly to ensure that workers are getting the right type of training for the jobs, which the company has not been granting, and it is an example of the kinds of regionally specific needs-based, demand driven enterprise that is in itself a political gesture towards transforming labour relations in a positive way.

Another promising project that is overseen by KLF is the True Women's Labour movement, organised by the Centre in Seoul of the same name. The use of the word 'true' is an approximate translation of the Korean term 'chamae', which means 'sisters'. The project offers training in dressmaking to seamstresses who are from underprivileged backgrounds and tend to be middle-aged as well as uneducated, who learn from entrepreneurs in Dongdemeun, a textile-heavy district of Seoul. The nine-person committee is made up of representatives from the True Women's Labour Centre, Dongdemeun

Merchants Association, the Seoul General Employment Centre, and other specialists from the PolyTech who are versed in women's employment, and researchers who have related expertise. The committee recommended to KLF that it would need USD200,000 for the project, and have so far trained 110 women into positions of higher skill in their industry. Women's garments are shown at fashion shows with the brand Sooda, and are also sold in one InsaDong store. Chun, Soonok is the sister of Chun Tae Il, who is well known for having protested and tragically incinerated himself outside a textiles plant during the disputes in 1970. Dr Chun worked at the Peace Market as a machinist when her brother also worked there and then committed suicide to protest the abominable working conditions. This amazing woman met with me in the summer of 2009 in Seoul to show me the Sooda sites of production and sales of the dresses and other garments created in ethical labs, and to discuss her work and how she is challenging the dominant paradigms of thought that control corporate/employee relationships. We visited her Sooda Academy and Sooda Factory. At the Sooda Gallery I was interviewed by Korean Broadcasting System journalists, who were there to create a documentary on the project in August 2009.

Dr Chun and I discussed the projects she has been running for many years and the work she is doing to combat sweatshop labour. Women who are involved in the training and then production activities have usually been working in the sweatshop industry for 20 years or more and have the basic skills for dressmaking that emphasise speed over quality. The projects teach quality over quantity and high skills, and allow women to become acquainted with the craft that is dressmaking. All women involved in the Sooda project have worked for the most part exclusively in sweatshops, which has prevented them from gaining skills beyond working quickly. The projects are an innovative method to combat underemployment and to demonstrate alternatives to sweatshop labour. As Mr Yeo who is also involved with the Sooda Factory, commented, 'these projects are about survival, you have to learn how to be employable'.

Machines, Marxism, and work

The invention and development of the computer is perhaps the most significant event of the twentieth and early twenty-first centuries, as it has transformed the way we interact, behave towards one another, and work. The media ecology of cyberspace has an impact on our understanding of the relationship between technology and people and results in a new 'perspective', one of 'contact at a distance' (Virilio 2005: 24). Characteristic of our present age is the almost universal embrace of the idea that technology is completely transforming our worlds and is the answer to most if not all of society's problems. 'Cybernetics is presented as the genie that, once liberated from the bottle, will possess the powers of an old time elixir, it can cure virtually any disease' (Aronowitz 2005: 133). The downside of this for people, however, is the scenario in which employers decide that employing labour is too much of a cost, and thus 'install a computer: watch heads roll and the bottom line soar' (ibid.). While technology should present alternatives and efficiencies, automation is the external affect of this historical explosion of events and is now a real and present danger.

On the other hand, there is a danger of technological determinism when considering our new world of work. Marx did not only resign all power to the machine but in fact saw empowerment through the machine, and his depiction of the general intellect in the *Grundrisse* is often forgotten. In 1858, in the section 'Fragment on Machines', as it has become known, within the *Grundrisse*, Marx takes a remarkable and almost prophetic position on the power of human intellect not only to invent fixed capital, but also to invent fixed capital that then becomes a 'direct force of production': a metaphor that becomes literal in the context of technology and the development of the computer. Our ability to create a machine that can then recreate our selves is both terrifying and empowering: 'The development of fixed capital indicates to what degree general social knowledge has become a direct force of production, and to what degree, hence, the conditions of the process of social life itself have come under the control of the general intellect and been transformed in accordance with it' (Marx 1858/1972: 143). Virno relates Marx's idea to Rousseau's *volonté générale*; to a 'materialist echo' of the Nous Poietikos, and the separate and impersonal 'active mind' that Aristotle pondered in De Anima. Labour time is the measure for value in most of Marx's work (seen in his 'law of value'), but as the production process becomes mechanised and automated, labour time is difficult to measure. Still, however, capital seeks to 'use labour time as the measuring rod for the giant social forces thereby created' (ibid.). But the pivotal shift in our era of cognitive capitalism is that the owners of the means of production are not as clearly defined. Thus, the subjectivity as well as social status of the capitalist him/herself can be challenged.

This chapter, with the general intellect in mind, challenges the idea of *one hegemonic subjectivity*, that is, the proscribed ideal type of 'subjectivity' that I have given substantial empirical data to identify (Moore 2009). This subjectivity is a fantasy that fuels substantial chunks of government policy, but it is not hegemonic, it exists within the context of a global passive revolution, because there is substantial evidence of 'fighting back', and a wholesale rejection of the ideas that are required to perpetuate capitalism. This chapter brings my argument into the wider contemporary context of a globalised knowledge-based economy for understanding subjectivities in the context of work and the measure of work in conjunction with the development of work emerging from the technology industries.

A relatively new political economic movement, the peer-to-peer production movement, originates in the computerised movement of free software and the Hackerspace community. This social movement is composed of a radical contingent of people who are committed to going beyond the strictures of capitalist production processes and of overcoming the measures of value that have controlled the employability (and thus subjectivity) discourse until now. While government-led employability and skills campaigns have created a specific ideal type of the seemingly employable worker, the peer production campaign identifies a model of interactivity that offers an alternative ecology for production to capitalism and one in which people are seen to be free to individually and/or collaboratively and cooperatively identify subjectivity, or subjectivities, or even intersubjectivities, that are not confined to the straightjacket of competition and profit-driven action and the associated values these activities require. Increasingly, networked computing has been used by the capitalist to centralize information and to attempt to devalue labour capital, and what we are seeing is a militarised global state monopolisation as states continue to gain on-average profit, while populations become poorer overall. Peer production can better manage these efficiencies and profit losses with use of an integrated platform better able to coordinate activities as well as information. Furthermore, people within these communities are interested in not only owning the means of production, but also driving tangible change to their own productivity and work. While other aspects of my work puts subjectivities into the context of the models of capitalism (Coates 2000), I argue that what we are seeing is the emergence of a peer-to-peer model of *post*-capitalist production.

Capitalists have realised that to capture surplus value from workers in the contemporary context of knowledge-based, information-driven economies, workplace-specific training for specific jobs and provision of a range of training programmes for specific tasks at work are not competitive or profitable moves. While Fordism and paternalist mass production were models that integrated all aspects of training and work and welfare, labour during the information age is apparently propelled by innovation and creativity. The perceived freedom that is required for ingenuity and resourcefulness seems to excuse employers from providing protections and safety nets for workers and their work (that is, in cases where *employers* exist). I do not romanticise the age of Fordism, but since the 1970s and the Treaty of Detroit, which also marks the launch of neoliberalism and paternalism without compensation, workers have been increasingly thrown into a flexibilised playing field for jobs, and protections against job loss and job insecurity have been all but eliminated.

While apprenticeships in the traditional sense still exist in a handful of craft professions, for the wider workforce training is increasingly rare. Not only could training suppress the innovation supposedly needed to drive the production of new technologies foreword but, in fact, the savvy profit-driven employer is aware that too much training, and in particular training en masse, can actually have results that would be detrimental to his/her profit incentive. Training could provide the physical space for the inculcation of what is considered in Marxist literature to be subjectivity in the sense of class consciousness, possible solidarity, and the resulting possibilities for uprisings and resistance. Social theorists including Hardt and Negri, Boutang, Lazzarato, Berardi, and Virno discuss the new technologies of appropriation of work as an immaterial and conceptual activity. The extraction of surplus value from work in the creative industries as well as any employment relationship that is defined and built on technologies is a new and unique category of exploitation that is interestingly also less bounded to the Fordist piece-rate work structures of management. However it is argued here that the creative and networked industries may be the space for creating post-capitalist ecologies of production and even societies that are built on tenets that contradict and challenge the very basis of capitalism.[1]

So far, postmodern and post-Marxist authors are usually those credited for looking at formulations of subjectivity as a recipe for emancipation, and as a recovery from the failures of the Enlightenment. While Marxist literature looks at the exploitation of subjects by the capitalist formula for property ownership that necessitates a profit-driven incentive also linked to individualism, it is committed to the final collapse of capitalism for exploitative relationships to be overcome and for the proletariat to gain class consciousness and then to take control of the means of production and so on. However, post-Marxist literatures and activists are also interested in how these relationships can be overcome, and do so through looking at multiplicities of narratives and interests. The friendship of Marxism and postmodernism is fraught, but scholars have much to learn from one another. While postmodern theorists look at the subject as being disciplined through bio-power and self-management, Marxists look at the human as *becoming* capital. Dissolution of the value-form of labour is the only way to dissolve capitalism, and this requires a uniting of individuals in solidarity against capital and against these value forms (Hill et al. 2002). Franco 'Bifo' Berardi sums up the issue nicely in a way that transcends these frictions: 'The transformation of the techno-cognitive environment redefines the possibilities and limits of individuation' (Berardi 2009: 13). Notwithstanding, the spectre haunting the world is none other than the ongoing spectre of capital.

Dyer-Witheford (1999) gives a convincing literature review assessing the way capital, capitalism, and work have been portrayed in the post-industrial and post-Fordist sociological, industrial relations, and IR/IPE literature, noting that *all* emergent arguments have been required in some way to deal with Marx and Marxist ideas. On *all* nodes of the spectrum from the far right to the radical left, changes to the workplace, the removal of job security and casualised professional work alongside the casualisation, and the rise of flexibilised precariat maintenance and/or types of service work, are issues that have been associated with the rise of technological developments and what has been called the age of information, 'new times', the global knowledge-based economy, high-technology societies, technetronic societies, and so on. We are now surviving the 'cancer stage of capitalism' (McMurtry 1999), as a result of thriving communications channels and interconnectivity both virtual and physical. If these connections are divorced from production, to the point wherein 'productive labour is now *that which produces society*' (Negri 1992, my italics); and capital has been able to reinvent and 'socialise' itself such as is seen in the restructuring of education around a perceived ideal type of employable and socialised worker, then we are seeing a conscious fusion of capital with society that can have a range of effects on people surviving within its grip.

In the 1960s, the glow of post-war affluence led to the claim that societies now could enjoy the 'end of ideology' (Bell 1960/2000), that is, the end of Marxism. This far right informed glow was snuffed out in the rise of civil dissent in the late 1960s and 1970s, and industrial society 'went into paroxysm' (Dyer-Witheford 2006), with the Vietnam war being fought over ideological and economic grounds, with the rising labour struggles in American automobile factories, and with women's rights activists and environmental groups on the rise. But Daniel Bell's ideas became a kind of prophecy of post-industrialism that connected intellectuals' investigation into the impact that the rise of information technologies would have on people and society: and the futurologist was born. *The Coming of Post-Industrial Society* (Bell 1976) is a portfolio of the ideas that fed US policy and corporate strategy, cooked in the kitchens of such think tanks as the RAND Corporation and the Hudson Institute (Dyer-Witheford 1999: 17). This post-industrial world could be defined by the rise of a service economy, the distribution of occupations moving to professionalised work rather than manual labour, the 'intellectual technology' embedded in systems analysis and games theory (ibid.: 18), and scientific discovery was becoming an increasingly powerful tool when linked to technology and application of technologies. This set of social, economic, political, intellectual, psychological, and physical transformations was not something to be taken lightly. Advocates of the determination of the future in this context were sure that there would be a new class of individuals emerging from the scenario of the future, a 'knowledge class', who would be the 'government and academia, bearers of the rationalist skills and virtues required by increasing organisational and technological complexity ... creat[ing] an epoch of rationalised integration and prosperity which ... would finally escape from the material want, economic crisis and class conflicts of the industrial era' (ibid.).

While Marx critiqued class oppression and the exploitation of labour through commodification and corruption of value in the industrial settings he saw in Germany, France, and Britain, he also wrote about machines and technology and the idea that they could eliminate the need for people's labour, through automation. The automation crisis thesis informs labour process theorists and neo-Luddites, who are wary of technology and its properties, and are sure that technology and the development of the machine is a serious threat to labour. Alvin Toffler, an influential ex-Marxist who popularised the idea of the new world order of information societies, mocked Marx for supposedly only writing about the worker as a brawny man in the factory and steel mill (Toffler 1990). With the decline of manufacturing, clearly this protagonist was not the most prominent and, supposedly, this would lead to the decline of the working class. Workers now supposedly own the means of production, since production occurs in the mind and the intellect. But the information age will not transform production alone but will also transform property ownership: 'since information constitutes the central resource of the new age these property-transcendent features herald the advent of an increasingly sharing, cooperative, equalitarian society' (ibid.). Supposedly, the Marxist 'obsession with ownership' is 'anachronistic in the era of info-property, non-material, non-tangible, and potentially infinite' (ibid.). If the future is beyond capital and ownership and looks like a 'computopia' (Masuda 1987) then indeed, the dissolution of capitalist relations could lead to the elimination of class, or at least to a 'better capital' or a 'universal opulent society' (Masuda 1990: 130). But these authors share a right-leaning technological determinism that is governed by the idea that capitalism can be improved, and not overcome, and certainly not replaced with socialism in the way that the traditional historical materialist desires. A distinct silence is apparent in these literatures on the topic of class struggle.

In response, Massimo De Angelis reminds information society gurus, and other advocates of the information society, that class will not disappear, but we should look at all classes for inspiration for change rather than the much-visited notion of the working class. Following a set of shared values, a class should not be condemned to an eternity of value identities seen during industrialisation. De Angelis highlights the way in which a specific class in society is a 'stratified field of subjectivity disciplined to a large degree to the norms of behaviour of a modern society in which capital has a fundamental role in organising social production through disciplinary markets, enclosures, governance and its profit seeking enterprises' (2009, 5), whose members are perfectly capable of reproducing the boundaries of the system it represents. Often, the literature condoning the activities of the creative classes and the triumphalism of the original free software advocates was snubbed due to its reliance on middle-class values, social capital as derived from privilege (within my own work I have alluded to this, see Moore and Taylor 2009).

However, as De Angelis points out, there *can* be an *outside* to capitalism, and to say that the working class or the subaltern class are the only groups likely to challenge capitalism is flawed. While the Middle Class (his capitalisation) has historically been a bourgeois outfit and accustomed to hegemonic power, De Angelis asks whether perhaps it is time for what he calls an explosion of the Middle Class ('if you read this section and think I am talking about you, you well you may be right. You are probably middle class' De Angelis 2008: 5). Since Middle-Class behaviour has set the value standard for capitalist norms over time, it is also capable of finding 'outsides' to capitalism and needs to reset standards in a way that can then overthrow the status quo. Through 'atomic re-appropriations of labour time and its products and space away from capital, or in molecular communities reproducing commons and their defence in factories, in the offices, in the neighbourhoods, in the homes, in the streets, in cyberspace' (ibid.), the middle class can continue to be the frontline of value struggles to look for ways to 'common', or 'commoning' in ways that are not disciplined to norms of capitalist behaviour. To overcome the confines of discussion of social conflict and class struggle against exploited labour by actually looking at the values that drive the hegemonic classes, which in turn drive expansive global capitalism, De Angelis looks at the explosion of the hegemonic Middle Classes, a political subjectivity that can be created as a result of the change in composition: 'suddenly the Middle Class finds that among itself there is an increasing section who either does not want to or cannot sustain its livelihoods as Middle Class [such as] the 1960s in which Middle Class youth battled against the authorities of fathers, police, university professors and politics ... a movement that was later integrated into the 'commons created by disciplinary markets' (ibid.13). While I see problems with this argument, the distinction between what is apparently 'outside' of capitalism, and arguments that do not allow for non-capitalist behaviour or values (such as Open Marxist arguments), is crucial. In fact, precarity, economic recession, exclusion, and value divisions have blurred the categories of class, from the way in which societies once knew them.

Marx has influenced authors in a variety of studies on work and the sociology of work as well as industrial relations and labour process theories, but these bodies of work could look more extensively at the social forces of capital that generate many of the antagonisms in the work setting and the surrounding policy and social and institutional changes.[2] Another body of literature by autonomist Marxists has constructed an ideological assault on capitalism, but these authors do not tend to discuss explicitly the post-capitalist model of society to the extent that some peer production practitioners and thinkers have begun to do. One *cannot* separate society from the workplace, one cannot see work outside of the wider context of capitalism, unless a new model for production is envisioned and consistently practised, thus creating a model for coherent and sustainable use value systems that challenge the exchange value of capital within the now hegemonic, capitalist model. This final chapter takes this challenge very seriously, and looks at a social movement that poses a serious challenge to capitalism and the related policy campaigns such as the skills 'revolutions' I have discussed (2009). Activists, scholars and practitioners are involved in the P2P movement, a movement that holds the potential to embody the next stage of global political economic history and a form of socialism in terms of shared resources and shared information, that is already demonstrating reciprocal behaviours as essential prerequisites for communism. Peer production is a post-capitalist political economic model in which production occurs within the commons, rather than the corporation or competitive environs.[3]

Peer production and the commons

Control of subjectivities of workers through the emerging relationships between the public and private sectors is becoming rampant through industry involvement in education under the rubric of neoliberal capitalism. After a detailed look at how the subjective elements of employability are portrayed in the relevant skills revolutions that these emerging sectoral links have created across the world, the final section of the book analyses what has become a very interesting resistance movement emerging from the creative industries and the 'creatives': the peer-to-peer production movement, which is one that transcends geographical and organisational boundaries and promises to challenge the core activities and premises of competitive capitalism. This alternative economic model originally emerged from those working in the software industry alongside the innovations of Linus Torvald and Richard Stallman et al., but it has become a model that is now being applied through immaterial labour as well as the production of hardware and relevant infrastructures as expressed in the new discipline of Open Manufacturing. The peer production model for hardware can replace the hegemonic ideational view of subjectivity that can be viewed as 'employability' into the hands of the producers themselves in a way that provides sustainable and personally owned futures.

This post-capitalist suggestion for communities that are dedicated to the 'commons' is one that is claimed to have far more possibilities of resilience against capitalist subsumption than previous suggestions. While market-based capitalism is based on the private ownership of the means of production and hierarchically organised corporations, the peer production model is based on shared ownership and shared upgrading/product development rights, activities that by their very nature do not allow proprietary behaviour. This is not to suggest a lack of individual ownership, but an enabler of personal possession, by presenting information and other resources. The contemporary capitalist model is attempting to subsume activities coming out of this movement (see Moore and Taylor 2009), through recognising that workers are becoming increasingly empowered, a group who 'unlike factory workers basically own or control their own means of production: i.e. their brains, computers, and access to the socialised network that is the internet' (Bauwens 2009: 2) and are thus able to create scenarios of co-creation which are decidedly 'not just about firms improving their social marketing, open innovation, community-building and learning efforts to generate new proprietary and valuable knowledge with/from their customers' (Lawer 2009).

However self-organising communities impose a threat to the hegemony of the traditional firm because their radical organisation by way of non-market production demonstrates that 'there is a limit to how far such firms can "own" channels of knowledge production and are able to manage engagement when they apply a market-based logic and its associated capabilities' (Lawer 2009; Benkler 2006). People who are interested in co-creation and peer production are producing in a way that should not be treated as a curiosity or as a fad. Passionate and intelligent people living in a multitude of locations are volunteering online, for example, to co-author Wikipedia, is to contribute to 'the most serious alternative to the Encyclopaedia Britannica, and then turn around and give it away for free ... 4.5 million volunteers contribute their leftover computer cycles to create the most powerful supercomputer on Earth, SETI@Home ... [this is a] new mode of production emerging in the middle of the most advanced economies in the world' (Benkler 2006: 5–6). This mode of production poses a real threat to the current dominant mode and the people involved are increasingly able to circumnavigate the supposed reflexive requirements for preparing themselves to become and remain employable. The autonomous worker of a networked information economy, as well as the producers of open manufacturing-based communities, have unprecedented power to cooperate across open spaces that were previously unavailable in the factory, and the emergent cultures are discussed as being more truly democratic for nearly a decade. Both consensus and democratic collaborative processes are applied to become individually or self-governed at best. This means consensus or democratic collaborative processes for vital infrastructure; the best and most widely adopted outcomes are from the adaptive systems created that enable individual freedom of adaptations without the knowledge or permission of core developers, as these adaptations do not endanger, but merely enrich, the core design. Peer production holds the possibility for a 'genuinely new form of production' that is based on 'permission-less self-aggregation around the creation of common value' (Bauwens 2009).

This chapter presents a depiction of a contemporary post-capitalist model that I argue allows workers to arrest their own self-management and perhaps return to a situation wherein people can again experience their own labour and means of production, rather than continue to be subordinated to management structures within the

new world of work. The self-organising communities of peer production threaten the status quo by owning the means of production,
and structuring capital output into a commons from which to adopt
and adapt personally or communally through the creation of a
licensing model (General Public Licensing) that renders obsolete the
intellectual property control of ideas.

Traditionally, studies on workers' uprisings and struggle have relied
on the 'control/resistance' capitalist model, one that is reliant on
the Marxist treatise of humans losing their control of production
in the sense of craft work. This model for the analysis of uprisings
relies on particular aspects of capitalism to exist, including capital's
control over workers and workers' resistance. Workers have no control over the means of production and their skills are very particular
to certain tasks, and management's use of technologies to separate
head-from-hand work. In the typical Marxist resistance formula, the
'ability to resist stems from the structural relations of capitalism, as
workers act out a role in an evolving historical script written into
the logic of capitalist development' (Geschwender 1999: 160). The
1970s and 1980s ushered in neoliberalism as a set of ideas and practices to replace Fordism. Gorz discusses the principle of an 'abolition
of work' as part of the ideological treatise of the post-Fordist world.
This world of 'destandardisation and demassification, the destatisa-
tion and debureaucratisation of social protection' (1999: 4–5) should
have opened the gates to self-organised, self-determined activity,
and perhaps even the doors to 'self-management' (Vanek 1975). But
the liberation of work and a new social concept that could provide
emancipatory relations between workers, management, and politics
(Wilken 1965) did not happen, because this would have required the
complete reinvention and liberation of social life.

The idealised post-Fordist world in the hands of the workerists
would require a new labour process, the overcoming of rationalised
strategies for economic growth, the eliminated mode of regulation or
transformation to self-regulation, as well as an unprecedented pattern
of social organisation for the successful reinvention or elimination
of capitalism. Massimo De Angelis points out that many Marxists
misunderstand the concept of capitalism and cannot see any social
relation outside of the confines of capitalism (2009). While this is
quite a dramatic claim, it is the case that capitalism is grounded
in the restriction of knowledge, land ownership, and production

techniques (information and machinery). Without these restrictions to these areas, capitalism does not, perhaps, exist, but something else does. Bruff also points out that Open Marxism, a currently growing school of ideas likewise 'ignores the possibility that human social practice is constituted by elements other than simply the need to extract surplus value from labour under conditions of the separation of labour from its means' (2009a: 340).

The infatuation with the new creative world of work or 'play-bour' hints at a seeming turn from labour in the traditional model wherein surplus value is owned by capitalists. But we must be careful, because the supposed abolition of work can look suspiciously like an attempt to abolish the working class; like a threat to solidarity and class subjectivity through a fragmentation and a blurring of the boundaries between classes, despite the fact that work remains a foundation for belonging and a crucial factor for people's subjectivities and sense of self-worth. Marx adapts Hegel's dialectic of productive forces and productive relations to contain an objective possibility of progress, and the stage of history that should follow capitalism involves the 'free association of producers', a model for production that overcomes the coercion of the state and overcomes property and profit-driven social relations. The general intellect is shared by producers in a way that advances society and overcomes the power relations inherent in capitalism. While capitalism relies on exploitation to thrive, this does not also mean that all relations in society today are exploitative and cannot exist outside of the seeming hegemony of capitalism. Marx saw labour in its original form as a self-validating activity, but the external form of the state is the reason labour cannot be free, so while I have not addressed the concept of the state here, it is fitting to point out that we should not become fatalistic about our understanding of the possibilities for beginning history (De Angelis 2007).

Bauwens (2009) separates the terms peer production, peer governance, and peer property to give a 'beginner's guide' to the political economy of peer-to-peer production:

1. Peer production: wherever a group of peers decides to engage in the production of a common resource;
2. Peer governance: the means by which they choose to govern themselves while they engage in such pursuit;

3. Peer property: the institutional and legal framework they choose to guard against the private appropriation of this common work; this usually takes the form of non-exclusionary forms of universal common property, as defined through the General Public License, some forms of the Creative Commons licences, or similar derivatives.

The practices within the community-based political economic model of work found within peer production differ significantly, indeed almost diametrically, from the traditional versions of firm-based capitalist exchanges and production. Participants within both forms of economic imaginaries are involved in constructing and reconstructing economic realities that appear ultimately to be objects of economic calculations. Participants' actions in community-based models, and their management formations and governance, need to be critically examined to understand whether these behaviours challenge the traditional understanding of property rights, ownership, motivation, and complexity, and the 'human firm' (Tomer 1999), and whether they de-legitimise neoclassical rational actor models. Does peer-to-peer production fundamentally challenge the ideologies of market norms within which the firm is a traditionally accepted actor? This section will look at the way in which the community-based movement can successfully realign economic identities and can produce an economic 'truth' regime of value. Cultural and macro-structural properties of community-based models of work must be contrasted to those of the firm to discern their relevance and implications for broader ethico-political changes within and across societies.

Intellectual property within the firm is managed by copyrights and patents, which ensure royalties are paid to individual innovators. In its early stages, around the 1950s–1960s, most IT innovation took place within universities, and software was simply released without any copyright or patents. Computer companies typically funded the work done in the universities and then bundled operative codes for 'free' with the hardware they sold (Levy 1984). Later, Microsoft was challenged for abusing its monopoly and dominance in the market in the antitrust trial United States v. Microsoft (87 F. Supp. 2d 30 D.D.C. 2000) filed in 1998, when the Department of Justice and 20 states filed a case against Microsoft. This firm had been bundling its own web browser Internet Explorer with the Windows operating system and designing its own computers to correspond to this browser most immediately rather than to competing browsers. The prosecutor claimed that this behaviour superseded accepted market competition. In late 1999, Judge Jackson found Microsoft guilty of dominance over personal computing systems and thus of being a monopoly in the market. Jackson ruled that Microsoft should be divided into two firms with different functions, one to make operating systems and the other to produce components. But in 2000 Microsoft appealed to the Supreme Court and Judge Colleen Kollar-Kotelly ruled that Microsoft would not be divided, and in November 2001 the case was settled. Microsoft was required to share application programming interfaces with some other companies, and to release previously undisclosed codes to a three-person panel. This meant that Microsoft was free to bundle its software with Windows, which infuriated those states still opposed to Microsoft's dominance over the market.

Several years earlier, in 1984, Richard Stallman had initiated the Free Software Foundation (FSF) with the aim to develop a Unix-like operating system named GNU that would operate under a very different code of conduct. Software developed by the FSF was released under a copyright licence called the General Public License (GPL), which unlike any other copyright licence provided the user with additional rights. This introduced the right to use, copy, modify, and redistribute the software. The only condition or limitation of the GPL was that any modification of the code should also be distributed under the GPL. While the FSF developed a quantity of useful software for their GNU project, they did not have a working kernel or the part of the operating system to control the resources for the computer and to assign tasks. In 1991, Linus Torvalds started developing a Unix-like kernel for the x86 PC architecture, which when combined with the GNU software provided a complete and free operating system. Torvalds released his code under the GPL licence primarily to receive feedback from users and encourage participation for maintenance and sophistication of the product. This behaviour completely elided the norms for knowledge management and control.

Free Software was, therefore, an antagonistic movement aimed at challenging copyright licence agreements, which were seen as restrictive and a hindrance to innovation, and it did this by creating something else, a form of amplification after the attenuation of antagonism, as Stallman expresses it. Participants in this movement protested that consumers pay for software but cannot study it and learn how it works, or improve its function, because they do not have the source code. Microsoft was a player in the global politics of domination with considerable 'success' through restrictions to code access, while the OS movement does not retain as obvious a place. If it does not hold this space, then how has it captured such a dominant place in the IT industry (Wheeler 2007)?

The term 'open source' surfaced after 3 February 1998 during a meeting in Palo Alto, California. The meeting aimed to create a new name for the flexibilisation, transparency, and adaptability of software development that was not as threatening to businesses as the word 'free' seemed to be. People in the business world associated the word free with cheap and thus not good, problematic, non-professional, and so on. Stallman did not attend the meeting, given that many people felt that his crusade against proprietary software would be damaging to the image of this new movement. As a result of this meeting, a non-profit organisation with the name Open Source Initiative was created alongside the trademark of the term 'open source'. This organisation published a formal definition of what OS is and approves or disapproves copyright licences according to that definition, and software published under one of the OS approved licences can use the term 'open source'. Despite this change, the FSF still exists and is very active, but is devoted to promoting the ideals on which it was founded, that is, freedom to run, study, redistribute, and improve the code. While Microsoft has a Shared Source initiative, by which they created more liberal copyright licences, only a handful that were released seem to be compatible with FS/OS.

Several questions emerge from a comparison of firm-based models of production, and community-based models. Figure 5.1 demonstrates their contrasting characteristics, and the FS/OS movement was seen as a subversive framework for knowledge sharing, which could potentially overthrow or at least challenge hierarchical relationships existing within the traditional economy of the firm. Is the OS movement 'emancipatory' for workers who have traditionally been bound by power relationships of exploitation of their labour, as within Marx's theory of labour value? While FS/OS overcomes some of the limitations and corruptions of firm-style knowledge sharing, are the measures for superiority of information fundamentally different from those within the firm, which propagate competition? While

Firm	Peer to peer collaborative platforms
Rational activity encouraged	Innovation encouraged
Perfect, pre-existing knowledge defines rules for interaction	Constant revision, knowledge creation
Static	Process
Profit-maximising	Ego-boo (a 'profit' without means for measure), individualistic, alluded peer review
Central authority	Decentralized authority
Hierarchical	Benevolent leaders with lieutenants
Competitive	Cultural norms as solution rather than elimination, 'cooking pot' market
Predictive	Unpredictable

Figure 5.1   Firm versus peer to peer production norms

firms are composed of hierarchies, what prevents leaders within the FS/OS movement from 'domination'? Weber shows that 'authority within a firm and the price mechanism across firms are standard means to efficiently coordinate specialised coordinate knowledge in complex division of labour – but neither is operative in open source' (Weber 2004). If 'domination' is then prevented, how? Without wages, what are the incentives for participation and contribution? And, could Mancur Olsen's 'free riding' be eliminated?

While workers' knowledge within companies in effect becomes the intellectual property of employers, FS/OS perhaps emancipates this relationship and allows a level of personal 'possession' of the product. Furthermore, if the OS movement is purely defined as a 'gift culture', or as a commons/capital hybrid, then some recommendations can be made in relation to transpositions of fairer and more democratic governance, but knowledge production within this context is still managed according to an unwritten curriculum of enlightenment norms, and 'within the history of capitalism itself' (ibid.).

Participation within the Open Source Communities

I now look at the day-to-day relevance that significant shifts in software development communities have accrued in relation to *employability*. The understanding of work in the KBE incorporates several unprecedented promises for life fulfilment and self-govern-ance. Appeals to human nature are complicit to the literature on employment in the KBE, to the extent that autonomy is considered the perfect rationality. The word 'autonomy' comes from two Greek words for 'self' and 'rule' and is the promise within knowledge-producing work environments. Negroponte celebrates the possibilities this promises workers who condone the 'self' as employer (Negroponte 1995). Strategies for management control have in recent history deemphasised specific types of labour power and physical behaviour, and increasingly investigate the 'mind-power and subjectivities of employees', which, if managed correctly, will result in corporate 'excellence' as well as personal fulfilment. Does the appeal to self-improvement and fulfilment fundamentally contradict the tenets of capitalism or negate state-involvement in economic affairs?

Jessop (2004) discusses critical semiotic analysis for a better under-standing of knowledge production that critiques the variation, selection, and retention model understood within the discussed Psychology circles. Jessop is interested in the way capitalism repro-duces itself via social and to a lesser extent material construction of historically specific networks of social relations and aggregations of institutions. Jessop initiates a discussion of CPE that marries critical political economy with semiotics, which specifically looks at 'argumentation, narrativity, rhetoric, hermeneutics, identity, reflex-ivity, historicity and discourse', and he looks at the 'intersubjective production of meaning [semiosis] to cover them all' (2004). It is thus appropriate to look at the production of knowledge regarding what makes employees employable and an investigation of the value ascribed to knowledge produced in the workplace that allows for critique rather than persistently passive acceptance of these ideas allowing elites to continue their ability to initiate neoliberal-driven policies. If OS is indeed a critical space for alternative exchange and creation that fundamentally contrasts with capitalism, then it has the potential to provide the momentum and blueprint for a 'hardware' world of distributed infrastructures as well. Radical ideas towards how the P2P production model can create sustainable societies despite climate change and global economic instability, are emerging from a body of researchers and practitioners, and are becoming increasingly contagious.

FS/OS is an open, evolutionary arena wherein hundreds and some-times thousands of users voluntarily explore design codes, spot bugs in codes, and make contributions to the code in a fashion that is completely unfamiliar to the otherwise hugely monopolised software market. This 'computerization movement' emerged as a challenge to the monopolisation of the software market by such mammoth firms as Microsoft and IBM, and is portrayed as being revolutionary (Elliot and Scacchi 2003; DiBona, Ockman, and Stone 1999; Kling and Iacono 1988) and an ultimate goal 'to provide free software to do all of the jobs computer users want to do, and thus make proprietary software obsolete' (Free Software Foundation 2005). However, if it is to succeed in bringing about a new social order (Kling and Iacono 1988) this movement must be re-evaluated from a critical standpoint through a look into the practices towards the knowledge production of participants themselves to understand users' incentives in a broader sense than is usually assumed within the triumphant claims that advocate this ideologically-driven movement. Free Software may be viewed as a social movement while Open Source is more of a development methodology, but it is not necessary to isolate our analysis to one or the other firstly due to the extensive overlap in software communities, and also because these roots lie within one intellectual and moral response to the exploitation of markets by powerful firms (see Elliot and Scacchi 2004).

At the University of Maine Law School's Fourth Annual Technology and Law Conference, Portland, Maine, professor Eben Moglen postulated that

> [F]ree software is an invocation for particular social purposes of the ability to develop resources in commons. This is not, as I have pointed out, an economic novelty. It is the single way in which we have produced the most important works of Western intellectual achievement since the Renaissance. It is also the way in which we have managed for all time fisheries, surface water resources, and large numbers of other forms of resource beyond human production. Free software presents an attempt to construct a commons in cyberspace with respect to executable computer code. It works.
>
> (Moglen 2003)

So, contributors to the media itself make the commons work. The model of the commons is nothing new, but it has not been hegemonic for some time. Gramsci wrote that the formation of organic intellectuals, who are individuals trained into reinforcing dominant production frameworks, is based on powerful ideas and these ideas provide a set of guidelines or a legal-institutional framework contributing to societies' common sense, which works to advocate its own version of appropriate practices for production (Gramsci 1929–1935/1999: 12; Cox 1983: 172–3). The comparison of modes of knowledge production and skills in the contemporary historical moment begs discussion of workers and the unemployed alike, within the remit of an unwritten curriculum supporting specific norms for production relations and participants' learning, which aids employability and other forms of status for participation. Skills towards production within firm-based models led to the reaffirmation of leading groups' ideological alignment and set the precedent for the development of production relations in a classical sense. There are particular requirements and expectations to ensure the durability of a dominant mode of social relations of production and in the process of *trasformismo*; another Gramscian idea that refers to rearticulations of dominant ideas to accommodate and effectively eliminate resistance to these ideas. All other modes are inferior and discredited.

P2P production and hardware

While P2P production has possibly made its name via software production that has overtaken traditional software production, it is becoming clear that the tenets for open source software can be applied within hardware production, alternative currencies, and ecological production for the planet's sustainable future. Several hardware projects have emerged in the recent years, some of which have been listed below.

Smari McCarthy, Director of Taj Fab Lab in Jalalabad, Afghanistan and native of Iceland, runs the following projects and fab labs:

Projects
- Peer escrow identity management system
- Crowdsourced democracy system
- Mutualist monetary system
- Economic information system (CyberSyn inspired)
- Natural resource mapping system

- Arbitrary arbitration protocol
- Peer-to-peer education system
- Distributed Healthcare system
- Executive authority management

Fab Labs
- Vestmannaeyjar Iceland Fab Lab
- FabFi wireless project
- Afghanistan Fab Lab
- Open Manufacturing
- FOME
- Icelandic Society for Digital Freedoms

Dr Eddie Kirkby has started up the Manchester FabLabs project at the Manufacturing Institute in Manchester. Paul Hartzog and Sam Rose are involved in the establishment of Twenty-First Century Wealth-Generating Ecologies and an Infrastructure for Open Everything (University of Salford, Media Ecologies and Postindustrial Production, November 2009). Massimo Menichinelli is interested in open design projects. Dr Marcin Jakubowski is Director for Permaculture and Open Manufacturing, which is the basis for his Factor e Farm Project using peer production methodologies.

> Open Source Ecology is a movement dedicated to the collaborative development of the world's first replicable, open source, modern off-grid 'global village'. By using permaculture and digital fabrication together to provide for basic needs and open source methodology to allow cheap replication of the entire village, we hope to empower anyone who desires to move beyond the struggle for survival and *evolve to freedom*.
>
> (Open Source Ecology 2009)

Factor e Farm is an experiment of putting theory into practice. Dr Jakubowski and several others have been applying peer-to-peer methodologies and codes of practice to their work since the Farm's inception. The aim is to create a 'global village construction set'; these activists are 'refining existing technologies and techniques into simple, easily replicated, open source designs with closed, zero-waste resource cycles' (ibid.). This movement's followers claim that communities that control their own manufacturing and production are advanced civilisations.

By our analysis, most of the technologies needed for a sustainable and pleasant standard of living could be reduced to the cost of scrap metal + labor. There is immense potential for social transformation once this technology is fully developed for building interconnected self-sufficient villages, since people will be freed from material constraints and able to seek self-actualization.

(Ibid.)

The Open Ecology peer production collaboration cycle and methodology is the following:

– Feedback throughout
– Fabrication, potentially in distributed locations
– Resource donations
– Quality markup
  • technical drawings
  • 3D computer models
  • economic analysis
– Further design
– Worknet workspace as initial development, ending in dedicated wiki webspace
– Technology administrator: for each product

(Ibid.)

So people working in the commons in both software and hardware production are dedicated to taking the means of production away from the elite digerati as well as corporate moguls who are the most recent examples of Gramsci's organic intellectuals. Bearing in mind that 'organic' in this sense is not the organic we often think of, regarding pesticide free, genetically authentic gardens or all-natural foods, and so on. Gramsci means that the elite are as capable of planting ideas as revolutionaries or subversives are, and have been able to cultivate their own species of intellectuals through forming corporate links and building alliances in ways that fuel capitalism. Lovink argues that the Internet and new media have both frightened and excited capitalists, frightened because they are in many ways still unexplored territory and provide a space that is less familiar with copyright and intellectual property restrictions; but also excited at the profit-making implications (Lovink 2002). The profit, however, is only enjoyed for the short run, aided by efficiencies or cost cutting, which ultimately result in labour devaluation followed by capital collapse.

In the contemporary 'information' age, managers within knowledge economies battle to capture the best talent for the most profitable production and accumulation. Is a transformation in skills needed that will in fact actually create the environments where people can labour and live in an interdependent and self-sustaining way, outside of capitalist modes and means of production? Can P2P values change users' incentives for participation in production that transcend competition and profit seeking? It appears that the image of dissidence and revolution is the only solution for the problems emerging with the global credit crisis. This pursuit also allows a critical view on the technological determinism that now pervades a tendency to place widespread reliance on human innovation immutably to coincide with the contemporary age of production (seen in 'enterprise' initiatives), which will transform traditional hierarchies within typified sites of production of the industrial age.

What are P2P collaborative spaces in the real world? They include:

- Media labs on the model of Access Space or the Brasilian Pontos de Cultura programme, which has applied this approach on a national scale;
- Coworking spaces and social media cafes (like London's Tuttle Club);
- Fab Labs for manufacturing, as already exist from Iceland to Afghanistan;
- Studio spaces like TenantSpin, the micro-TV station in Liverpool based in a flat in a towerblock – and like many other examples in the world of Community Media (Hine 2009);
- Hackerspaces;
- Intentional Communities.

These radical spaces are based on the following principles:

Our mission is to extend the Open Source model to the provision any goods and services – Open Source Economics. This means opening access to the information and technology which enables a different economic system to be realized, one based on the integration of natural ecology, social ecology, and industrial ecology. This economic system is based on open access – based on widely accessible information and associated access to productive capital – distributed into the hands of an increased number of people. We believe that a highly distributed, increasingly participatory model of production is the core of a democratic society, where stability is established naturally by the balance of human activity with sustainable extraction of natural resources. This is the opposite of the current mainstream of centralized economies, which have a structurally built-in tendency towards of overproduction.

(P2P Foundation 2009)

Commoning, De Angelis claims, is a political strategy, based on the following principles:

1. A constituent process of new social relations: This can only be a process of commoning, able to keep at bay and push back the form of commoning predicated on capitalist relations and, therefore, capitalist value practices.
2. On creating lines of flight, without capitalist landing: The setting of a limit to the 'beast' and the problematic of how to constitute and sustain the 'outside' which is brought to life by the many struggles are two inescapable strategic coordinates of the beginning of history.
3. Value struggles: Commoning is not only based on pre-existent values, preexistent 'ethical' choices. The commoning we seek is also and most importantly a field of production of values, and the precondition for this production is that a wide range of different ethics, different cultures, different life-styles, and, as we will see, different power positions within the planetary wage hierarchy participate in the co-production of new systems of values, of producing what is of common value together.
4. A beginning of history: The bottom line of the discussion so far is that the minimum condition for alternatives to be able to both reproduce themselves and set a limit to capital is that they constitute processes of commoning through which cooperating subjects seek, establish, represent, and communicate a field of value production which is not only opposed to that of capital, but also propositive and constituent of new social relations at

every occasion of struggle. In this sense, the process of common-ing beyond capital is a process of destructive creation as opposed to the process of creative destruction of Schumpeterian memory. While for the latter the creation of the new and the correspond-ent destruction of the old is concerned with the mutation of the forms of capitalist social relations, we can understand the concern of destructive creation the destruction of these very capitalist rela-tions and the correspondent creation of new forms of commoning predicated on different value productions. Here the emphasis is on the constituent processes of commoning other than capital, rather than on mutated forms of capitalist commoning.

(De Angelis 2008: 2–5)

Through 'commoning' and through the production of hardware and sustainable living environments, it has become possible to chal-lenge capitalism and to create new forms of labouring subjects in a way that casts aside the wage relation and the invasive externally imposed 'skills' required in capitalist recipes for success. The global passive revolution requires passive subjects, and the P2P movement is a veritable revolutionary threat.

Conclusion

The key to the argument is that the production of knowledge occurs within a rapidly changing arena and holds the potential to become a site for contestation, or for a reconsideration of how intersubjectivities are formed. Because the value of labour is increas-ingly difficult to measure quantitatively or in exchange value terms with the developments of technology and with the transformation from the reliance on full-time employment to a flexibilised notion of employability, workers are thrown into a completely new playing field that must be met with more abundant resources in vital life sup-port areas to flourish. Demands on labour and conditions of produc-tion have a tendency to change rapidly and unpredictably and thus often remain uncontested. This volume has looked at how the idea of employability is consistently used to exploit the subjective nature of people's skills through the universalisation of certain ideas, in particular through education and training policy reform, and there-fore through perpetual reform of the discourse that informs concrete policy initiatives. I have demonstrated empirically grounded case studies of skills revolutions in the form of employability campaigns in both hemispheres. But to resist geographical parameters, I look at a resistance movement that is based on Marx's concept of the general intellect that may, I argue, overcome class struggle and empower people in ways that labour struggle previously has not been able to do. If producers in the P2P environment are in fact creators of value, and are able successfully to challenge the tenets of capitalism that paralyse our societies today, then it is a very real, albeit radical, model we must investigate, understand, and embrace. The global economic crisis does not even need to be mentioned as an obvious reason for this urgent investigation.

I have argued that the new technologies for management control have taken the form of dominant discourses of employability and lifelong learning, but these discourses are less powerful than the technologies manipulated in both the physical and the cognitive sense in peer-to-peer production environments. Producers of software in the open source communities as well as productive communities based on peer-to-peer tenets operate to some extent on an ethos similar to that seen in the rhetoric of the skills revolutions: while they are groups of entrepreneurs and are some of the most precariat workers in the contemporary world of work, they are also some of the most revolutionary in their ideas for knowledge production as well what we are seeing within eminent hardware and infrastructural production projects.

Rather than focusing on the worker revolutions in South Korea, simmering unrest in the UK, or the nascent signs of resistance in Singapore, while they are extremely relevant, I have chosen in this book to propose to the wider IPE community an idea that will look quite provocative and contest the supposed hegemonic subjectivity of the proposed subordinate learner worker. Actual producers' involvement in what is often unpaid production in the arena of open source and peer-to-peer models of production appears to be a voluntary and a very much enjoyed arena of resistance to dominant models of capitalism. After introducing the concept of P2P production, developed in the software industry and through the development of the Linux operating system, I have briefly looked at a handful of projects that are adopting peer-to-peer methods as well as the production methodologies of the Sooda movement in South Korea to create a very realistic new form of society, one that is based on 'commoning' or 'producing in commons' which advocates a political strategy that requires a new subjectivity of producers. This subjectivity is one that will overcome the seemingly required subjectivity of employability, which as De Angelis (2007) notes is very much a symptom of the growth of a contemporary middle class who are educated but who are being forced to exist in a career lifestyle of the precariat and are thus expected to find ways to survive through self-management in a way that is as yet prostrate to government policy.

In the critical IPE literature – even in the English school, which is typically sympathetic to critical approaches – we are too reliant on traditional perceptions of how transformation occurs and can occur. We need to start thinking about new sites for revolution, emerging from the shared wisdom Marx referred to in his depiction of the general intellect. The P2P arena as well as alternative production arrangements as demonstrated by the Sooda factory can allow workers space to explore what it *can* mean to be a 'lifelong learner', that is, to cultivate class consciousness and a subjectivity of multitude. Rather than becoming individuals who are subordinate to flexible work situations and changing labour markets, people can become learners who become empowered in a way that eliminates even the need for the concept 'employability', as workers become more powerful according to their shared alternative value systems. Is the future of work really based in the subjectivity proselytised by the skills revolutions depicted across geographical boundaries? Or is this recent challenge one that will in fact instigate a revolution of people who will find the power to dictate their own destinies through the formation of work communities not reliant on a wage, such as those producers in open source communities? Could a new 'ethical economy' (Arvidsson and Peitersen 2011 forthcoming), or an economy of reciprocity (Orsi 2006) arise from these communities, and create a genuine crisis for the current capitalist passive revolution?

Notes

1 The International Political Economy of Work

1. Carl Dahlman is Program Manager, Knowledge for Development in the World Bank Institute of the World Bank since 1999. He was Staff Director of the *World Development Report 1998/99 Knowledge for Development.*
2. Each site of development in this regard experiences control of labour with these soft touch programmes of limited safety-net capacity.
3. See for example Cox (1981, 1983, 1987, 1989, 2000, 2001); Gills (1993); Worth (2005, 2008); Bieler (2000, 2002); Bieler and Morton (2001, 2003, 2006); Taylor (2001); Showstack-Sassoon (1982); Moore (2005, 2006, 2007); Morton (2010).
4. One editorial board member, Adam D. Morton, is creating a special issue on passive revolution for the journal *Capital and Class* (2010).
5. See Sklair (1997, 2001a); van der Pijl (1997, 1998) and Cox (1987). Cox (1987) refers to a managerial class of a similar calibre. See also my discussion of the concept of transnational capitalist networks in Moore (2007) to incorporate the idea of contemporary organisations of capital in the technological age that appear to transcend and overcome outdated notions of 'class', but fail to do so in the last instance.

2 Work, Employability, Subjectivity

1. 'The employment rate for people of working age [in the UK] was 74.1 per cent for the three months to December 2008, down 0.3 from the previous quarter and down 0.7 over the year. The number of people in employment for the three months to December 2008 was 29.36 million, down 45,000 over the quarter and down 37,000 over the year. While there has been a fall over the quarter of 78,000 people in full-time employment, the number of people in part-time employment has increased by 33,000' (UK National Statistics 2009).
2. Perhaps the idea of 'play-bour' originates in the gaming industry, wherein, for example, the modification of games, or 'modding' is seen as something IT developers do as a leisurely pastime. However, developers often are not able to translate their activity into something personally useful, and the output of modding is frequently used by the industry or by salaried developers to advance the quality of games, while modders remain in precarious forms of work. 'The relationship between work and play is changing, leading, as it were, to a hybrid form of "playbour"' (Kücklich 2005).
3. In Australia, a country that has recently had significant fallouts with its labour unions, the subjectivity of workers was explicitly avoided in any

related policy until recently, when competent 'learner-workers' were expected to also acquire 'employability skills'. Williams (2005) warns that this kind of intervention will necessarily lead to ambiguities towards what is expected of workers, and contradicts previous commitments to keep personal attributes out of policy discussion. Events in Australasia reflect a similar redefinition of workers' relationship with employment in nations that reflect each of Coates' defined models of capitalism.

3 Skills Revolutions in the 'West'

Portions of this text have been published in Phoebe Moore, 'UK Education, Employability, and Everyday Life', *Journal for Critical Education Policy Studies*, 7:1 (2009), 242–74.

1. In this piece, Williams discusses the way in which the Australian government did not permit the use of character or competency specific terminologies in the compilation of personal skills related policy but that, over time, worker subjectivities became increasingly insinuated within proposed policy, contrasting earlier regulation.

2. Typically, in cases of increasing unemployment, as is happening in the UK, the state will pay for training, and if a company refuses to pay for training generally the state may impose increased taxes onto the company as an incentive to cooperate. In 2007, there were two industrial boards in the UK that placed a training levy on the sectors of construction, and engineering. A third levy was predicted as well, to be imposed within the film industry in order to maintain talent in large media companies such as the BBC, Sky, and Granada, which rely on microbusinesses for talent and only make voluntary contributions to the SSC. The Train to Gain programme was not completely providing the skills needed within this sector, so the question of information regarding what is needed in terms of skills, as well as a clear message for who is paying for what training, needs to be made clear. Otherwise, the danger is that the costs fall onto individuals to maintain a personal project for employability, which functions to place increased responsibilities onto workers rather than provide safety nets in the increasingly unstable job market.

4 Skills Revolutions in the 'East'

My sincere gratitude is extended to Professor Dr Dae-Bong Kwon, President of the Korea Research Institute for Vocational Education and Training (KRIVET) based in Seoul, Korea, and the KRIVET researchers who met with me in 2002, 2004, and 2009 for their kind assistance with gathering data for this chapter.

All names of interviewees have been changed to retain anonymity.

1. The emergence and expansion of a 'managerial class' (Cox 1981: 126–55), or the transnational capitalist class (TCC) (Sklair 2001) is a phenomenon

of 'globalization' (Gills 2000). Gills states that 'capital is ... always a class position and associated with a "capitalist class"' (Gills 2002: 147) that is, in the contemporary age, increasingly transnationally networked. The TCC consists of transnational corporate executives and local affiliates, internationalising politicians and bureaucrats, globalising professionals, and the media (Sklair 2001: 17). These groups are involved in leading the process of globalisation of NICs, and likewise play a key role in nations' economic restructuring.

2. This information was gathered from a semi-structured interview with the Vice Director of the MOL, at the MOL offices in Seoul, on 4 December 1999.

3. The notion of convergence, or nations' abilities to replicate industrialised countries' development trajectories, was both implicitly and explicitly a part of IMF restructuring schemes such as that applied to South Korea in 1998 and onward. Members of the 'convergence club' are advanced industrial countries, and the benchmarking of best practices for the creation of wealth emanate from those sites. There are various reasons given for the non-successes of convergence strategies, which result from several discrepancies discussed by Rowley and Bae (2002) that include particular cultural value systems. These discrepancies need to be considered carefully in order to increase success rates for VET programmes.

4. Statistics provided within an interview I conducted with a senior researcher at the KRIVET Asia Pacific regional headquarters in Seoul, on 9 August 2002.

5. The Vice Director of the MOL (whose interview is discussed in previous sections) predicted that if labour were to fight with management, businesses would surely 'disappear'.

5   Employability as Renewed Subjectivity: Sooda Korea, and Peer Production

My sincere thanks to Andrew Robinson, Jussi Parikka, Matthew Fuller and Michael Goddard for their kind and helpful comments on drafts of this chapter.

Thanks to Nathan Cravens for discussions on this section of the book.

1. As Dyer-Witherford (2006, 1) notes, 'the cellular form of communism is the common, a good produced to be shared in association. The circuit of the common traces how shared resources generate forms of social cooperation – associations – that coordinate the conversion of further resources into expanded commons. ... A twenty-first century communism can, again by analogy, be envisioned as a complex unity of terrestrial, state and networked commons, but the strategic and enabling point in this ensemble is the networked commons. These must however, also be seen in their dependency on, and even potential contradiction, with the other

commons sectors. The concept of a complex, composite communism based on the circulation between multiple but commons forms is opens possibilities for new combinations of convivial custom, planetary planning and autonomous association'.

2. In the labour process literature, Braverman was accused of overlooking the possibilities for resistance to management control through a reclaiming of the subjective, despite his seminal work on deskilling and Taylorist scientific management and the 'degradation of work'. In fact, Braverman shows that capitalists consciously divorce the subjective factors of the labour process from the physical act of production, because 'not only is capital the property of the capitalist, but labour itself has become part of capital'. Braverman refers to Taylor's claim that 'not only do the workers lose control over their instruments of production, but they must now lose control over their own labour and the manner or its performance' (1974, 116). While Burawoy (1979) is congratulated for updating these ideas through extensive anthropological work in factories, he is also critiqued for his neglect to take into the account external factors that affect work and the workplace.

3. Peer production differs from cooperatives. While cooperatives own collective capital and have a democratic decision-making structure in place, they are still subject to the dynamics of the firm and corporate regulation, so Bauwens calls this a 'variant to the market' (2009).

Bibliography

Abbott, J. and O. Worth (eds), *Critical Perspectives on International Political Economy* (Palgrave Macmillan, 2002).

Amnesty International, 'Republic of Korea (South Korea) Arrests of Trade Union Leaders' (21 July 1998). Online, Available (27/04/10) http://web.amnesty.org/library/Index/ENGASA250241998?open&of=ENG-KOR.

Amoore, L., *Globalisation Contested: An International Political Economy of Work* (Manchester University Press, 2002).

Amsden, A., 'Why Isn't the Whole World Experimenting with the East Asian Model to Develop?: Review of the East Asian Miracle', *World Development* 22: 4 (1994), 627–33.

Anderson, N. R. and N. A. West, 'Measuring Climate for Work Group Innovation', *Journal of Organisational Behaviour* 19 (1998), 235–58.

Australian National Training Authority (ANTA) and Department of Education, Training and Youth Affairs (DETYA), *Training Package Assessment Materials Kit* (2005). Online, Available (03/08/09) http://www.atpl.net.au/itemdetail.aspx?piid=8188.

Apple, M., 'Between Good Sense and Bad Sense: Race, Class, and Learning from Learning to Labour', in N. Dolby and G. Dimitriadis with P. Willis (eds), *Learning to Labour in New Times* (Routledge, 2004), 61–82.

Arendt, H., *The Human Condition* (University of Chicago Press, 1970).

Aronowitz, S. and W. DiFazio, *The Jobless Future: Sci-Tech and the Dogma of Work* (Regents of the University of Minnesota, 1994).

Arvidsson, A., *Brands: Meaning and Value in Media Culture* (Routledge, 2006).

Arvidsson, A. and N. Peitersen, *The Ethical Economy: Business and Society in the 21st Century* (Columbia University Press, 2011, forthcoming).

Ashton, D., F. Green, J. Sung and D. James, 'The Evolution of Education and Training Strategies in Singapore, Taiwan and S. Korea: a Development Model of Skill Formation', *Journal of Education and Work* 15: 1 (2002), 1–30.

AsiaPulse, 'South Korean Unemployment Benefit Filings Hit Record High in Jan', (Seoul, 09 Feb 2009). Online, Available (03/03/09) http://www.zibb.com/article/4851085.

Atkinson, J., 'Changing Work Patterns: How Companies Achieve Flexibility to Meet New Needs' (National Economic Development Office London, 1986).

Avis, J., '(Im)possible Dream: Post-Fordism, Stakeholding and Post-Compulsory Education', *Journal of Education Policy* 13: 2 (1998), 251–63.

Axtell, C. M., D. J. Holman, K. Unsworth, T. D. Wall, P. E. Waterson, and E. Harrington, 'Shopfloor Innovation: Facilitating the Suggestion and Implementation of Ideas', *Journal of Occupational and Organizational Psychology* 73: 3 (2000), 265–85.

BBC, 'UK Unemployment Hits 1.92 Million' (BBC, 21 January 2009). Online, Available (01/08/09) http://news.bbc.co.uk/1/hi/business/7841349. stm.

Bain, A., *The Senses and the Intellect*, third edition (Appleton, 1874).

Bandura, A., 'Self-Efficacy Mechanism in Human Agency', *The American Psychologist* 37: 2 (1982), 122–47.

Barfuss, T., 'Active Subjects, Passive Revolution: Agility, Cleverness and Irony in Contemporary Society', *Cultural Studies* 22: 6 (2008), 837–49.

Bauwens, M., 'The Emergence of Open Design and Open Manufacturing', *We-Magazine 2*. Online, Available (21/04/09) http://www.we-magazine.net/we-volume-02/the-emergence-of-open-design-and-open-manufacturing/.

Beatty, C., S. Fothergill, T. Gore, and R. Powell, 'The Real Level of Unemployment 2007', occasional paper, Centre for Regional Economic Social Research, Sheffield Hallam University, 2007.

Beckmann, A. and C. Cooper, 'Conditions of Domination: Reflections on Harms Generated by the British Education System', *British Journal of Sociology of Education* 26: 4 (2005), 475–89.

Benkler, Y., *The Wealth of Networks: How Social Production Transforms Markets and Freedom* (Yale University Press, 2006).

Berardi, F. 'Bifo', *Precarious Rhapsody: Semiocapitalism and the Pathologies of the Post-Alpha Generation* (Minor Compositions, 2009).

Berardi, F. B., *The Soul at Work: From Alienation to Autonomy* (Semiotex(e), 2009).

Bercuson, K. (ed.), *Singapore: A Case Study in Rapid Development* (International Monetary Fund, 1995).

Berend, Ivan T., 'Foucault and the Welfare State', *European Review* 13: 2 (2005), 551–6.

Berger, P. L. and T. Luckmann, *The Social Construction of Reality: A Treatise in the Sociology of Knowledge* (Anchor, 1967).

Berger, S. and R. Dore (eds), *National Diversity and Global Capitalism* (Cornell University Press, 1996).

Bernard, N., *Multilevel Governance in the European Union* (Kluwer Law International, 2002).

Berntson, E., M. Sverke, and S. Marklund, 'Predicting Perceived Employability: Human Capital or Labour Market Opportunities?', *Economic and Industrial Democracy* 27: 2 (2006), 223–44.

Beynon, H., D. Grimshaw, J. Rubery, and K. Ward, *Managing Employment Change: The New Realities of Work* (Oxford University Press, 2002).

Bieler, A., *Globalisation and Enlargement of the European Union: Austrian and Swedish Social Forces in the Struggle over Membership* (Routledge, 2000).

Bieler, A., 'Austria's and Sweden's Accession to the European Union: A Comparative Neo-Gramscian Analysis', in S. Breslin, C. W. Hughes, N. Phillips, and B. Rosamond (eds), *New Regionalism(s) in the Global Political Economy: Theories and Cases* (Routledge, 2002), 150–62.

Bieler, A. and A. D. Morton (eds), *Social Forces in the Making of the New Europe: The Restructuring of European Social Relations in the Global Political Economy* (Palgrave Macmillan, 2001).

Bieler, A. and A. D. Morton, 'Globalisation, the State and Class Struggle', *British Journal of Politics and International Relations* 5: 4 (2003), 467–99.

Bieler A. and A. D. Morton (eds), *Images of Gramsci: Connections and Contentions in Political Theory and International Relations* (Routledge, 2006).

Birdsall, N., D. Ross, and R. Sabot, 'Inequality and Growth Reconsidered: Lessons from East Asia', *World Bank Economic Review* 9 (1995), 477–508.

Blackler, F. and S. McDonald, 'Power, Mastery and Organizational Learning', *Journal of Management Studies* 37: 6 (2000), 833–51.

Blunkett, D., 'Foreword', *The Learning Age: A Renaissance for a New Britain* (1998). Online, Available (06/03/09) http://www.leeds.ac.uk/educol/documents/000000654.htm.

'Bologna Seminar on Employability in the Context of the Bologna Process, Conclusions and Recommendations' (October 2004). Online, Available (21/10/08) http://www.bologna-bergen2005.no/EN/Bol_sem/Seminars/041022-23Bled/041023Conclusions.pdf.

Bomberg, E. and J. Peterson, 'Policy Transfer and Europeanisation: Passing the Heineken Test?', Queen's Papers on Europeanisation, No. 2, 2000. Online, Available (06/03/09) http://www.qub.ac.uk/ies/.

Brain Korea 21(BK21)/New University for Regional Innovation (NURI) (2006). Online, Available (03/08/09) http://bnc.nrf.go.kr/home/eng/bnc/chairman.jsp.

Braverman, H., 'Which Way to a New American Radicalism?', *American Socialist* (1956). Online, Available (05/03/09) http://www.marxists.org/archive/braverman/1956/04/radicalism.htm.

Braverman, H., *Labour and Monopoly Capital: The Degradation of Work in the Twentieth Century* (Monthly Review Press, 1974).

Brook, P., 'In Critical Defense of Emotional Labour, Refuting Bolton's Critique of Hoschild's Concept', *Work, Employment and Society* 23: 531 (2009), 531–48.

Brown, G., Speech for Confederation of British Industry Annual Conference (Birmingham, November 2004). Online, Available (06/03/09) http://business.timesonline.co.uk/article/016849-1351062,00.html.

Brown, G., Speech for the Trades Union Congress Annual Conference (Warwick, Sept. 2005). Online, Available (06/03/09) http://www.tuc.org.uk/congress/tuc-10552-f0.cfm.

Brown, P. and A. Hesketh, *The Mismanagement of Talent: Employability and Jobs in the Knowledge Economy* (Oxford University Press, 2004).

Brown, P., A. Hesketh, and S. Williams, 'Employability in a Knowledge-Driven Economy', *Journal of Education and Work* 16: 2 (2003), 107–26.

Bruff, I., *Culture and Consensus in European Varieties of Capitalism: A 'Common Sense' Analysis* (Palgrave Macmillan, 2008).

Bruff, I., 'The Totalisation of Human Social Practice: Open Marxists and Capitalist Social Relations, Foucauldians and Power Relations', *The British Journal of Politics and International Relations* 11 (2009a), 332–51.

Bruff, I., *Culture and Consensus in European Varieties of Capitalism: A 'Common Sense' Analysis* (Palgrave Macmillan, 2009b).

Bulmer, S. and S. A. Padgett, 'Policy Transfer in the European Union; An Institutionalist Perspective', *British Journal of Political Science*, 35: 1 (2005), 103–26.

Burawoy, M., *Manufacturing Consent: Changes in the Labour Process under Monopoly Capitalism* (University of Chicago Press, 1979).

Burawoy, M., *The Politics of Production: Factory Regimes Under Capitalism and Socialism* (Verso, 1985).

Burnham, P., 'Neo-Gramscian Hegemony and the International Order', *Capital and Class* 45 (1991).

Burnham, P., 'The Recomposition of National States in the Global Economy: From Politicised to Depoliticised forms of Labour Regulation', in P. Edwards and T. Elgar (eds), *The Global Economy, National States and the Regulation of Labour* (Mansell, 1999), 42–63.

Cammack, P., 'Making the Poor Work for Globalisation?', *New Political Economy* 63 (2001), 397–408.

Cammack, P., 'The Mother of All Governments: The World Bank's matrix for Global Governance', in R. Wilkinson and S. Hughes (eds), *Global Governance: Critical Perspectives* (Routledge, 2002a), 36–53.

Cammack, P., 'Attacking the Poor', *New Left Review* 2: 13 (2002b), 125–34.

Campbell, D. T., 'Blind Variation and Selective Retention in Creative Thought as in Other Knowledge Processes', *Psychological Review* 67 (1960), 380–400.

Casey, T., 'Comparative Disadvantage: Models of Capitalism and Economic Performance in the Global Era', presented at 2004 Political Studies Association conference, University of Lincoln, 2004.

Chartered Institute of Personnel and Development (CIPD), 'Labour Market Outlook survey 2006', *Online Magazine of the Chartered Institute of Personnel and Development* (31 August, 2006). Online, Available (06/03/09) http://www.peoplemanagement.co.uk.

Cheng, S. M. and A. H. Chang, 'Quality of Working Life and Employee Participation in Singapore', in I. Nish, G. Redding and N. Sek-hong (eds), *Work and Society: Labour and Human Resources in East Asia* (Hong Kong University Press, 1996), 199–218.

Chappel, C., C. Rhodes, N. Solomon, M. Tennant, and L. Yates, *Reconstructing the Learner Worker: Pedagogy and Identity in Individual, Organisational and Social Change* (RoutledgeFalmer, 2003).

Choy, C. L. and C. Yeoh, 'Technological Transformation and Society', in Chong Li Choy, C. H. Tan, K. C. Wong, and C. Yeoh (eds), *Business, Society and Development in Singapore* (Times Academic Press, 1990).

Chun, S.O., *They are Not Machines: Korean Women Workers and their Fight for Democratic Trade Unionism in the 1970s* (Ashgate, 2003).

Chung, J. S., 'Diversification of Training Pathways through the Credit Bank System in the Republic of Korea', paper presented at International Policy Seminar on Making Lifelong Learning a Reality, IIEP/KRIVET/NCVER/NIER collaborative project, Seoul, 24–26 June 2003.

Clough, P. T., *Autoaffection: Unconscious Thought in the Age of Teletechnology* (University of Minnesota Press 2000).

Coates, D., *Models of Capitalism: Growth and Stagnation in the Modern Era* (Polity Press, 2000).

Cockburn, C., *Brothers: Male Dominance and Technological Change* (Pluto, 1983).

Cohen, B. J., *International Political Economy: An Intellectual History* (Princeton University Press, 2008).

Committee of Vice-Chancellors and Principals/Department for Education and Employment, *Skills Development in Higher Education* (London/CVCP, 1998).

Confederation of British Industry (CBI), *Future Fit: Preparing Graduates for the World of Work* (CBI, 208).

Contu, A., C. Grey, and A. Örtenblad, 'Against Learning', *Human Relations* 56: 8 (2003), 931–52.

Cooley, C. H., *Social Process* (Southern Illinois University Press, 1966).

Cooley, R., 'Taylor in the Office', in R. Ottaway (ed.), *Humanising the Workplace* (Croom Helm, 1977), 65–77.

Cox, R. W., 'Social Forces, States and World Orders: Beyond International Relations Theory', *Millennium: Journal of International Studies* 10: 2 (1981), 126–55.

Cox, R. W., 'Gramsci, Hegemony and International Relations: An Essay in Method', *Millennium: Journal of International Studies* 12: 2 (1983), 162–75.

Cox, R. W., *Production, Power, and World Order: Social Forces in the Making of History* (Columbia University Press, 1987).

Cox, R. W., 'Production, the State, and Change in World Order', in E. O. Czempiel and J. Rosenau (eds), *Global Changes and Theoretical Challenges* (DC Heath, 1989).

Cox, R. W., 'Gramsci, Hegemony and International Relations: An Essay in Method', in S. Gills (ed.), *Gramsci, Historical Materialism and International Relations* (Cambridge University Press, 1993), 49–66.

Cox, R. W., 'Civil Society at the Turn of the Millennium: Prospects for an Alternative World Order', *Review of International Studies* 25:2 (1999), 162–75.

Cox, R. W., 'Political Economy and World Order: Problems of Power and Knowledge at the Turn of the Millennium', in R. Stubbs and G. Underhill (eds), *Political Economy and the Changing Global Order* (Oxford University Press, 2000), 25–37.

Cox, R. W., 'The Way Ahead: Toward a New Ontology of World Order', in R. Wyn Jones (ed.), *Critical Theory and World Politics* (Lynne Rienner Publishers, 2001), 45–59.

Cranmer, S., 'Enhancing Graduate Employability: Best Intentions and Mixed Outcomes', *Studies in Higher Education* 31: 2 (2006), 169–84.

Crouch, C. and W. Streeck (eds), *Political Economy of Modern Capitalism: Mapping Convergence and Diversity* (Sage, 1997).

Cubitt, S., *Digital Aesthetics* (Sage, 1998).

Crouch, C. and W. Streeck (eds), *The Political Economy of Modern Capitalism: Mapping Convergence and Diversity* (Sage, 1999).

Cuglesan, N., 'Multilevel Governance in the EU: What Model for Romania?', *Eurojournal.org* (October 2006). Online, Available (06/03/09) http://www.ceeol.com/aspx/getdocument.aspx?logid=5&id=8bf80d82-535a-4eff-bdbf-adff20f9a579.

Curson, C. (ed.), *Flexible Patterns of Work* (Institute of Personnel Management, 1986).

Cutler, T., 'The Romance of Labour', *Economy and Society* 7:1 (1978), 74–95.

Daguerre, A., 'Importing Workfare Policy Transfer of Social and Labour Market Policies from the USA to Britain under New Labour', *Social Policy and Administration* 38: 1 (2004), 41–56.

Dale, I. (ed.), *Labour Party General Election Manifestos 1900–1997 (Vol. 2)* (Routledge, 2002).

Darlington, R., *What's the Point of Industrial Relations? In Defence of Critical Social Science* (British Universities Industrial Relations Association, 2009).

Davies, M., *International Political Economy and Mass Communication in Chile: National Intellectuals and Transnational Hegemony* (Macmillan, 1999).

Davies, M., 'The Spatial Architectonics of International Political Economy: Work, Body, Aesthetics', paper presented at World Politics and Popular Culture Conference, Tynemouth, United Kingdom, 19 November 2009.

Davies, M. and M. Ryner (eds), *Poverty and the Production of World Politics: Unprotected Workers in the Global Political Economy* (Palgrave Macmillan, 2007).

De Angelis, A., 'The Production of Commons and the "Explosion" of the Middle Class' (2008). Online, Available (29/04/10) http://www.taller-commons.com/downloads/angelis.pdf.

De Angelis, M., *The Beginning of History: Value Struggles and Global Capital* (Pluto Press, 2007).

De Certeau, M., *The Practice of Everyday Life*, translated by S. Rendall (University of California Press, 1984).

De Certeau, M., J. Doherty, and T. Leven, 'Evaluation of the Technical and Vocational Education Initiative (TVEI) Extension', No. 52 (Interchange, the Scottish Office Education and Industry Department, 1998).

Deen, T., 'United Nations: Advocates "Social Safety Net" in Third World', Third World Network (2003). Online, Available (27/04/10) http://www.twnside.org.sg/title/safety-cn.htm

DfEE (Department for Education and Employment), *Meet the Challenge, Education Action Zones* (Department for Education and Employment London, 1999).

DfEE, *The Learning Age: A Renaissance for a New Britain* (26 July 1998). Online, Available (24/02/09) http://www.lifelonglearning.co.uk/greenpaper/.

DIUS (Department for Innovation, Universities and Skills), *World Class Skills: Implementing the Leitch Review of Skills in England* (HM Government, Crown Copyright 2007).

DWP (Department for Work and Pensions), *New Employability Skills Programme to Help People Back into Work* (1 August 2007). Online, Available (19/09/08) http://www.gnn.gov.uk/Content/Detail.asp?ReleaseID=304329&NewsAreaID=2.

DiBona, C., S. Ockman, and M. Stone, *Open Sources: Voices from the Open Source Revolution* (O'Reilly and Associates Inc., 1999).

Dolby, N. and G. Dimitriadis with P. Willis (eds), *Learning to Labour in New Times* (Routledge, 2004), 61–82.

Drainville, A. C., 'International Political Economy in the Age of Open Marxism', *Review of International Political Economy* 1: 1 (1994), 105–32.

du Gay, P. and M. Pryke, 'Cultural Economy: An Introduction', in *Cultural Economy: Cultural Analysis and Commercial Life* (Sage, 2002), 1–19.

Dyer-Witheford, N. 'The Circulation of the Common', paper presented at Immaterial Labour, Multitudes and New Social Subjects, Class Composition in Cognitive Capitalism, King's College, Cambridge, 29–30 April 2006. Online, Available http://www.fims.uwo.ca/people/faculty/dyerwitheford/Commons2006.pdf.

Dyer-Witheford, N., *Cyber-Marx: Cycles and Circuits of Struggle in High-Technology Capitalism* (University of Illinois Press, 1999).

Easterby-Smith, M., R. Snell and S. Gherardi, 'Organisational Learning: Diverging Communities of Practice?', *Management Learning* 29: 3 (1998), 259–72.

Elliot, L., 'Britain has Three Times the Official Number of Jobless, Study Finds', *The Guardian* Wednesday (13 June 2007), 29.

Elliot, M. S. and W. Scacchi, 'Free Software Development: Cooperation and Conflict in a Virtual Organisational Culture', in S. Koch (ed.), *Free Open Source Software Development* (Idea Group Publishing, 2003), 152–7.

Elliot, M. S. and W. Scacchi, 'Mobilisation of Software Developers' (Institute for Software Research, August 2004). Online, Available (08/06/09) http://www.ics.uci.edu/%7Ewscacchi/Papers/New/Elliott-Scacchi-Free-Software-Movement.pdf.

EU (European Union), 'A Memorandum on Lifelong Learning', Commission of the European Communities (2003). Online, Available (31/05/10) http://www.bologna-berlin2003.de/pdf/MemorandumEng.pdf.

European Communities, 'Creating an Innovative Europe: Report of the Independent Expert Group on R&D and Innovation (appointed following the Hampton Court Summit and chaired by Mr Esko Aho) (January 2006). Online, Available (08/06/09) http://ec.europa.eu/invest-in-research/pdf/download_en/aho_report.pdf.

European Employment Task Force, 'Jobs, Jobs, Jobs: Creating More Employment in Europe', report chaired by Win Kok (2003). Online, Available (08/06/09) http://ec.europa.eu/employment_social/employment_strategy/pdf/etf_en.pdf.

European Ministers of Education (joint declaration), 'The European Higher Education Area', meeting convened in Bologna (19 June 1999). Online, Available (24/02/09) http://www.oest.oas.org/engineering/ingles/documentos/reference/Doc_03_Bologna%20Declaration.pdf.

EURASHE, 'Policy Statement on the Bologna-Prague-Berlin Process' (Mat 2002). Online, Available (09/11/08) http://www.bologna-berlin2003.de/pdf/Eurashe_Policy_Statement_Declaration.pdf.

Farr, J. L. and C. M. Ford, 'Individual Innovation', in M. A. West and L Farr (eds), *Innovation and Creativity at Work: Psychological and Organisational Strategies* (John Wiley and Sons, 1990), 63–80.

Felstead, A., D. Gallie, and F. Green, *Work Skills in Britain 1986–2001* (DfES/SKOPE, 2002).

Fine, B., *Social Capital versus Social Theory: Political Economy and Social Science at the Turn of the Millennium* (Routledge, 2001).

Fine, B., *The World of Consumption: The Material and Cultural Revisited* (Routledge, 2002).

Fine, B. and Milonakis, D., *From Political Economy to Economics: Method, the Social and the Historical in the Evolution of Economic Theory* (Routledge, 2008).

Fletcher, S., *NVQs, Standards and Competence* (Kogan, 1991).

Florida, R., *The Rise of the Creative Class and How It's Transforming Work, Leisure, Community, and Everyday Life* (Basic Books, 2002).

Florida, R., *Creative Intelligence* (Joint publication of Catalytix, Inc. and the Richard Florida Creativity Group, December 2002) 1: 1. Online, Available (13/02/06) http://www.catalytix.biz/acrobat/vol1issue1.pdf.

Florida, R., 'Creative Class War: How the GOP's Anti-Elitism Could Ruin America's Economy', *Washington Monthly* (January/February 2004). Online, Available (05/09/09) http://www.washingtonmonthly.com/features/2004/0401.florida.html.

Forrester, K., 'Learning for Revival: British Trade Unions and Workplace Learning', *Studies in Continuing Education* 27: 3 (2005), 257–70.

Foucault, M., *The History of Sexuality. Volume I: An Introduction*, translated by Robert Hurley (Vintage Books, 1990).

Foucault, M., 'The Subject and Power', in James D. Faubion (ed.), *Michel Foucault: Essential Works of Foucault 1954–1984* (Penguin, 2000), 326–48.

Foucault, M., Madness and Civilization: A History of Insanity in the Age of Reason (Routledge, 2001).

Fox, A., 'Managerial Ideology and Labour Relations', *British Journal of Industrial Relations* 4 (1966), 366–78.

Fox, S., 'Communities of Practice, Foucault and Actor-Network Theory', *Journal of Management Studies* 37: 6 (2000), 853–67.

Free Software Foundation, 'Overview of the GNU System' (27 September 2005). Online, Available (14/12/05) http://www.gnu.org/gnu/gnu-history.html.

Garsten, C. and K. Jacobsson, *Learning to be Employable: New Agendas on Work, Responsibility and Learning in a Globalising World* (Palgrave Macmillan, 2004).

Germain, R. and M. Kenny, 'Engaging Gramsci: International Relations Theory and the New Gramscians', *Review of International Studies* 24: 1 (1998), 3–21.

Geschwender, J. A. with L. Geschwender, 'Gender, Occupational. Sex Segregation and the Labour Process', in *Rethinking the Labour Process* (State University of New York Press, 1999), 149–88.

Gill, S., *American Hegemony and the Trilateral Commission* (Cambridge University Press, 1990).

Gill, S. (ed.), *Gramsci, Historical Materialism and International Relations* (Cambridge University Press, 1993a).

Gill, S., 'Epistemology, Ontology and the "Italian School"', in S. Gill (ed.), *Gramsci, Historical Materialism and International Relations* (Cambridge University Press, 1993b) 21–48.

Gill, S., 'Globalisation, Market Civilisation and Disciplinary Neoliberalism', *Millennium: Journal of International Studies* 24: 3 (1995), 399–423.

Gill, S., *Power and Resistance in the New World Order* (Palgrave Macmillan, 2003).

Gills, B. K., 'The Hegemonic Transition in East Asia', in S. Gill (ed.), *Gramsci, Historical Materialism and International Relations* (Cambridge University Press, 2008).

Glenn, E. N. and R. L. Feldberg, 'Proletarianising Clerical Work: Technology and Organisation Control in the Office', in A. Zimbalist (ed.), *Case Studies in the Labour Process* (Monthly Review Press, 1979).

Gorz, A., *Capitalism, Socialism, Ecology* (Verso, 1994).

Gorz, A., *Reclaiming Work: Beyond the Wage-based Society* (Polity Press, 1999).

Gramsci, A., *Selections from the Prison Notebooks* (Lawrence & Wishart, 1971).

Gramsci, A., *Selections from the Cultural Notebooks* (Lawrence & Wishart, 1985).

Gramsci, A., *Further Selections from the Prison Notebooks* (Minnesota University Press, 1995).

Green, F., D. Ashton, D. James, and J. Sung, 'The Role of the State in Skill Formation: Evidence from the Republic of Korea, Singapore, and Taiwan', *Oxford Review of Economic Policy* 15: 1 (1999), 82–96.

Grubb, W. N. and M. Lazerson, *The Education Gospel: The Economic Power of Schooling* (Harvard University Press, 2004).

Hall, P. A. and D. Soskice, *Varieties of Capitalism: The Institutional Foundations of Comparative Advantage* (Oxford University Press, 2001).

Hall, S., 'Gramsci's Relevance for the Study of Race and Ethnicity', *Journal of Communication Enquiry* 10: 5 (1986), 1–24.

Han, S. H., 'Asian Lifelong Learning in the Context of a Global Knowledge Economy: A Task Re-visited', *Asia Pacific Education Review* 8: 3 (2007), 478–86.

Harding, J., 'Creating Incurable Learners: Building Learner Autonomy through Key Skills', in S. Fallows and C. Steven (eds), *Integrating Key Skills into Higher Education: Employability, Transferable Skills and Learning for Life* (Kogan Page, 2000), 77–86.

Harrod, J., *Power Production and the Unprotected Worker* (Columbia University Press, 1987).

Harrod, J., 'Social Forces and International Political Economy: Joining the Two IRs', in S. Gill and J. H. Mittelman (eds), *Innovation and Transformation in International Studies* (Cambridge University Press, 1997), 105–14.

Harrod, J., 'Towards an International Political Economy of Labour', in J. Harrod and R. O'Brien (eds), *Globalised Unions: Theory and Strategy of Organised Labour in the Global Political Economy* (Routledge, 2001), 50–63.

Harrod, J. and R. O'Brien, *Global Unions?: Theory and Strategy of Organized Labour in the Global Political Economy* (Routledge, 2002).

Harvey, D., *The Condition of Postmodernity* (Blackwell Publishers, 1994).

Harvey, L., 'Employability and Diversity'. Online, Available (04/02/09) www2.wlv.ac.uk/webteam/confs/socdiv/sdd-harvey-0602.doc.

Harvey, L. and T. Bowers-Brown, 'Employability Cross-Country Comparisons Graduate Market Trends Winter 2004/5' (2004). Online, Available (06/03/09) http://www.prospects.ac.uk/cms/Show-Page/Home_page/p!emplid.

Harvey, L. and Morey, A., *Enhancing Employability, Recognising Diversity* (Universities UK and Higher Education Careers Services Unit, 2003). Online, Available (24/02/09) http://209.85.229.132/search?q=cache:_ZmUJhzBGrIJ:www2.wlv.ac.uk/webteam/confs/socdiv/sdd-harvey0602.doc+Harvey,+L.+and+

Morey,+A.+Enhancing+Employability,+Recognising+Diversity&hl=en&ct=clnk&cd=1&gl=uk&client=firefox-a. Also a Universities UK Main Report, Online, Available (24/02/09) http://www.universitiesuk.ac.uk/Publications/Documents/employability.pdf.

HEFCE (Higher Education Funding Council for England), 'How Much Does Higher Education Enhance the Employability of Graduates?', summary report (2003). Online, Available (21/11/08) HEFCE, http://www.hefce.ac.uk/pubs/RDreports/2003/rd13_03/.

Hendrick, J. D., 'Globalization, Islamic Activism, and Passive Revolution in Turkey: The Case of Fethullah Gulen', *Journal of Power* 2: 3 (2009), 343–68.

Hillage, J. and E. Pollard, *Employability: Developing a Framework for Policy Analysis* (Department for Education and Employment 1999).

Heller, A. with F. Fehér and G. Markus, *Dictatorship over Needs* (Basil Blackwell, 1983).

Hill, D., P. McLaren, M. Cole, and G. Rikowski, *Marxism against Postmodernism in Educational Theory* (Lexington Books, 2002).

Hillage, J. and E. Pollard, *Employability: Developing a Framework for Policy Analysis* (Department for Education and Employment, 1999).

Hine, D., 'The Future of Unemployment: The Situation', *Agit8* (09 February 2009). Online, Available (25/04/09) http://agit8.org.uk/?p=307.

HM Treasury, 'Skills in the Global Economy', *The Pre-Budget Report* (Crown copyright 2004).

HM Treasury, UK Budget 2007, *Increasing Employment Opportunity for All* (2007). Online, Available (06/03/09) http://www.hmtreasury.gov.uk/media/A/2/bud07_chapter4_267.pdf.

Holman D., S. Frenkel, O. Sørensen and S. Wood, 'Work Design Variation and Outcomes in Call Centers: Strategic Choice and Institutional Explanations', *Industrial Labour Relations Review* 62 (2009), 510–32.

Holman, D., D. Martinez-Iñigo, and P. Totterdell, 'Emotional Labour, Well-Being and Performance', in C. L. Cooper and S. Cartwright (eds), *The Oxford Handbook of Organizational Well-Being* (Oxford University Press, 2008), 331–55.

Holman, O., 'Asymmetrical Regulation and Multidimensional Governance in the European Union', *Review of International Political Economy* 11: 4 (2004), 714–35.

Hood, C., 'A Public Management for All Seasons?', *Public Administration* 69 (1991), 3–19.

Hochschild, A. R., *The Managed Heart: Commercialisation of Human Feeling* (University of California, 1983).

Humphreys, P. J. and S. A. Padgett, 'Globalization, the European Union, and Domestic Governance in Telecoms and Electricity', *Governance* 19: 3 (2006), 383–406.

HRDK (Human Resources Development Korea), *Introduction to HRD Korea* (HRD Korea, 2009).

ILO (International Labour Organisation), 'Impact of Flexible Labour Market Arrangements in the Machinery Electrical and Electronic Industries', Report for discussion at the Tripartite Meeting on the Impact of Flexible

Labour Market Arrangements in the Machinery, Electrical and Electronic Industries (Geneva, 26–30 October 1998). Online, Available (06/03/09) http://www.ilo.org/public/english/dialogue/sector/techmeet/tmmei98/tmmeir1.htm.

ILO, 'Learning and Training for Work in the Knowledge Society', Report 4 (1) (International Labour Organisation, 2002).

ILO, Guidelines for Development of Regional Model Competency Standards (RMCS) (ILO 2006). Online, Available (27/04/10) http://www.ilo.org/public/english/region/asro/bangkok/skills-ap/docs/rmcs_guide.pdf.

ILO, 'ILO Global Employment Trends Report 2009 – Unemployment, Working Poor, Vulnerable Employment to Increase Dramatically due to Global Employment Crisis' (29 January 2009). Online, Available (03/03/09) http://www.ilo.org/asia/info/public/pr/lang—en/WCMS_101494/index.htm.

ILO, 'World Employment Report 1998–99', press release (1998). Online, Available (23/07/09) http://www.ilo.org/global/About_the_ILO/Media_and_public_information/Press_releases/lang—en/WCMS_007996/index.htm.

IMD (Institute for Management Development), *The World Competitiveness Yearbook 1996* (1996).

IMF (International Monetary Fund), 'Statement by the Hon. Gordon Brown, Governor of the Fund and Alternate Governor of the Bank for the United Kingdom, at the Joint Annual Discussion' (Washington DC, 1998). Online, Available (06/03/09) http://www.imf.org/external/am/1998/speeches/pr54gbe.pdf.

IMF, 'Mission Concluding Statement, United Kingdom—2002 Article IV' (9 December 2002). Online, Available (06/03/09) http://www.imf.org/external/np/ms/2002/120902a.htm.

Index Mundi, 'Singapore Unemployment Rate' (2009). Online, Available (06/03/09) http://www.indexmundi.com/singapore/unemployment_rate.html.

Institute for Public Policy Research, *Building Better Partnerships: The Final Report of the Commission on Public Private Partnerships* (Institute for Public Policy Research, 2001), 72.

International Herald Tribune, The Associated Press, 'Singapore Unemployment Jumps to 2.6 Percent' (30 January 2009). Online, Available (06/03/09) http://singaporenewsalternative.blogspot.com/2009/01/singapore-unemployment-jumps-to-26.html.

Jessop, B., 'Thatcherism and Flexibility: The White Heat of a Post-Fordist Revolution', in B. Jessop, H. Kastendiek, K. Nielsen, and O. Pedersen (eds), *The Politics of Flexibility: Restructing State and Industry in Britain, Germany and Scandinavia* (Edward Elgar Publishing House, 1991), 135–61.

Jessop, B., 'Critical Semiotic Analysis and Cultural Political Economy', *Critical Discourse Studies* 1: 2 (2004), 159–74.

Jessop, B., 'Hollowing Out the "Nation-State" and Multilevel Governance', in P. Kennet (ed.), *A Handbook of Comparative Social Policy* (Edward Elgar, 2004), 11–25.

Joerges, C., 'Deliberative Political Processes Revisited: What Have We Learnt about the Legitimacy of Supranational Decision-Making', *Journal of Common Market Studies* 44: 4 (2006), 779–802.

Jung, C. C., 'Wind of Change in Korean Labour Movement', *Korea Labour Review* 5: 26 (May–June 2009), 6–9.

Jung, I. and I. Rha, 'A Virtual University Trial Project: Its Impact on Higher Education in South Korea', *Innovations in Education and Teaching International* 38: 1 (2000), 31–41.

Kennett, P., *Comparative Social Policy* (Open University Press, 2001).

Kim, D. J., 'Address to the Nation', December 19 1997, Article 6 #2' (translated by the Blue House), in C.-H. Sohn and J. Yang (eds), *Korea's Economic Reform Measures under the IMF Program: Government Measures in the Critical First Six Months of the Korean Economic Crisis* (Korea Institute for International Economic Policy, 1997).

Kim, J.-H., *New Paradigm of Human Resources Development: Government Initiatives for Economic Growth and Social Integration in Korea* (KRIVET, 2005).

Kim, M. S. and T. S. Chung, 'Structural Transformation for Demand-Oriented Vocational Training', in J. H. Kim (ed.) *New Paradigm of Human Resources Development, Government Initiatives for Economic Growth and Social Integration in Korea* (KRIVET, Seoul, 2005), 79–96.

Kim, S. S. and D. Briscoe, 'Globalization and a New Human Resource Policy in Korea: Transformation to a Performance-Based HRM', *Employee Relations* 19: 4 (1997), 298–308.

Kingston, P., 'Leitch Set to Get Top Marks for Report', *Guardian* (12 June 2007), 9.

Klein, N., *No Logo* (Flamingo, 2001).

KLI (Korea Labour Institute), 'Learning for Work in the Knowledge Society', project for ILO Revision of the Human Resources Development Recommendations: Infocus Programme on Skills, Knowledge and Employment (2003). Online, Available (03/08/09) http://www.logos-net.net/ilo/150_base/en/report/rep_toc.htm.

KLF (Korea Labour Foundation), Homepage. Online, Available (03/08/09) http://www.nosa.or.kr/eng/info/vision.jsp.

Kling, R. and S. Iacono, 'The Mobilisation of Support for Computerization: The Role of the Computerization Movements', *Social Problems* 35: 3 (1988), 226–42.

Knights, D., 'Subjectivity, Power and the Labour Process', in D. Knights and H. Wilmott (eds), *Labour Process Theory* (Macmillan, 1990).

Koh, G. and O. Giok-Ling (eds), *State-Society Relations in Singapore* (Oxford University Press, 2000).

KOILAF (Korea International Labour Foundation), 'Changes in the Employment Structure: Recent Developments, Current Labour Situation in Korea' (KOILAF, 1999a). Online, Available (18/08/09) http://www.koilaf.org/publication/link16.htm#4.

KOILAF, '1999 Guidelines for Collective Bargaining: Labor, Management and the Government' (KOILAF, 1999b).

KOILAF, *Labour Relations in Korea* (KOILAF, 1999c).

KOILAF, '2002 Collective Guidelines for Collective Bargaining: Labour, Management and the Government' (KOILAF, 2002).

KOILAF, '61% of Personnel or HRM Managers Predict "Unstable Labor-Management Relations for 2005"', *Labour Today* 239, (31 December 2004a). Online, Available (18/08/09) http://www.koilaf.org/index2.htm.

KOILAF, 'Unemployment Unchanged at 3.5 Per Cent' (2004b). Online, Available (18/08/09) http://www.koilaf.org/index2.htm korea herald 2004.

KOILAF, 'Support for Workers' Vocational Skills Development at SMEs', *Korea Labour Review* 5: 25 (May–June 2009), 20–1.

KRIVET (Korea Research Institute for Vocational Education and Training), 'Korea's Centennial History of Vocational Education and Training' (KRIVET, 1999).

KRIVET, 'Participation Factor of Training Programmes' (KRIVET, 2000).

KRIVET, 'Educational and Training Program Situation In Korea' (KRIVET, 2000b) (in Korean).

KRIVET, website (2008). Online, Available (31/05/10) http://www.krivet.re.kr/.

KRIVET UNESCO Regional Centre Project, *KRIVET International Workshop on Official Development Assistance and Technical Vocational Education and Training* (KRIVET, 2008).

KRF (Korea Research Foundation) BK21/NURI Committee, website. Online Available (18/08/09) http://bnc.krf.or.kr/home/eng/.

Kücklich, J., 'Precarious Playbour: Modders and the Digital Games Industry', *Journal of FibreCulture*, 5 (September 2005). Online, Available (27/02/09) http://journal.fibreculture.org/issue5/kucklich.html.

Kuruvilla, S., C. Erickson, and A. Hwang, 'Developing an Assessment of the Singapore Skills Development System: Does It Constitute a Viable Model for Other Developing Countries?', *World Development* 30: 8 (2002), 1461–76.

Labour Party Manifesto (1992). Online, Available (27/02/09) http://www.psr.keele.ac.uk/area/uk/man/lab92.htm

Labour Party Manifesto (1998). Online, Available (27/02/09) http://www.psr.keele.ac.uk/area/uk/man/lab97.htm.

Landau, I., 'Law and Civil Society in Cambodia and Vietnam: A Gramscian Perspective', *Journal of Contemporary Asia* 38: 2 (2008), 244–58.

Landy, M., 'Gramsci, Passive Revolution, and Media', *Boundary 2* 35: 3 (2008), 99–131.

Lash, S. and J. Urry, *The End of Organised Capitalism* (Polity Press, 1987).

Lash, S. and J. Urry, *Economies of Signs and Space* (Sage, 1994).

Launch of Manpower 21 Plan Press Release, Singapore (31 August 1999). Online, Available (07/08/99) http://www.gov.sg/mom/news/news99/990831.html.

Law, S. S., 'Dynamics and Challenges of a Vocational Training System – the Singapore Experience', ITE paper no. 2, 1996.

Lawer, C., 'Market and Non-Market Co-Creation', in *The Empty Whitecoat* (2009). Online, Available (21/04/09) http://chrislawer.blogs.com/chris_lawer/2009/04/market-and-nonmarket-cocreation.html.

Layard, R., *Happiness: Lessons from a New Science* (Penguin, 2005).

Lazzarato, M., 'Immaterial Labour', in P. Virno and M. Hardt (eds), *Radical Thought in Italy: A Potential Politics* (University of Minnesota Press, 1996).

Leadbeater, C., 'Who Will Own the Knowledge Economy?', *Political Quarterly* 69: 4 (October–December 1998), 375–85.

Leadbeater, C., 'It's Not Just the Economy, Stupid', *New Statesman* (27 September 1999), iv–vi.

LSC (Learning and Skills Council), 'Entrepreneurial Spirit Sweeps the Nation', news release, publication number 446 (30 July 2007). Online, Available (27/02/09) http://readingroom.lsc.gov.uk/lsc/National/nat-entrepreneurial-nation.doc.

LSC (Learning and Skills Council), 'Our Future. It's in Our Hands', *What We Do* (July 2007). Online, Available (07/07/07) http://www.lsc.gov.uk/whatwedo/ourfuture.htm.

Lee, K., 'New Direction of Korea's Vocational Education and Training Policy', paper presented at International Conference on TVET, Adelaide, Australia, 2001.

Lee, Y.-H., *Workforce Development in the Republic of Korea: Policies and Practices* (Asia Development Bank Institute, 2007).

Lefebvre, H., *The Survival of Capitalism: Reproduction of the Relations of Production* (Allison & Busby, 1973).

Lefebvre, H., *Critique of Everyday Life Volume I*, translated by John Moore (Verso, 1958/1991).

Leitch Report, 'Leitch Review of Skills: Prosperity for All in the Global Economy – World Class Skills, Final Report (London: Her Majesty's Stationery Office, 2006). Online, Available (06/03/09) http://www.hm-treasury.gov.uk/media/523/43/leitch_finalreport051206.pdf.

Levy, S., *Hackers: Heroes of the Computer Revolution* (Penguin, 1984).

Lim, K., 'Singapore Wages Council Predicts Unemployment to Soar', *Reuters* (15 January, 2009). Online, Available (06/03/09) http://www.reuters.com/article/idUSSIN37377020090116.

Lim, L. and P. E. Fong, *Trade, Employment and Industrialisation in Singapore* (Geneva: International Labour Organisation, 1986).

Lissauer, R. and P. Robinson (eds), *A Learning Process: Public Private Partnerships in Education* (London: Institute for Public Policy Research, 2000), 4.

Littler, C., 'The Labour Process Debate: A Theoretical Review', in D. Knights and H. Willmott (eds), *Labor Process Theory* (Macmillan, 1990).

Lloyd, C. and J. Payne, 'On the Political Economy of Skill: Assessing the Possibilities for a Viable High Skills Project in the United Kingdom', *New Political Economy* 7: 3 (2002), 367–95.

Lovink, G., *Uncanny Networks: Dialogues with the Virtual Intelligentsia* (The MIT Press, 2002).

Low, L., *The Political Economy of a City-State: Government-Made Singapore* (Oxford University Press, 1998).

Lynch, L. M. (ed.), *Training and the Private Sector: International Comparisons* (University of Chicago Press, 1994).

Mach, E., 'On the Part Played by Accident in Invention and Discovery', *Monist* 6 (1896), 161–75.

Magariños, C. A.,'Managing UN Reform: UNIDO's Need-Driven Approach', presentation at the Royal Institute for International Affairs, Chatham House, London, 21 September 2001.

Marks, G., L. Hooghe, and K. Blank, 'European Integration from the 1980s: State-Centric V. Multi-level Governance', *Journal of Common Market Studies* 34: 3 (1996), 341–78.

Marx, K., *The Grundrisse*, edited and translated by David McLellan (Harper Torchbooks, 1972).

Marx, K., *Capital: A Critique of Political Economy*, Volume I (Penguin, 1976).

Mandeville, B., *The Fable of the Bees: Or Private Vices, Publick Benefits* (Penguin Classics, 1714/1989).

Mason, G, G. Williams, and S. Cranmer, 'Employability Skills Initiatives in Higher Education: What Effects Do They have on Graduate Labour Market Outcomes?', National Institute of Economic and Social Research, London (2006). Online, Available (24/02/09) http://www.niesr.ac.uk/pubs/DPS/dp280.pdf.

Masuda, Y., 'A Vision of Computopia', *Futurist* 21: 2 (Mar/April 1987), 61.

Masuda, Y., *Managing in the Information Society: Releasing Synergy Japanese Style* (Blackwell, 1990).

Mayer Report, 'Employment-Related Key Competencies: A Proposal for Consultation / the Mayer Committee' (Mayer Committee, 1992).

McMurtry, J., *Unequal Freedoms: The Global Market as an Ethical System* (Garamond, 1998).

McQuade, E. and T. Maguire, 'Individuals and Their Employability', *Journal of European Industrial Training* 29: 6 (2005), 447–56.

Meager, N., *Temporary Work in Britain: Its Growth and Changing Rationales* (Institute of Manpower Studies, 1985).

Meyer, J. W., J. Boli, G. M. Thomas, and F. O. Ramirez, 'World Society and the Nation-State', *The American Journal of Sociology* 103: 1 (1997), 144–81.

Middelton, J., A. Ziderman, A. Van Adams, *Skills for Productivity* (Oxford University Press, 1993).

Mintel International Group Ltd, 'Changing Work Patterns United Kingdom, 2003' (CT: Global Information Ltd., 2003).

Moglen, Eben, 'Freeing the Mind: Free Software and the Death of Proprietary Culture', keynote address at the University of Maine Law School's Fourth Annual Technology and Law Conference (Portland, Maine, 29 June 2003). Online, Available (25/04/09) http://old.law.columbia.edu/publications/maine-speech.html.

MOL (Ministry of Labour South Korea), 'Labour Sector Reforms Gaining Speed: MOL Decides to Operate the 2nd Term Labour Reform Task Force' (International Co-operation Division, 1999). Online, Available (20/08/09) http://www.molab.go.kr/English/English.html.

MOL, 'Vocational Ability Development Overview', *Labour Policy* (2005). Online, Available (06/07/08) http://www.molab.go.kr:8787/labor/labor_06_01_01.jsp.

Montgomerie, J., 'Bridging the Critical Divide: Global Finance, Financialisation and Contemporary Capitalism', *Contemporary Politics* 14: 3 (2008), 233–52.

Moore, P., 'Revolutions from Above: Worker Training as *Trasformismo* in South Korea', *Capital and Class* 86 (2005), 39–72.

Moore, P., 'Global Knowledge Capitalism, Self-woven Safety Nets, and the Crisis of Employability', *Global Society* 20: 4 (2006), 453–73.

Moore, P., *Globalisation and Labour Struggle in Asia: A Neo-Gramscian Critique of South Korea's Political Economy* (I.B. Tauris, 2007).

Moore, P. and A. Karatzogianni (eds), *Parallel Visions of P2P Production Governance, Organisation and the New Economies*, special issue for *Capital and Class* 97 (January 2009).

Moore, P. and P. A. Taylor, 'Exploitation of the Self in Community-Based Software Production – Workers' Freedoms or Firm Foundations?', *Capital and Class* 97 (2009), 99–120.

Morley, L., *Organising Feminisms: The Micropolitics of the Academy* (Macmillan, 1999).

Morley, L., 'Producing New Workers: Quality, Equality and Employability in Higher Education', *Quality in Higher Education* 7: 2 (2001), 131–8.

Morton, A. D, 'Structural Change and Neoliberalism in Mexico: "Passive Revolution" in the Global Political Economy', *Third World Quarterly* 24: 4 (2003), 631–54.

Morton, A. D., *Unravelling Gramsci: Hegemony and Passive Revolution in the Global Political Economy* (Pluto Press, 2007).

Morton, A. D, *Approaching Passive Revolutions, Capital & Class* Special Issue 34: 3 (2010).

Morton, A. D., 'Reflections on Uneven Development: Mexican Revolution, Primitive Accumulation, Passive Revolution', *Latin American Perspectives* 37: 1 (2010), 7–34.

National Statistics, 'Unemployment Rate Rises to 6.1%' (2009). Online, Available (06/03/09) http://www.statistics.gov.uk/CCI/nugget.asp?ID=12.

National Statistics and Office for National Statistics (ONS), 'ILO Unemployment Rates for selected EU countries, 1990–98' (1998). Online, Available (06/03/09) http://www.publications.parliament.uk/pa/ld199899/ldhansrd/vo990614/text/90614w01.htm.

Negri, A., *Marx Beyond Marx: Lessons on the Grundrisse* (Autonomedia, 1992).

Negri, A., 'Interpretation of the Class Situation Today: Methodological Aspects', in W. Bonefeld, R. Gunn, and K. Psychopedis (eds), *Open Marxism Vol. 2, Theory and Practice* (Pluto, 1992), 69–105.

Negri, A., *Time for Revolution* (Continuum International Publishing Group, 2003).

Negroponte, N., *Being Digital* (Coronet/Hodder and Stoughton, 1995).

Nish, I., G. Redding, and N. Sek-hong (eds), *Work and Society: Labour and Human Resources* (Hong Kong: Hong Kong University Press, 1996).

Nunn, A., 'What Next for the New Labour Project after Blair?', *State of Nature* (Nov/Dec 2006). Online, Available (12/02/09) http://www.stateofnature.org/whatNextForNewLabour.html.

Nouse, *Britain's Personal Debt Crisis Escalates* (2008). Online, Available (12/02/09) http://www.nouse.co.uk/2008/06/10/britains-personal-debt-crisis-escalates-2/.

Nyhan, B. (ed.), *Taking Steps towards the Knowledge Society: Reflections on the Process of Knowledge Development* (Office for Official Publications of the European Communities, 2002).

O'Brien, R., 'Labour and IPE: Rediscovering Human Agency', in R. Palan (ed.), *Global Political Economy: Contemporary Theories* (Routledge, 2000), 89–99.

O'Brien, R., A. M. Goetz, J. Aart Scholte, and M. Williams, *Contesting Global Governance: Multilateral Economic Institutions and Global Social Movements* (Cambridge University Press, 2000).

O'Doherty, D. and H. Willmott, 'Debating Labour Process Theory: The Issue of Subjectivity and the Relevance of Poststructuralism', *Sociology* 35: 2 (2001), 457–76.

O'Donoghue, J. and T. Maguire, 'The Individual Learner, Employability and the Workplace: A Reappraisal of Relationships and Prophecies', *Journal of European Industrial Training* 29: 6 (2005), 436–46.

OECD, *Technology, Productivity and Job Creation*, Paris; OECD (1996).

OECD, *Knowledge Management in the Learning Society: Education and Skills* (OECD, 2000).

OECD Public Governance and Territorial Development Directorate, *Defining the Borders between the Public and the Private Sectors* (OECD, 2005).

Open Source Ecology. Online, Available (08/06/09) http://openfarmtech.org/index.php?title=Main_Page.

Orenstein, M. A. and H. P.Schmitz, 'The New Transnationalism and Comparative Politics', *Comparative Politics* 38: 4 (2006).

Orsi, C., *The Value of Reciprocity: Arguing for a Plural Political Economy* (Federico Café Centre, 2006).

Oyen, E., Comparative Methodology: Theory and Practice in International Social Research (Sage, 1990).

Panitch, L., 'Globalisation and the State', in R. Miliband and L. Panitch (eds), *Socialist Register* (The Merlin Press, 1994), 60–93.

Park, D. J., J. Park, and G.-C. Yu, 'Assessment of Labour Market Response to the Labour Law Changes Introduced in 1998', in F. Park, Y.-B. Park, G. Betcherman, and A. Dar (eds), *Labour Market Reforms in Korea: Policy Options for the Future* (World Bank and Korea Labour Institute, 2001), 125–50.

Pascail, L. 'The Emergence of the Skills Approach in Industry and Its Consequences for the Training of Engineers', *European Journal of Engineering Education* 31: 1 (2006), 55–61.

Pedagogy for Employability Group, *Learning and Employability Series One: Pedagogy for Employability* (The Higher Education Academy/Enhancing Student Employability Co-ordination Team, 2006).

Pedagogy for Employability Group, *Pedagogy for Employability* (The Higher Education Academy/Enhancing Student Employability Coordination Team ESECT) (2006). Online, Available (25/04/09)http://www.heacademy.ac.uk/assets/York/documents/ourwork/tla/employability/id383_pedagogy_for_employability_357.pdf.

Peters, T. and R. Waterman, *In Search of Excellence: Lessons from America's Best-Run Companies* (Harper and Row, 1982).

Philpott, J. and G. Davies, 'No Turning Back?', *People Management Magazine* (14th September 2006).

Phillips, L., 'Employers Go for Soft Option', *Online Magazine of the Chartered Institute of Personnel and Development* (31 August 2006). Online, Available (06/03/09) http://www.peoplemanagement.co.uk.

Promberger, M.,'The Recoil of Globalisation: Flexibility and Social Inequality within Metropolitan Societies', paper presented at The Transformation of Work in a Global Knowledge Economy: Towards a Conceptual Framework, Chania, Crete, September 2006. Online, Available (24/02/09) http://www.worksproject.be/documents/workschaniaconferencereportfinal.pdf.

P2P Foundation, 'Open Source Ecology'. Online, Available (25/04/09) http://p2pfoundation.net/Open_Source_Ecology (2009).

Quah, J. S. T. (ed.), *In Search of Singapore's National Values* (Times Academic Press, 1990).

Radaelli, C. M., 'Policy Transfer and Europeanisation: Institutional Isomorphism as a Source of Legitimacy', *Governance* 13 (2000), 25–43.

Ransome, P., *Antonio Gramsci: A New Introduction* (Harvester Wheatsheaf, 1992).

Reilly, P., *Flexibility at Work: Balancing the Interests of Employer and Employee* (Gower, 2001).

Resnick, S. and R. Wolff, *Knowledge and Class* (University of Chicago Press, 1987).

Rifkin, J., *The End of Work: The Decline of the Global Labour Force and the Dawn of the Post-Market Era* (Tarcher Putnam, 1992).

Ritzy, F. and B. Lingard, 'Globalisation and the Changing Nature of the OECD's Educational Work', in H. Lauder, P. Brown, J. Dillabough, and A. H. Halsey (eds), *Education, Globalisation, and Social Change* (Oxford University Press, 2006), 247–60.

Robinson, W., A Theory of Global Capitalism Production, Class, and State in a Transnational World (Johns Hopkins University Press, 2004).

Robinson, W., 'Gramsci and Globalisation: From Nation-State to Transnational Hegemony', *Critical Review of International Social and Political Philosophy* 8:4 (2005), 1–16.

Robinson, A. and S. Tormey, 'New Labour's Neoliberal Gleichschaltung: The Case of Higher Education', *The Commoner* 7 (Spring/Summer 2003). Online, Available (24/02/09) http://www.commoner.org.uk/07robinson&tormey.pdf.

ROK (Republic of Korea), 'Human Resources Development Strategies for Korea: Human Resources Knowledge New Take-Off' (Republic of Korea, 2001).

Rooney, P., P. Kneale, B. Gambini, A. Keiffer, B. Vandrasek, and S. Gedye, 'Variations in International Understandings of Employability for Geography', *Journal of Geography in Higher Education*, 30: 1 (2006), 133–45.

Rose, N., *Governing the Soul: The Shaping of the Private Self* (Free Association Books, 1999).

Rosenberg, G., *Careers Advisory Services and HEI-Business Interactions* (2001). Online, Available (04/05/01) http://www.dfes.gov.uk/hecareersservice-review/docs/g_01.doc.

Rothstein, B., 'Critique de l'Etat-providence', in J. P. Durand (ed), *La Fin du modele suedois* (Syros, 1994).

Rubery, J. and M. Grimshaw, *The Organisation of Employment: An International Perspective* (Palgrave Macmillan, 2003).

Rupert, M., *Producing Hegemony: The Politics of Mass Production and American Global Power* (Cambridge University Press, 1995).

Rupert, M., *Ideologies of Globalization: Contending Visions of a New World Order* (Routledge, 2000).

Sakolsky, R., 'Disciplinary Power in the Labour Process', in A. Sturdy, D. Knights and H. Willmott (eds), *Skill and Consent* (Routledge, 1992).

Salmon, M., *Delivering Skills for Business* (Sector Skills Development Agency, Department for Education and Skills, 2002). Online, Available (25/08/09) http://www.ssda.org.uk/pdf/delivery-remit.pdf.

Sanderson, G., 'International Education Developments in Singapore', *International Education Journal* 3: 2 (2002), 85–102.

Scholz, T., 'Downtime'. Online, Available (03/11/09) http://www.collectivate.net/journalisms/2005/11/19/downtime.html.

SDF (Singapore Skills Development Fund) (2003). Online, Available (06/03/09) http://www.sdf.gov.sg/.

Seex, P., 'Leitch Review of Skills: Initial Reactions Centre for Cities Reaction' (Institute for Public Policy Research, 06 December 2006). Online, Available (25/08/09) http://www.ippr.org/centreforcities/articles/archive.asp?id=2473&fID=178 21.

Sen, C. S., 'The Singapore Government and Civil-Society', in G. Koh and O.G. Ling (eds), *State-Society Relations in Singapore* (Oxford University Press, 2000), 122–30.

Showstack-Sassoon, A., *Approaches to Gramsci* (Writers and Readers, 1982).

Si, Min-Seok, 'Support for Workers' Vocational Skills Development at SMEs', *Korea Labour Review* 5:26 (2009), 20–1.

Singapore Ministry of Trade and Industry, 'Minister Lim Hng Kiang's Oral Reply to Parliament Questions on Employment Forecast and Growth Sectors 19/01/2009' (2009). Online, Available (06/03/09) http://app.mti.gov.sg/default.asp?id=148&articleID=17182.

Sklair, L., 'Social Movements for Global Capitalism: The Transnational Capitalist Class in Action', *Review of International Political Economy* 4:3 (1997), 514–38.

Sklair, L., *The Transnational Capitalist Class* (Blackwell, 2001a).

Sklair, L., 'The Transnational Capitalist Class and the Discourse of Globalization' (Global Dimensions, LSE Centre for the Study of Global Governance, 2001b). Online, Available (06/03/09) http://www.globaldimensions.net/articles/sklair/LSklair.html.

Smith, C., 'Technical Workers: A Class and Organisational Analysis', in S. Clegg (ed.), *Organization Theory and Class Analysis: New Approaches and New Issues* (Walter de Gruyter, 1990), 233–56.

Smith, L., 'World Class Skills for a World Class Nation' (Further Education News, 2007). Online, Available (25/08/09) http://www.fenews.co.uk/newsview.asp?n=2540.

Spencer, D., *The Political Economy of Work* (Routledge, 2009).

Steinfels, P., *The Neo-Conservatives: The Men Who Are Changing America's Politics* (Simon and Schuster, 1979).

Storey, J. and N. Bacon, 'Individualism and Collectivism: Into the 1990s', *International Journal of Human Resource Management* 4: 3 (1993), 655–84.

Sturdy, A., D. Knights, and H. Willmott (eds), *Skill and Consent: Contemporary Studies in the Labour Process* (Routledge, 1992).

Sturdy, A., 'Clerical Consent: "Shifting" Work in the Insurance Office', in A. Sturdy, D. Knights and H. Willmott (eds), *Skill and Consent: Contemporary Studies in the Labour Process* (Routledge, 1992), 115–48.

SWSQ (Singapore Workforce Skills Qualifications), *Generic Skills* (Centre for Employability Skills, 2005). Online, Available (04/09/09) http://wsq.wda.gov.sg/GenericSkills/English+Employability+Skills+System+(ESS)/Training+Modules/.

Tan, E. K-B., 'Law and Values in Governance: The Singapore Way', *Hong Kong Law Journal* 30: 1 (2000), 91–119.

Tan, K. Y. L., 'Understanding and Harnessing Ground Energies in Civil Society', in G. Koh and O. Giok-Ling (eds), *State-Society Relations in Singapore* (Oxford University Press, 2000), 98–121.

Tamkin, P. and J. Hillage, 'Employability and Employers: The Missing Piece of the Jigsaw', Report 361, Institute for Employment Studies (Brighton: Institute of Employment Studies, November 1999). Online, Available (15/06/10) http://www.employment-studies.co.uk/pubs/summary.php?id=361.

Taylor, F. W., 'Shop Management', *Scientific Management* (Dover Publications, 1903/1998).

Taylor, I., *Stuck in Middle GEAR: South Africa's Post-Apartheid Foreign Relations* (Praeger Publishers, 2001).

Toffler, A., *Power Shift: Knowledge, Wealth, and Violence at the Edge of the 21st Century* (Bantam, 1990).

Tomer, J., *The Human Firm: A Socio-Economic Analysis of Its Behaviour and Potential in a New Economic Age* (Routledge, 1999).

Tong, G. C., Launch of Singapore 21 Vision Saturday, 24 April 1999. Online, Available (01/02/08) http://www.singapore21.org.sg/speeches_240499.html.

Tremewan, C., *The Political Economy of Social Control in Singapore* (Palgrave Macmillan, 1994).

Tripartite Commission, *National Initiatives Concerning Social Dialogue on Training* (Republic of Korea, 31 July, 2001). Online, Available (08/08/07) http://www.logosnet.net/ilo/150_base/en/topic_n/t23_kor.htm.

Tugal, C., *Passive Revolution: Absorbing the Islamic Challenge to Capitalism* (Stanford University Press, 2009).

Turnbull, C. M., *A History of Singapore 1918–1975* (Oxford University Press, 1989).

Twaakyondo, H. M., E. P. Bhalalusesa, J. L. Ndalichako, 'Factors Shaping Successful Public Private Partnership in the ICT Sector in Developing Countries' (Commonwealth Policy Studies Unit, 2002). Online, Available (24/08/08) http://www.cpsu.org.uk/downloads/Annex3.pdf.

UK Budget 2007, Online, Available (23/04/10) http://webarchive.national archives.gov.uk/+/http://www.hm-treasury.gov.uk/budget/budget_07/bud_bud07_index.cfm.

United Nations Development Programme (UNDP), *Social Safety Net for the Most Vulnerable Groups in the Republic of Korea* (UNDP, 1999).

UK National Statistics Online, 'Unemployment Rate Rises to 6.3%' (03 March 2009). Online, Available (03/03/09) http://www.statistics.gov.uk/cci/nugget.asp?ID=12.

Universities UK. Online, Available (25/08/09) http://www.universitiesuk.ac.uk/knowledgetransfer/Default.asp?11=1&.

UNESCOa, 'Establishment of a Long Term Programme for the Development of TVET', General Conference 30th Session, Paris 1999.

UNESCOb, 'Country Report: Education for All, the Year 2000 Assessment' (2001). Online, Available (06/03/09) http://www2.unesco.org/wef/countryreports/korea/contents.html#cont.

UNEVOC (United Nations Education and Vocational Training Council), 'Restructuring TVET: Current Approaches' (2002). Online, Available (11/05/10) http://www.unevoc.unesco.org/donors/background/restructt-vet.htm.

van Apeldoorn, B., *Transnational Capitalism and the Struggle over European Integration* (Routledge, 2002).

van der Pijl, K., *The Making of an Atlantic Ruling Class* (Verso, 1984).

van der Pijl, K., *Transnational Classes and International Relations* (Routledge, 1998).

van der Pijl, K., 'Transnational Class Formation and State Forms', in S. Gill and J. H. Mittelman (eds), *Innovation and Transformation in International Studies* (Cambridge University Press, 1997) 118–33.

van der Pijl, K., 'Historical Materialism and the Emancipation of Labour', in M. Rupert and H. Smith (eds), *Historical Materialism and Globalization* (Routledge, 2002).

van Der Ryn, S. and S. Cowan, *Ecological Design – 10th Anniversary Edition* (Island Press, 2007).

Vanek, J. (ed.), *Self-Management: Economic Liberation of Man* (Penguin, 1975).

Virilio, P., 'Speed and Information: Cyberspace Alarm!', in D. Trend (ed.), *Reading Digital Culture* (Blackwell Publishers, 2005), 23–7.

Virno, P., 'On General Intellect', in A. Zadini and U. Fadini (eds), *Lessico Postfordista* (Feltrinelli, 2001).

Virno, P., *A Grammar of the Multitude* (Semiotext(e), 2002).

Wade, R., *Governing the Market: Economic Theory and the Role of Government in East Asian Industrialization* (Princeton, 2003).

Walker, P. (ed.), *Between Labour and Capital* (Harvester Press, 1979).

Walker, R. and K. Kellard, *Staying in Work: Policy Overview* (Department for Education and Employment London, 2001).

Watson, M., *The Foundations of International Political Economy* (Palgrave Macmillan, 2005).

Weber, S., *The Success of Open Source* (Harvard University Press, 2004).

Wellington, J., 'Skills for the Future?: Vocational Education and New Technology', in M. Holt (ed.), *Skills and Vocationalism* (Open Uni Press, 1987), 21–42.

Welshman, J., 'The Concept of the Unemployable', *Economic History Review* 59: 3 (2006), 578–606.

Wheeler, D. A., 'Why Open Source Software / Free Software (OSS/FS, FLOSS, or FOSS)? Look at the Numbers!' (2007). Online, Available (08/06/09) http://www.dwheeler.com/oss_fs_why.html.

Wilken, F., *The Liberation of Work: The Elimination of Strikes and Strife in Industry through Associative Organisation of Enterprise* (Routledge, 1965).

Williams, H., 'Property Reform and Legitimacy', *Journal of Contemporary Asia* 28: 2 (1998), 159–74.

Williams, C., 'The Discursive Construction of the Competent Learner-Worker, from Key Competencies to "Employability Skills"', *Studies in Continuing Education* 27: 1 (2005), 33–49.

Williams, R., 'Base and Superstructure in Marxist Cultural Theory', in *Problems in Materialism and Culture: Selected Essays* (Verso, 1980).

Willmott, Hugh, 'Subjectivity and the Dialectics of Praxis: Opening up the Core of Labour Process Analysis', in D. Knights and H. Willmott (eds), *Labour Process Theory* (Macmillan, 1990).

Wood, S., *The Degradation of Work? Skill, Deskilling and the Labour Process* (Hutchinson, 1982).

Wood, S. (ed.), *The Transformation of Work?* (Unwin Hyman, 1989).

Worth, O., *Hegemony, International Political Economy and Post-Communist Russia* (Ashgate Publishing, 2005).

Worth, O., 'The Poverty and Potential of Gramscian Thought in International Relations', *International Politics* 45: 6 (2008), 633–49.

Worth, O., 'Beyond World Order and Transnational Classes: The (Re)Application of Gramsci in Global Politics', in M. McNally and J. Schwarzmantel (eds), *Gramsci and Contemporary Politics* (Routledge, 2009), 31–56.

Worth, O. and P. Moore (eds), *Globalisation and the New Semi-Peripheries in the 21st Century* (Palgrave Macmillan, 2009).

Worth, S., 'Adaptability and Self-Management: A New Ethic of Employability for the Young Unemployed?', *Journal of Social Policy* 32: 4 (2003), 607–21.

Wright, C. and J. Kitay, 'Spreading the Word: Gurus, Consultants and the Diffusion of the Employee Relations Paradigm in Australia', *Management Learning* 35: 3 (2004), 271–86.

Wrigley, T., 'Rethinking Education in an Era of Globalisation', *Journal for Critical Education Policy Studies* 5: 2 (2007). Online, Available (24/08/09) http://www.jceps.com/index.php?pageID=article&articleID=95.

Yahoda, M., *Marienthal: The Sociography of an Unemployed Community* (Transaction Publishers, 1932/2002).

Yeoman, D., 'Constructing Vocational Education: From TVEI to GNVQ' (1996). Online, Available (06/03/09) http://www.leeds.ac.uk/educol/documents/00002214.htm.

Young, B., 'Disciplinary Neo-Liberalism in the European Union and Gender Politics', *New Political Economy* 5: 1 (2000), 77–98.

Zimbalist, A. (ed.), *Case Studies on the Labour Process* (Monthly Review Press, 1979).

Index